Spanish

phrasebooks

Spanish phrasebook
2nd edition – April 2003
First published –August 1997

Published by
Lonely Planet Publications Pty Ltd ABN 36 005 607 983
90 Maribyrnong St, Footscray, Victoria 3011, Australia

Lonely Planet Offices
Australia Locked Bag 1, Footscray, Victoria 3011
USA 150 Linden St, Oakland CA 94607
UK 72-82 Rosebery Ave, London, EC1R 4RW

Cover illustration
They dance on tables by Daniel New

ISBN 0 86442 719 0

10 9 8 7

Printed through Colorcraft Ltd, Hong Kong
Printed in China

acknowledgments

Lonely Planet Language Products and editor Meg Worby would like to thank this cast of thousands for living *la vida loca* ...

Publishing manager Jim 'Gaudí' Jenkin, whose great vision saw the series develop from the ground up

Project manager Fabrice 'Don Qixote' Rocher

Series designer Yukiyoshi 'Ibiza' Kamimura

Commissioning editors Karin 'Macarena' Vidstrup Monk and Karina 'Las Ketchup' Coates and acting senior editor Emma 'Carmen' Koch

New managing editor Annelies 'Flamenco' Mertens who offered grammar and general Spanish expertise and editor Ben 'Rumba' Handicott for leading the way

Editor Piers 'Matador' Kelly for a gallant effort in sourcing regional languages and cultural information and editor Francesca 'Spanish Fly' Coles for assistance with the index

Layout designer Sally 'Arriba!' Morgan for super speedy layout

Layout designers Sonya 'Carnaval' Brooke and Katie 'Catalan' Cason for putting in the finishing touches

Freelance designer Patrick *'Jamón Jamón'* Marris for the ace illustrations throughout

Designer Daniel 'Picasso' New for the cover illustration

Cartographer Natasha 'Basque-ing' Velleley for the map, with finishing touches by *los amigos*, special projects managing cartographer Paul Piaia and map editor Wayne Murphy

Design manager Nina 'Tapas' Sturges for coordinating layout checks

Freelance proofer Adrienne 'Castanets' Costanzo

Peter and Marta Gibney for careful proofing of the Spanish

Special thanks to contracted author Marta López, who also produced baby James during this book. Marta thanks Graciela Recogzy, David García Campelo and Andrew Tsirigotis.

make the most of this phrasebook ..

Anyone can speak another language! It's all about confidence. Don't worry if you can't remember your school language lessons or if you've never learnt a language before. Even if you learn the very basics (on the inside covers of this book), your travel experience will be the better for it. You have nothing to lose and everything to gain when the locals hear you making an effort.

> finding things in this book

For easy navigation, this book is in sections. The Tools chapters are the ones you'll thumb through time and again. The Practical section covers basic travel situations like catching transport and finding a bed. The Social section gives you conversational phrases, pick-up lines, the ability to express opinions – so you can get to know people. Food has a section all of its own: gourmets and vegetarians are covered and local dishes feature. Safe Travel equips you with health and police phrases, just in case. Remember the colours of each section and you'll find everything easily; or use the comprehensive Index. Otherwise, check the two-way traveller's Dictionary for the word you need.

> being understood

Throughout this book you'll see coloured phrases on the right hand side of each page. They're phonetic guides to help you pronounce the language. You don't even need to look at the language itself, but you'll get used to the way we've represented particular sounds. The pronunciation chapter in Tools will explain more, but you can feel confident that if you read the coloured phrase slowly, you'll be understood.

> communication tips

Body language, ways of doing things, sense of humour – all have a role to play in every culture. 'Local talk' boxes show us common ways of saying things, or everyday language to drop into conversation. 'Listen for ...' boxes supply the phrases you may hear. They start with the phonetic guide (because you'll hear it before you know what's being said) and then lead in to the language and the English translation.

introduction..6

tools...11

practical...37

social...89

food...143

safe travel...175

dictionaries.......................................189

index..249

contents

5

United States
of America

Mexico

Cuba

Dominican Republic
Puerto Rico

Guatemala
El Salvador

Nicaragua

Honduras

Venezuela

Costa Rica

Panama

Ecuador

Colombia

Peru

Bolivia

Paraguay

Uruguay

Chile Argentina

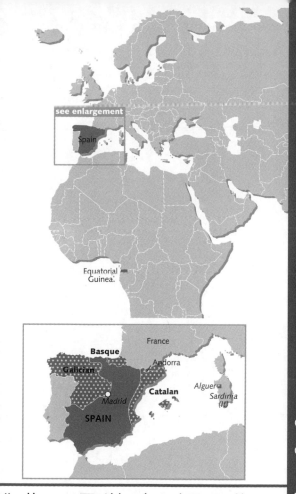

see enlargement

Spain

Equatorial
Guinea.

France

Basque

Galician

Andorra

Alguera
Sardinia
(It)

Catalan

Madrid

SPAIN

national language ▓ widely understood ▒▒ regional language
For more details see the **introduction**.

language map

Spanish, or Castilian, as it's also called in Spain, is the most widely spoken of the Romance languages, the group of languages derived from Latin which includes French, Italian and Portuguese. Outside Spain, it's the language of most of Latin America and the West Indies and is also spoken in the Philippines and Guam, as well as in some areas of the African coast and in the US. Worldwide, there are more than 30 countries or territories where Spanish is spoken.

Spanish is derived from Vulgar Latin, which Roman soldiers and merchants brought to the Iberian Peninsula during the period of the Roman conquest (3rd to 1st century BC). By 19 BC Spain had become totally Romanised and Latin became the language of the peninsula in the four centuries that followed. Today's Castilian is spoken in the north, centre and south of Spain.

People are intensely proud of their language and generally expect visitors to know at least a little. English is less widely spoken in Spain than in many other European countries, especially outside the major cities.

This book gives you the practical words and phrases you need to get by, and the fun, spontaneous phrases that lead to a better experience of Spain and its people. Need more encouragement? Remember, the contact

at a glance ...

language name: Spanish

name in language:
Español es·pa·*nyol*

language family: Romance

key country: Spain

approximate number of speakers:
over 390 million worldwide

close relatives: Latin American Spanish, Portuguese, Italian

donations to english: alligator, bonanza (lit: fair weather), canyon, guerilla, rodeo, ranch, stampede, tornado and many more familiar words ...

introduction

you make through using Spanish will make your travels unique. Local knowledge, new relationships and a sense of satisfaction are on the tip of your tongue, so don't just stand there, say something!

> basque, catalan & galician

We also give you the basics of these languages because they are each considered official in Spain, even though Spanish, or Castilian, covers by far the largest territory.

Basque, a non-latin language, is spoken in parts of the north. Catalan is spoken in the east and Galician in the north-west. These last two are also Romance languages, so are closer in origin to Spanish.

If you're travelling widely in Spain, see the special section on these regional languages for some basic expressions, page 100.

> abbreviations used in this book

f	feminine
inf	informal
m	masculine
sg	singular
pl	plural
pol	polite

TOOLS > pronunciation
herramientas de pronunciación

- Spanish pronunciation isn't hard, as many sounds are similar to sounds used in English.
- There are some easy rules to follow and once you learn them it's likely you'll be understood.
- The relationship between Spanish sounds and their spelling is straightforward and consistent.
- Like most languages, pronunciation can vary according to region. This book focuses on Castilian Spanish.

word stress

énfasis

- There is stress in Spanish, which means you emphasise one syllable over another. Rule of thumb: when a written word ends in *n*, *s* or a vowel, the stress falls on the second-last syllable. Otherwise, the final syllable is stressed.
- If you see an accent mark over a syllable, it cancels out these rules and you just stress that syllable instead.

vowel sounds

vocales

symbol	english equivalent	spanish example
a	alms	*agua*
e	red	*número*
ee	bee	*día*
o	go	*ojo*
oo	book	*gusto*
ai	aisle	*bailar*
ow	cow	*autobús*
oy	boy	*hoy*

pronunciation

11

consonant sounds

symbol	english equivalent	spanish example
b	big	*barco*
ch	chilli	*chica*
d	din	*dinero*
f	fun	*fiesta*
g	go	*gato*
k	kick	*cabeza/queso*
kh	loch	*jardín/gente*
l	loud	*lago*
ly	million	*llamada*
m	man	*mañana*
n	no	*nuevo*
ny	canyon	*señora*
p	pig	*padre*
r	run, but stronger and rolled	*ritmo/burro*
s	so	*semana*
t	tin	*tienda*
th	thin	*Barcelona/manzana*
v	soft 'b', somewhere between 'v' and 'b'	*abrir*
w	win	*guardia*
y	yes	*viaje*

There are some key things to remember about consonants in Spanish writing:

- the letter *c* is pronounced with a lisp, bar·the·*lo*·na (Barcelona), except when it comes before *a*, *o* and *u* or a consonant, when it's hard like *k* in 'king'.
- when ending a word, the letter *d* is also soft, like a *th*, or it's so slight it doesn't get pronounced at all.
- the Spanish letter *j* stands for a harsh and gutteral sound, so we use a kh symbol in our phonetic guides.
- try to roll your double *r*'s.
- the letter *q* is pronounced hard like a k.
- the letter *v* sounds more like a b, said with the lips pressed together.
- there are a few letters which don't appear in the English alphabet: *ch*, *ll* and *ñ*. You'll see these have their own entries in the spanish–english dictionary.

spanish alphabet

a	*A*	a	*b*	*B*	be	*c*	*C*	the
ch	*CH*	che	*d*	*D*	de	*e*	*E*	e
f	*F*	e·fe	*g*	*G*	khe	*h*	*H*	a·che
i	*I*	ee	*j*	*J*	*kho*·ta	*k*	*K*	ka
l	*L*	e·le	*ll*	*LL*	e·lye	*m*	*M*	e·me
n	*N*	e·ne	*ñ*	*Ñ*	e·nye	*o*	*O*	o
p	*P*	pe	*q*	*Q*	koo	*r*	*R*	e·re
s	*S*	e·se	*t*	*T*	te	*u*	*U*	oo
v	*V*	oo·ve	*w*	*W*	oo·ve do·vle	*x*	*X*	e·kees
y	*Y*	ee·*grye*·ga	*z*	*Z*	*the*·ta			

false friends

Beware of false friends – those words that sound like familiar English, but could land you in a bit of trouble if you use them unwittingly in Spanish. Here are some mistakes it's a little too easy to make:

el suburbio el soo·*boor*·byo **slum district**
   not 'suburb' which is *el barrio*, el *ba*·ryo

Estoy es·*toy* **I have a cold.**
constipado/a. m/f kons·tee·*pa*·do/a
   not 'I'm constipated' which is *estoy estreñido/a* m/f
   es·*toy* es·tre·*nyee*·do/a

Estoy es·*toy* **I'm pregnant.**
embarazada. em·ba·ra·*tha*·da
   not 'I'm embarassed' which is *estoy avergonzado/a* m/f
   es·*toy* a·ver·gon·*tha*·do/a

la injuria la een·*khoo*·ree·a **insult**
   not 'injury' which is *la herida*, la e·*ree*·da

largo/a m/f *lar*·go/a **long**
   not 'large' which is *grande*, *gran*·de

los parientes los pa·ree·*yen*·tes **relatives**
   not 'parents' which is *los padres*, los *pa*·dres

sensible sen·*thee*·ble **sensitive**
   not 'sensible' which is *prudente*, proo·*den*·te

a–z phrasebuilder
construyendo frases

This chapter is designed to help you make your own sentences. It's arranged alphabetically for ease of navigation. If you can't find the exact phrase you need in this book, remember, there are no rules, only particular ways to say things! A little grammar, a few gestures, a couple of well-chosen words and you'll generally get the message across.

a/an & some

I'd like a ticket and a postcard.
Quisiera un billete y   kee·*sye*·ra oon bee·*lye*·te ee
una postal.   oo·na pos·*tal*
(lit: I-would-like a ticket
and a postcard)

Spanish has two words for 'a/an': *un* and *una*. The gender of the noun determines which one you use. *Un* and *una* have plural forms, *unos* and *unas*, meaning 'some'.

masculine	*un* sg	*un huevo* oon *hwe*·vo	an egg
	unos pl	*unos huevos* oo·nos *hwe*·vos	some eggs
feminine	*una* sg	*una casa* oo·na *ka*·sa	a house
	unas pl	*unas casas* oo·nas *ka*·sas	some houses

adjectives see describing things

be

Spanish has two words for the English verb 'be': *ser* and *estar*.

use SER to express	examples	
permanent characteristics of persons/things	*Liz es muy guapa.* leez es mooy gwa·pa	**Liz is very beautiful.**
occupations or nationality	*Ana es de España.* a·na es de e·spa·nya	**Ana is from Spain.**
the time and location of events	*Son las tres.* son las tres	**It's 3 o'clock.**
possession	*De quién es esta mochila?* de kyen es es·ta mo·chee·la	**Whose backpack is this?**

use ESTAR to express	examples	
temporary characteristics of persons/things	*La comida está fría.* la ko·mee·da es·ta free·ya	**The food is cold.**
the time & location of persons/things	*Estamos en Madrid.* es·ta·mos en ma·dree	**We are in Madrid.**
the mood of a person	*Estoy contento.* es·toy kon·ten·to	**I'm happy.**

I	am	an anarchist	yo	soy	anarquisto
you sg inf	are	from Spain	tú	eres	de España
you sg pol	are	an artist	Usted	es	artista
he/she	is	an artist	él/ella m/f	es	artista
we	are	single	nosotros/as m/f	somos	solteros/as
you pl inf	are	kind	vosotros/as m/f	sois	simpáticos/as
you pl pol	are	students	Ustedes	son	estudiantes
they	are	students	ellos/as m/f	son	estudiantes

I	am	well	yo	estoy	bien
you sg inf	are	angry	tú	estás	enojado
you sg pol	are	drunk	Usted	está	borracho
he/she	is	drunk	él/ella m/f	está	borracho
we	are	happy	nosotros/as m/f	estamos	felices
you pl inf	are	on holiday	vosotros/as m/f	estáis	de vacaciones
you pl pol	are	learning	Ustedes	están	estudiando
they	are	learning	ellos/as m/f	están	estudiando

describing things

I'm looking for a comfortable hotel.

Estoy buscando un   es·*toy* boos·*kan*·do oon
hotel cómodo.   o·*tel* ko·mo·do
(lit: I-am looking-for a
hotel comfortable)

When using an adjective to describe a noun, you need to use a
different ending depending on whether the noun is masculine or
feminine, and singular or plural. Most adjectives have four forms
which are easy to remember:

	singular	plural
masculine	fantástico	fantásticos
feminine	fantástica	fantásticas

un hotel fantástico	oon o·*tel* fan·*tas*·tee·ko	a fantastic hotel
una comida fantástica	oo·na ko·*mee*·da fan·*tas*·tee·ka	a fantastic meal
unos libros fantásticos	oo·nos *lee*·bros fan·*tas*·tee·kos	some fantastic books
unas tapas fantásticas	oo·nas ta·pas fan·*tas*·tee·kas	some fantastic tapas

Adjectives generally come after the noun in Spanish. However, 'adjectives' of quantity (such as 'much', 'a lot', 'little/few', 'too much') and adjectives expressing possession ('my' and 'your') always precede the noun.

muchos turistas	moo·chos too·*rees*·tas	many tourists
primera clase	pree·*me*·ra *kla*·se	first class
mi coche	mee ko·che	my car

gender

In Spanish, all nouns – words which denote a thing, person or idea – are either masculine or feminine.

The dictionary will tell you what gender a noun is, but here are some handy tips to help you determine gender:
* gender is masculine when talking about a man and feminine when talking about a woman
* words ending in -*o* are often masculine
* words ending in -*a* are often feminine
* words ending in -*d*, -*z* or -*ión* are usually feminine

See also **a/an & some**, **describing things**, **possession** and **the**.

have

I have two brothers.

Tengo dos hermanos.　　　　　ten·go dos er·ma·nos
(lit: I-have two brothers)

Possession can be indicated in various ways in Spanish. The easiest way is by using the verb *tener*, 'have'.

I	have	a ticket	*yo*	*tengo*	*un billete*
you sg inf	have	the key	*tú*	*tienes*	*la llave*
you sg pol	have	the key	*Usted*	*tiene*	*la llave*
he/she	has	aspirin	*él/ella* m/f	*tiene*	*aspirinas*
we	have	matches	*nosotros/as* m/f	*tenemos*	*cerillas*
you pl inf	have	tapas	*vosotros/as* m/f	*tenéis*	*tapas*
you pl pol	have	tapas	*Ustedes*	*tienen*	*tapas*
they	have	problems	*ellos/as* m/f	*tienen*	*problemas*

See also **my & your** and **somebody's**.

is & are see be

location see this & that

more than one

I'd like two tickets.

Quisiera dos billetes.　　　　　kee·sye·ra dos bee·lye·tes
(lit: I-would-like two tickets)

In general, if the word ends in a vowel, you add *-s* for a plural. If the noun ends in a consonant (or *y*), you add *-es*:

| bed | *cama* | *ka·ma* | beds | *camas* | *ka·mas* |
| woman | *mujer* | *moo·kher* | women | *mujeres* | *moo·khe·res* |

my & your

This is my daughter.
  Ésta es mi hija.   es·ta es mee ee·kha
  (lit: this is my daughter)

A common way of indicating possession is by using possessive adjectives before the noun they describe. As with any other adjective, they always agree with the noun in number (singular or plural) and gender (masculine or feminine).

	singular		plural	
	masculine	**feminine**	**masculine**	**feminine**
	gift	**room**	**friends**	**glasses**
my	*mi regalo*	*mi habitación*	*mis amigos*	*mis gafas*
your sg inf	*tu regalo*	*tu habitación*	*tus amigos*	*tus gafas*
your sg pol	*su regalo*	*su habitación*	*sus amigos*	*sus gafas*
his/her/its	*su regalo*	*su habitación*	*sus amigos*	*sus gafas*
our	*nuestro regalo*	*nuestra habitación*	*nuestros amigos*	*nuestras gafas*
your pl inf	*vuestro regalo*	*vuestra habitación*	*vuestros amigos*	*vuestras gafas*
your pl pol	*su regalo*	*su habitación*	*sus amigos*	*sus gafas*
their	*su regalo*	*su habitación*	*sus amigos*	*sus gafas*

See also **have** & **somebody's**.

negative

Just add the word *no* before the main verb of the sentence:

I'm not going to try the speciality.
>*No voy a probar*   no voy a pro·*bar*
>*la especialidad.*   la es·peth·ya·lee·*da*
>(lit: not I-go to try
>the speciality)

planning ahead

As in English, you can talk about your plans or future events by using the verb *ir* (go) followed by the word *a* (to) and the infinitive of another verb, for example:

Tomorrow, I'm going to travel to Madrid.
>*Mañana, yo voy a viajar*   ma·*nya*·na yo voy a vya·*jar*
>*a Madrid.*   a ma·*dree*
>(lit: tomorrow I go to travel
>to Madrid)

I	am going	to call	yo	voy	a llamar
you sg inf	are going	to sleep	tú	vas	a dormir
you sg pol	are going	to dance	Usted	va	a bailar
he/she	is going	to drink	él/ella m/f	va	a beber
we	are going	to sing	nosotros/as m/f	vamos	a cantar
you pl inf	are going	to eat	vosotros/as m/f	vais	a comer
you pl pol	are going	to write	Ustedes	van	a escribir
they	are going	to learn	ellos/as m/f	van	a aprender

plural see more than one

pointing something out

To point something out, the easiest phrases to use are *es* (it is), *esto es* (this is) or *eso es* (that is).

Es una guía de Sevilla.	es *oo*·na *gee*·a de se·*vee*·lya	It's a guide to Seville.
Esto es mi pasaporte.	es·to es mee pa·sa·*por*·te	This is my passport.
Eso es gazpacho.	e·so es gath·*pa*·cho	That is gazpacho.

See also **this & that**.

possession see have, my & your and somebody's

questions

Is this the right stop?
Es esta la parada?   es es·ta la pa·*ra*·da
(lit: is this the stop)

When asking a question, simply make a statement, but raise your intonation towards the end of the sentence, as you can do in English. The inverted question mark in written Spanish prompts you to do this.

question words		
Who?	*¿Quién?* sg	kyen
	¿Quiénes? pl	*kye*·nes
Who is it?	*¿Quién es?*	kyen es
Who are those men?	*¿Quiénes son estos hombres?*	*kye*·nes son es·tos *om*·bres
What?	*¿Qué?*	ke
What are you saying?	*¿Qué está Usted diciendo?* pol	ke es·*ta* oo·*ste* dee·*thyen*·do

Which?	¿Cuál? sg ¿Cuáles? pl	kwal kwa·les
Which restaurant is the cheapest?	¿Cuál restaurante es el más barato?	kwal res·tow·ran·te es el mas ba·ra·to
Which local dishes do you recommend?	¿Cuáles platos típicos puedes recomendar?	kwa·les pla·tos tee·pee·kos pwe·des re·ko·men·dar
When?	¿Cuándo?	kwan·do
When does the next bus arrive?	¿Cuándo llega el próximo autobús?	kwan·do lye·ga el prok·see·mo ow·to·boos
Where?	¿Dónde?	don·de
Where can I buy tickets?	¿Dónde puedo comprar billetes?	don·de pwe·do kom·prar bee·lye·tes
How?	¿Cómo?	ko·mo
How do you say this in Spanish?	¿Cómo se dice ésto en español?	ko·mo se dee·the es·to en es·pa·nyol
How much?	¿Cuánto?	kwan·to
How much is it?	¿Cuánto cuesta?	kwan·to kwes·ta
How many?	¿Cuantos?	kwan·tos
For how many nights?	¿Por cuántas noches?	por kwan·tas no·ches
Why?	¿Por qué?	por ke
Why is the museum closed?	¿Por qué está cerrado el museo?	por ke es·ta the·ra·do el moo·se·o

some see a/an & some

somebody's

In Spanish, ownership is expressed through the word *de* (of).

That's my friend's backpack.

Esa es la mochila de mi amigo.
(lit: that is the backpack of my friend)

e·sa es la mo·*chee*·la de mee a·*mee*·go

See also **have** and **my & your**.

this & that

There are three 'distance words' in Spanish, depending on whether something is close (this), away from you (that) or even further away in time or distance (that over there).

masculine	singular	plural
close	*éste* (this)	*éstos* (these)
away	*ése* (that)	*ésos* (those)
further away	*aquél* (that over there)	*aquéllos* (those over there)
feminine		
close	*ésta* (this)	*éstas* (these)
away	*ésa* (that)	*ésas* (those)
further away	*aquélla* (that over there)	*aquéllas* (those over there)

See also **pointing something out**.

the

The Spanish articles *el* and *la* both mean 'the'. Whether you use *el* or *la* depends on the gender of the thing, person or idea talked about, which in Spanish will always be either masculine or feminine. The gender is not really concerned with the sex of something, for example a fox is a masculine noun, even if it's female! There's no rule as to why, say, the sea is masculine but the beach is feminine.

When talking about plural things, people or ideas, you use *los* in stead of *el* and *las* instead of *la*.

	singular	plural
masculine	*el*	*los*
feminine	*la*	*las*

el coche	el *ko·*che	the car
los coches	los *ko·*ches	the cars
la tienda	la *tyen·*da	the shop
las tiendas	las *tyen·*das	the shops

See also **gender** and **a/an** & **some**.

word order

Sentences in Spanish have a basic word order of subject-verb-object, just as English does.

I study business.

Yo estudio comercio.   yo es·*too·*dyo ko·*mer·*thyo
(lit: I study business)

However, Spanish often omits a subject pronoun: '*Estudio comercio*' is enough.

yes/no questions

It's not impolite to answer questions with a simple *sí* (yes) or *no* (no) in Spanish. There's no way to say 'Yes it is/does', or 'No, it isn't/doesn't'.

See also **questions**.

you

When talking to people familiar to you or younger than you, it's usual to use the informal form of you, *tú*, too, rather than the polite form, *Usted*, oo·*ste*. The plural versions are we, *vosotros/vosotras*, vo·so·*tros*/vo·so·*tras* and (all of) you, *Ustedes*, oo·*ste*·des. Phrases in this book use the form of 'you' that is appropriate to the situation.

For more on polite language, see the box in **business**, page 77.

m (masculine) or f (feminine)?

In this book, masculine forms appear before the feminine forms. If you see a word ending in -o/a, it means the masculine form ends in -o, and the feminine form ends in -a, (that is, you replace the -o ending with the -a ending to make it feminine). The same goes for the endings -os/as (the plural endings). If you see an (a) between brackets on the end of a word, it means you have to add it in order to make that word feminine. In other cases we spell out the whole word.

There are two words for 'Spanish': *español* and *castellano*. *Español* is used in Spain, whereas *castellano* is more likely to be used by South Americans.

I speak a little Spanish.
 *Hablo un poco de
 español.*
 ab·lo oon po·ko de
 es·pa·nyol

Do you speak English?
 ¿Habla inglés?
 ab·la een·gles

Does anyone speak English?
 *¿Hay alguien que hable
 inglés?*
 ai al·gyen ke ab·le
 een·gles

Do you understand?
 ¿Me entiende?
 me en·tyen·de

I (don't) understand.
 (No) Entiendo.
 (no) een·tyen·do

How do you pronounce this word?
 *¿Cómo se pronuncia
 esta palabra?*
 ko·mo se pro·noon·thya
 es·ta pa·lab·ra

How do you write 'ciudad'?
 *¿Cómo se escribe
 'ciudad'?*
 ko·mo se es·kree·be
 thee·oo·da

What does ... mean?
 ¿Qué significa ...?
 ke seeg·nee·fee·ka ...

Could you repeat that?
 ¿Puedes repetir?
 pwe·des re·pe·teer

listen for ...		
ko·mo	*¿Cómo?*	**Pardon?**
no	*No.*	**No.**
see	*Sí.*	**Yes.**

Could you please ...?	¿Puedes ... por favor?	pwe·des ... por fa·vor
speak more slowly	hablar más despacio	ab·lar mas des·pa·thyo
write it down	escribirlo	es·kree·beer·lo

dirty latin

Over the last 500 years, the Spanish spoken in Latin America has developed differently to the Spanish spoken in Europe. Variations in pronunciation, vocabulary and even grammar can lead to confusion or embarrassment. Here are two examples that could get you into trouble.

Quiero coger el autobús.
I want to catch the bus.
   (Latin America: I want to bonk the bus.)

Hay un gran bicho en el baño.
There's a huge bug in the bathroom.
   (Latin America: There's a big prick in the bathroom.)

cardinal numbers

		los números cardinales
0	*cero*	*the·*ro
1	*uno*	*oo·*no
2	*dos*	dos
3	*tres*	tres
4	*cuatro*	*kwa·*tro
5	*cinco*	*theen·*ko
6	*seis*	seys
7	*siete*	*sye·*te
8	*ocho*	*o·*cho
9	*nueve*	*nwe·*ve
10	*diez*	dyeth
11	*once*	*on·*the
12	*doce*	*do·*the
13	*trece*	*tre·*the
14	*catorce*	ka·*tor·*the
15	*quince*	*keen·*the
16	*dieciséis*	dye·thee·*seys*
17	*diecisiete*	dye·thee·*sye·*te
18	*dieciocho*	dye·thee·*o·*cho
19	*diecinueve*	dye·thee·*nwe·*ve
20	*veinte*	*veyn·*te
21	*veintiuno*	veyn·tee·*oo·*no
22	*veintidós*	veyn·tee·*dos*
30	*treinta*	*treyn·*ta
40	*cuarenta*	kwa·*ren·*ta
50	*cincuenta*	theen·*kwen·*ta
60	*sesenta*	se·*sen·*ta
70	*setenta*	se·*ten·*ta
80	*ochenta*	o·*chen·*ta
90	*noventa*	no·*ven·*ta
100	*cien*	thyen

101	ciento uno	thyen·to oo·no
102	ciento dos	thyen·to dos
500	quinientos	kee·nyen tos
1,000	mil	mil
1,000,000	un millón	oon mee·lyon

ordinal numbers

los números ordinales

1st	primero/a m/f	pree·me·ro/a
2nd	segundo/a m/f	se·goon·do/a
3rd	tercero/a m/f	ter·the·ro/a
4th	cuarto/a m/f	kwar·to/a
5th	quinto/a m/f	keen·to/a

fractions

las fracciones

a quarter	un cuarto	oon kwar·to
a third	un tercio	oon ter·thyo
a half	un medio	oon me·dyo
three-quarters	tres cuartos	tres kwar·tos
all	todo	to·do
none	nada	na·da

amounts

las cantidades

a little	un poquito	oon po·kee·to
many	muchos/as m/f	moo·chos/as
some	algunos/as m/f	al·goo·nos/as
more	más	mas
less	menos	me·nos

time & dates
la hora & la fecha

telling the time

English	Spanish	Pronunciation
What time is it?	*¿Qué hora es?*	ke o·ra es
It's (one) o'clock.	*Es (la una).*	es (la oo·na)
It's (ten) o'clock.	*Son (las diez).*	son (las dyeth)
Quarter past one.	*Es la una y cuarto.*	es la oo·na ee kwar·to
Twenty past one.	*Es la una y veinte.*	es la oo·na ee veyn·te
Half past one.	*Es la una y media.*	es la oo·na ee me·dya
Twenty to one.	*Es la una menos veinte.*	es la oo·na me·nos veyn·te
Quarter to one.	*Es la una menos cuarto.*	es la oo·na me·nos kwar·to
It's early.	*Es temprano.*	es tem·pra·no
It's late.	*Es tarde.*	es tar·de
am	*de la mañana*	de la ma·nya·na
pm	*de la tarde*	de la tar·de

days of the week

English	Spanish	Pronunciation
Monday	*lunes*	loo·nes
Tuesday	*martes*	mar·tes
Wednesday	*miércoles*	myer·ko·les
Thursday	*jueves*	khwe·ves
Friday	*viernes*	vyer·nes
Saturday	*sábado*	sa·ba·do
Sunday	*domingo*	do·meen·go

time & dates

31

the calendar

> months

January	*enero*	e·*ne*·ro
February	*febrero*	fe·*bre*·ro
March	*marzo*	*mar*·tho
April	*abril*	a·*breel*
May	*mayo*	*ma*·yo
June	*junio*	*khoo*·nyo
July	*julio*	*khoo*·lyo
August	*agosto*	a·*gos*·to
September	*septiembre*	sep·*tyem*·bre
October	*octubre*	ok·*too*·bre
November	*noviembre*	no·*vyem*·bre
December	*diciembre*	dee·*thyem*·bre

> seasons

summer	*verano*	ve·*ra*·no
autumn	*otoño*	o·*to*·nyo
winter	*invierno*	een·*vyer*·no
spring	*primavera*	pree·ma·*ve*·ra

dates

What date?
¿Qué día?   ke *dee*·a

What date is it today?
¿Qué día es hoy?   ke *dee*·a es oy

It's (18 October).
Es (el dieciocho de   es (el dye·thee·o·cho de
octubre).   ok·*too*·bre)

present

now	*ahora*	a·o·ra
right now	*ahora mismo*	a·o·ra *mees*·mo
this ...		
afternoon	*esta tarde*	es·ta *tar*·de
month	*este mes*	es·te mes
morning	*esta mañana*	es·ta ma·*nya*·na
week	*esta semana*	es·ta se·*ma*·na
year	*este año*	es·te *a*·nyo
today	*hoy*	oy
tonight	*esta noche*	es·ta *no*·che

past

el pasado

... ago	*hace ...*	a·the ...
(three) days	*(tres) días*	(tres) *dee*·as
half an hour	*media hora*	*me*·dya o·ra
a while	*un rato*	un *ra*·to
(five) years	*(cinco) años*	(*theen*·ko) *a*·nyos
day before yesterday	*anteayer*	an·te·a·*yer*
last ...		
month	*el mes pasado*	el mes pa·*sa*·do
night	*anoche*	a·*no*·che
week	*la semana pasada*	la se·*ma*·na pa·*sa*·da
year	*el año pasado*	el *a*·nyo pa·*sa*·do
since (May)	*desde (mayo)*	*des*·de (*ma*·yo)
yesterday	*ayer*	a·*yer*
yesterday ...	*ayer por la ...*	a·*yer* por la ...
afternoon	*tarde*	*tar*·de
evening	*noche*	*no*·che
morning	*mañana*	ma·*nya*·na

future

in ...	dentro de ...	den·tro de ...
(six) days	(seis) días	(seys) dee·as
an hour	una hora	oo·na o·ra
(five) minutes	(cinco)	(theen·ko)
	minutos	mee·noo·tos
a month	un mes	oon mes
next ...	... que viene	... ke vye·ne
month	el mes	el mes
week	la semana	la se·ma·na
year	el año	el a·nyo
tomorrow	mañana	ma·nya·na
day after	pasado	pa·sa·do
tomorrow	mañana	ma·nya·na
tomorrow ...	mañana por la ...	ma·nya·na por la ...
afternoon	tarde	tar·de
evening	noche	no·che
morning	mañana	ma·nya·na
until (June)	hasta (junio)	as·ta (khoo·nyo)

during the day

durante el día

afternoon	tarde f	tar·de
dawn	madrugada f	ma·droo·ga·da
day	día m	dee·a
evening	noche f	no·che
midday	mediodía m	me·dyo·dee·a
midnight	medianoche f	me·dya·no·che
morning	mañana f	ma·nya·na
night	noche f	no·che
sunrise	amanecer m	a·ma·ne·ther
sunset	puesta f del sol	pwes·ta del sol

Where's the nearest ATM?
¿Dónde está el cajero automático más cercano?
don·de es·ta el ka·khe·ro ow·to·ma·tee·ko mas ther·ka·no

Can I use my credit card to withdraw money?
¿Puedo usar mi tarjeta de crédito para sacar dinero?
pwe·do oo·sar mee tar·khe·ta de kre·dee·to pa·ra sa·kar dee·ne·ro

What's the exchange rate?
¿Cuál es el tipo de cambio?
kwal es el tee·po de kam·byo

What's the charge for that?
¿Cuánto hay que pagar por eso?
kwan·to ai ke pa·gar por e·so

How much is this?
¿Cuánto cuesta esto?
kwan·to kwes·ta es·to

The price is too high.
Cuesta demasiado.
kwes·ta de·ma·sya·do

Can you lower the price?
¿Podría bajar un poco el precio?
po·dree·a ba·khar oon po·ko el pre·thyo

I'd like to change ...	Me gustaría cambiar ...	me goos·ta·ree·a kam·byar ...
money	dinero	dee·ne·ro
a travellers cheque	un cheque de viajero	oon che·ke de vya·khe·ro

Do you accept ...?	*¿Aceptan ...?*	a·*thep*·tan ...
credit cards	*tarjetas de crédito*	tar·*khe*·tas de kre·dee·to
debit cards	*tarjetas de débito*	tar·*khe*·tas de de·bee·to
travellers cheques	*cheques de viajero*	che·kes de vya·*khe*·ro

Do I need to pay up front?
¿Necesito pagar por adelantado?
ne·the·*see*·to pa·*gar* por a·de·lah·*ta*·do

Could I have a receipt please?
¿Podría darme un recibo por favor?
po·*dree*·a dar·me oon re·*thee*·bo por fa·*vor*

I'd like my money back.
Quisiera que me devuelva el dinero.
kee·*sye*·ra ke me de·*vwel*·va el dee·*ne*·ro

getting around

desplazándose

What time does the ... leave?	¿A qué hora sale el ...?	a ke o·ra sa·le el ...
boat	barco	bar·ko
bus (city)	autobús	ow·to·boos
bus (intercity)	autocar	ow·to·kar
plane	avión	a·vyon
train	tren	tren
tram	tranvía	tran·vee·a
What time's the ... (bus)?	¿A qué hora es el ... (autobús)?	a ke o·ra es el ... (ow·to·boos)
first	primer	pree·mer
last	último	ool·tee·mo
next	próximo	prok·see·mo
I'd like a/an ... seat.	Quisiera un asiento ...	kee·sye·ra oon a·syen·to ...
aisle	de pasillo	de pa·see·lyo
non-smoking	de no fumadores	de no foo·ma·do·res
smoking	de fumadores	de foo·ma·do·res
window	junto a la ventana	khoon·to a la ven·ta·na

asking for an address

What's the/your address?
¿Cuál es la/su dirección?		kwal es la/soo dee·rek·thyon
avenue	avenida f	a·ve·nee·da
lane	callejón m	ka·lye·khon
street	calle f	ka·lye

Is there (a) ...?	*¿Hay ...?*	ai ...
air-conditioning	*aire acon-*	*ai*·re a·kon·
	dicionado	dee·thyo·*na*·do
blanket	*una manta*	oo·na *man*·ta
toilet	*servicios*	ser·*vee*·thyos
video	*vídeo*	*vee*·de·o

The ... is delayed/cancelled.
El ... está retrasado/   el ... es·*ta* re·tra·*sa*·do/
cancelado.   kan·the·*la*·do

How long will it be delayed?
¿Cuánto tiempo se   *kwan*·to *tyem*·po se
retrasará?   re·tra·sa·*ra*

Is this seat free?
¿Está libre este asiento?   es·*ta lee*·bre *es*·te a·*syen*·to

That's my seat.
Ése es mi asiento.   *e*·se es mee a·*syen*·to

Can you tell me when we get to ...?
¿Me podría decir   me po·*dree*·a de·*theer*
cuándo lleguemos a ...?   *kwan*·do lye·*ge*·mos a ...

I want to get off here!
¡Quiero bajarme aquí!   *kye*·ro ba·*khar*·me a·*kee*

buying tickets

comprando billetes

Do I need to book?
¿Tengo que reservar?   *ten*·go ke re·ser·*var*

How much is it?
¿Cuánto cuesta?   *kwan*·to *kwes*·ta

Where can I buy a ticket?
¿Dónde puedo comprar   *don·de pwe·do kom·prar*
un billete?   oon bee·*lye*·te

It's full.
Está completo.   es·*ta* kom·*ple*·to

How long does the trip take?
¿Cuánto se tarda?   *kwan*·to se *tar*·da

Is it a direct route?
¿Es un viaje directo?   es oon *vya*·khe dee·*rek*·to

Can I get a stand-by ticket?
¿Puede ponerme en la   *pwe*·de po·*ner*·me en la
lista de espera?   *lees*·ta de es·*pe*·ra

I'd like to ...	*Me gustaría ...*	me goos·ta·*ree*·a ...
my ticket.	*mi billete.*	mee bee·*lye*·te
cancel	*cancelar*	kan·the·*lar*
change	*cambiar*	kam·*byar*
confirm	*confirmar*	kon·feer·*mar*

A one-way ticket to (Barcelona).
Un billete sencillo   oon bee·*lye*·te sen·*thee*·lyo
a (Barcelona).   a (bar·the·*lo*·na)

Two ... tickets,	*Dos billetes ...,*	dos bee·*lye*·tes ...
please.	*por favor.*	por fa·*vor*
child's	*infantil*	een·fan·*teel*
return	*de ida y vuelta*	de *ee*·da ee *vwel*·ta
student's	*de estudiante*	de es·too·*dyan*·te
1st-class	*de primera clase*	de pree·*me*·ra *kla*·se
2nd-class	*de segunda clase*	de se·*goon*·da *kla*·se

luggage

el equipaje

My luggage has been ...	Mis maletas han sido ...	mees ma·*le*·tas an *see*·do ...
damaged	dañadas	da·*nya*·das
lost	perdidas	per·*dee*·das
stolen	robadas	ro·*ba*·das

My luggage hasn't arrived.
Mis maletas se han perdido.
mees ma·*le*·tas se an per·*dee*·do

I'd like a luggage locker.
Quisiera un casillero de consigna.
kee·*sye*·ra oon ka·see·*lye*·ro de kon·*seeg*·na

Can I have some coins/tokens?
¿Me podía dar monedas/fichas?
me po·*dee*·a dar mo·*ne*·das/*fee*·chas

plane

el avión

When's the next flight to ...?
¿Cuándo sale el próximo vuelo para ...?
kwan·do *sa*·le el *prok*·see·mo *vwe*·lo *pa*·ra ...

What time do I have to check in?
¿A qué hora tengo que facturar mi equipaje?
a ke *o*·ra *ten*·go ke fak·too·*rar* mee e·kee·*pa*·khe

bus

el autobús

Which city/intercity bus goes to ...?
¿Qué autobús/autocar   ke ow·to·*boos*/ow·to·*kar*
va a ...?   va a ...

This/That one.
Éste/Ése.   es·te/e·se

Bus number ...
El autobús número ...   el ow·to·*boos* noo·me·ro ...

Please tell me when we get to ...
¿Puede avisarme   pwe·de a·vee·*sar*·me
cuando lleguemos a ...?   kwan·do lye·*ge*·mos a ...

train

el tren

What station is this?
¿Cuál es esta estación?   kwal es *es*·ta es·ta·*thyon*

What's the next station?
¿Cuál es la próxima   kwal es la *prok*·see·ma
estación?   es·ta·*thyon*

Does this train stop at (Madrid)?
¿Para el tren en (Madrid)?   pa·ra el tren en (ma·*dree*)

Do I need to change trains?
¿Tengo que cambiar de tren?   ten·go ke kam·*byar* de tren

Which carriage is ...?	*¿Cuál es el coche ...?*	kwal es el *ko*·che ...
1st class	*de primera clase*	de pree·*me*·ra *kla*·se
for (Madrid)	*para (Madrid)*	pa·ra (ma·*dree*)
for dining	*comedor*	ko·me·*dor*

boat

el barco

Are there life jackets?
¿Hay chalecos salvavidas?   ai cha·*le*·kos sal·va·*vee*·das

What's the sea like today?
¿Cómo está el mar hoy?   *ko*·mo es·*ta* el mar oy

I feel seasick.
Estoy mareado.   es·*toy* ma·re·a·do

taxi

el taxi

I'd like a taxi ...	*Quisiera un taxi ...*	kee·*sye*·ra oon *tak*·see ...
at (9am)	*a (las nueve de la mañana)*	a (las *nwe*·ve de la ma·*nya*·na)
now	*ahora*	a·o·ra
tomorrow	*mañana*	ma·*nya*·na

Is this taxi free?
¿Está libre este taxi?   es·*ta lee*·bre es·te *tak*·see

Please put the meter on.
Por favor, ponga el taxímetro.   por fa·*vor pon*·ga el tak·*see*·me·tro

How much is it to ...?
¿Cuánto cuesta ir a ...?   *kwan*·to *kwes*·ta eer a ...

Please take me to (this address).
Por favor, lléveme a (esta dirección).   por fa·*vor lye*·ve·me a (es·ta dee·rek·*thyon*)

I'm really late.
Voy con mucho retraso.   voy kon *moo*·cho re·*tra*·so

How much is the final fare?
¿Cuánto es en total?   *kwan*·to es en to·*tal*

Please ...	*Por favor ...*	por fa·*vor* ...
slow down	*vaya más*	*va*·ya mas
	despacio	des·*pa*·thyo
wait here	*espere aquí*	es·*pe*·re a·*kee*
Stop ...!	*¡Pare ,,,!*	*pa*·re
at the corner	*en la esquina*	en la es·*kee*·na
here	*aquí*	a·*kee*

car & motorbike hire

alquiler de coches & motos

Where can I hire a ...?
¿Dónde se puede   *don*·de se *pwe*·de
alquilar ...?   al·*kee*·lar ...

Does that include insurance/mileage?
¿Incluye el seguro/   een·*kloo*·ye el se·*goo*·ro/
kilometraje?   kee·lo·me·*tra*·khe

I'd like to	*Quisiera*	kee·*sye*·ra
hire a/an ...	*alquilar ...*	al·*kee*·lar ...
4WD	*un todoterreno*	oon to·do·te·*re*·no
automatic car	*un coche*	oon *ko*·che
	automático	ow·to·*ma*·tee·ko
manual car	*un coche*	oon *ko*·che
	manual	ma·*nwal*
motorbike	*una moto*	*oo*·na *mo*·to

with ...	*con ...*	kon ...
air conditioning	*aire acon-*	*ai*·re a·kon·
	dicionado	dee·thyo·*na*·do
a driver	*chófer*	*cho*·fer

How much for	*¿Cuánto cuesta*	*kwan*·to *kwes*·ta
... hire?	*el alquiler por ...?*	el al·*kee*·ler por ...
daily	*día*	*dee*·a
hourly	*hora*	*o*·ra
weekly	*semana*	se·*ma*·na

transport

43

on the road

Is this the road to ...?
   ¿Se va a ... por esta   se va a ... por es·ta
   carretera?   ka·re·te·ra

Where's a petrol station?
   ¿Dónde hay una   don·de ai oo·na
   gasolinera?   ga·so·lee·ne·ra

What's the ...	*¿Cuál es el límite*	kwal es el *lee*·mee·te
speed limit?	*de velocidad ...?*	de ve·lo·thee·*da* ...
city	*en la ciudad*	en la thyoo·*da*
country	*en el campo*	en el *kam*·po

signs

Acceso	ak·*the*·so	**Entrance**
Aparcamiento	a·par·ka·*myen*·to	**Parking**
Ceda el Paso	*the*·da el *pa*·so	**Give Way**
Desvío	des·*vee*·o	**Detour**
Dirección Única	dee·rek·*thyon* oo·nee·ka	**One Way**
Frene	*fre*·ne	**Slow Down**
Peaje	pe·*a*·khe	**Toll**
Peligro	pe·*lee*·gro	**Danger**
Prohibido Aparcar	pro·ee·*bee*·do a·par·*kar*	**No Parking**
Prohibido el Paso	pro·ee·*bee*·do el *pa*·so	**No Entry**
Stop	es·*top*	**Stop**
Vía de Acceso	*vee*·a de ak·*the*·so	**Exit Freeway**

Please fill it up.
Por favor, lléneme el depósito.
por fa·*vor* lye·ne·me el de·*po*·see·to

I'd like (20) litres of ...
Quiero (veinte) litros de ...
kye·ro (veyn·te) lee·tros de ...

petrol (gas)	*gasolina*	ga·so·*lee*·na
diesel	*diesel*	*dye*·sel
leaded (regular)	*gasolina normal*	ga·so·*lee*·na nor·*mal*
unleaded	*gasolina sin plomo*	ga·so·*lee*·na seen *plo*·mo

Please check the ...	*Por favor, revise ...*	por fa·*vor* re·*vee*·se ...
oil	*el nivel del aceite*	el nee·*vel* del a·*they*·te
tyre pressure	*la presión de los neumáticos*	la pre·*syon* de los ne·oo·*ma*·tee·kos
water	*el nivel del agua*	nee·vel del a·gwa

petrol
gasolina f
ga·so·*lee*·na

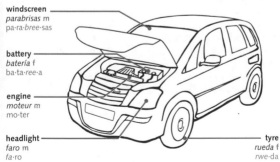

windscreen
parabrisas m
pa·ra·*bree*·sas

battery
batería f
ba·ta·*ree*·a

engine
moteur m
mo·ter

headlight
faro m
fa·ro

tyre
rueda f
rwe·da

de ke *mar*·ka es
¿*De qué marca es?*   **What make/model is it?**

(How long) Can I park here?
¿*(Por cuánto tiempo)*   (por kwan·to *tyem*·po)
Puedo aparcar aquí?   pwe·do a·par·*kar* a·*kee*

Where do I pay?
¿*Dónde se paga?*   *don*·de se pa·ga

problems

problemas

I need a mechanic.
Necesito un/una   ne·the·*see*·to oon/*oo*·na
mecánico/a. m/f   me·*ka*·nee·ko/a

The car has broken down (at ...).
El coche se ha averiado   el *ko*·che se a a·ve·*rya*·do
(en ...).   (en ...)

I had an accident.
He tenido un   e te·*nee*·do oon
accidente.   ak·thee·*den*·te

The motorbike won't start.
No arranca la moto.   no a·*ran*·ka la *mo*·to

I have a flat tyre.
Tengo un pinchazo.   *ten*·go oon peen·*cha*·tho

I've lost my car keys.
He perdido las llaves   e per·*dee*·do las *lya*·ves
de mi coche.   de mee *ko*·che

I've locked my keys inside.
He cerrado con las llaves   e the·*ra*·do kon las *lya*·ves
dentro.   *den*·tro

I've run out of petrol.
Me he quedado sin gasolina.
me e ke·*da*·do seen ga·so·*lee*·na

Can you fix it (today)?
¿Puede arreglarlo (hoy)?
pwe·de a·re·*glar*·lo (oy)

How long will it take?
¿Cuánto tardará?
kwan·to tar·da·*ra*

bicycle

la bicicleta

Where can I hire a bicycle?
¿Dónde se puede alquilar una bicicleta?
don·de se *pwe*·de al·kee·*lar* oo·na bee·thee·*kle*·ta

Where can I buy a (second-hand) bike?
¿Dónde se puede comprar una bicicleta (de segunda mano)?
don·de se *pwe*·de kom·*prar* oo·na bee·thee·*kle*·ta (de se·*goon*·da *ma*·no)

How much is it per ...?	*¿Cuánto cuesta por ...?*	*kwan*·to *kwes*·ta por ...
afternoon	*una tarde*	oo·na *tar*·de
day	*un día*	oon *dee*·a
hour	*una hora*	oo·na *o*·ra
morning	*una mañana*	oo·na ma·*nya*·na

I have a puncture.
Se me ha pinchado una rueda.
se me a peen·*cha*·do oo·na *rwe*·da

local transport

People usually walk around cities and municipalities, but if you want to catch a bus, you could ask:

Are you waiting for more people?

¿Está esperando a	es·ta es·pe·ran·do a
más gente?	mas khen·te

Can you take us around the city please?

¿Nos puede llevar por	nos pwe·de lye·var por
la ciudad?	la thyoo·da

For phrases on disabled access, see **disabled travellers**, page 85.

signs

Aduana	a·dwa·na	**Customs**
Artículos	ar·tee·koo·los	**Duty-Free**
Libres de	lee·bres de	**Goods**
Impuestos	eem·pwes·tos	
Salida	sa·lee·da	**Exit/Way Out**
Control de	con·trol de	**Passport**
Pasaporte	pa·sa·por·te	**Control**

passport control

control de pasaporte

listen for ...

soo ... por fa·*vor*	*Su ... por favor.*	**Your ... please.**
pa·sa·*por*·te	*pasaporte*	**passport**
vee·*sa*·do	*visado*	**visa**
es·*ta*	*¿Está*	**Are you**
vya·*khan*·do ...	*viajando ...?*	**travelling ...?**
en oon *groo*·po	*en un grupo*	**in a group**
kon *oo*·na	*con una*	**with a family**
fa·*mee*·lya	*familia*	
so·lo	*solo*	**on your own**

I'm here ...	*Estoy aquí ...*	es·*toy* a·*kee* ...
on business	*de negocios*	de ne·*go*·thyos
on holiday	*de vacaciones*	de va·ka·*thyo*·nes
in transit	*en tránsito*	en *tran*·see·to
I'm here for ...	*Estoy aquí por ...*	es·*toy* a·*kee* por ...
days	*días*	*dee*·as
months	*meses*	*me*·ses
weeks	*semanas*	se·*ma*·nas

customs

I have nothing to declare.
*No tengo nada que
declarar.*

no *ten*·go *na*·da ke
de·kla·*rar*

I have something to declare.
Quisiera declarar algo.

kee·sye·ra de·kla·*rar al*·go

I didn't know I had to declare it.
*No sabía que tenía
que declararlo.*

no sa·*bee*·a ke te·*nee*·a
ke de·kla·*rar*·lo

filling in forms

Apellido(s)	surname(s) – many Spanish use two surnames, their father's and their mother's
Domicilio	address (residence)
Exp. en	issued at
Fecha	date
Fecha di nacimiento	date of birth
Firma	signature
Lugar de nacimiento	place of birth
Nacionalidad	nationality
Nombre	given name
Pasaporte	passport
Profesión	occupation

finding accommodation

buscando alojamiento

Where's a ...?	¿Dónde hay ...?	don·de ai ...
bed & breakfast	una pensión con desayuno	oo·na pen·syon kon de·sa·yoo·no
camping ground	terreno de cámping	te·re·no de kam·peeng
guesthouse	una pensión	oo·na pen·syon
hotel	un hotel	oon o·tel
youth hostel	un albergue juvenil	oon al·ber·ge khoo·ve·neel

Can you recommend somewhere ...?	¿Puede recomendar algún sitio ...?	pwe·de re·ko·men·dar al·goon see·tio ...
cheap	barato	ba·ra·to
nice	agradable	a·gra·da·ble
luxurious	de lujo	de loo·kho
nearby	cercano	ther·ka·no
romantic	romántico	ro·man·tee·ko

What's the address?
¿Cuál es la dirección?   kwal es la dee·rek·thyon

For more on how to get there, see **directions**, page 61.

local talk

dive	tugurio m	too·goo·ryo
rat-infested	plagado de ratas	pla·ga·do de ra·tas
top spot	lugar m guay	loo·gar gwai

booking ahead & checking in

haciendo una reserva & registrándose

I'd like to book a room, please.
Quisiera reservar una habitación.
kee·sye·ra re·ser·var oo·na a·bee·ta·thyon

I have a reservation.
He hecho una reserva.
e e·cho oo·na re·ser·va

My name's ...
Me llamo ...
me lya·mo ...

For (three) nights/weeks.
Por (tres) noches/ semanas.
por (tres) no·ches/ se·ma·nas

From (July 2) to (July 6).
Desde (el dos de julio) hasta (el seis de julio).
des·de (el dos de khoo·lyo) as·ta (el seys de khoo·lyo)

Do I need to pay upfront?
¿Necesito pagar por adelantado?
ne·the·see·to pa·gar por a·de·lan·ta·do

listen for ...

lo *syen*·to es·ta kom·*ple*·to *Lo siento, está completo.*	I'm sorry, we're full.
por *kwan*·tas *no*·ches *¿Por cuántas noches?*	For how many nights?
soo pa·sa·*por*·te por fa·*vor* *Su pasaporte, por favor.*	Your passport, please.

How much is it per ...?	¿Cuánto cuesta por ...?	kwan·to kwes·ta por ...
night	noche	no·che
person	persona	per·so·na
week	semana	se·ma·na
Can I pay by ...?	¿Puedo pagar con ...?	pwe·do pa·gar con ...
credit card	tarjeta de crédito	tar·khe·ta de kre·dee·to
travellers cheque	cheques de viajero	che·kes de vya·khe·ro

For other methods of payment, see **money**, page 35.

air-conditioning
aire acondicionado m
ai·re a·kon·dee·thyo·na·do

toilet
retrete m
re·tre·te

bed
cama f
ka·ma

key
llave f
lya·ve

TV
televisión f
te·le·vee·syon

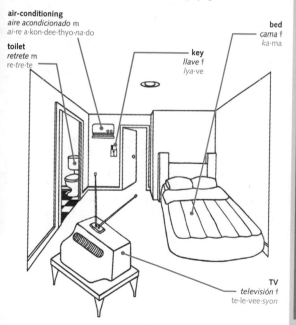

Do you have a ... room?	¿Tiene una habitación ...?	tye·ne oo·na a·bee·ta·thyon ...
double	doble	do·ble
single	individual	een·dee·vee·dwal
twin	con dos camas	kon dos ka·mas

with/without (a) ...	con/sin ...	kon/seen ...
Can I see it?	¿Puedo verla?	pwe·do ver·la
It's fine. I'll take it.	Vale, la alquilo.	va·le la al·kee·lo

requests & queries

las peticiones & las preguntas

When/Where's breakfast served?
¿Cuándo/Dónde se sirve el desayuno?
kwan·do/don·de se seer·ve el de·sa·yoo·no

Please wake me at (seven).
Por favor, despiérteme a (las siete).
por fa·vor des·pyer·te·me a (las sye·te)

Can I get another ...?
¿Puede darme otro/a ...? m/f
pwe·de dar·me o·tro/a ...

Can I use the ...?	¿Puedo usar ...?	pwe·do oo·sar ...
kitchen	la cocina	la ko·thee·na
laundry	el lavadero	el la·va·de·ro
telephone	el teléfono	el te·le·fo·no

Is there a/an ...?	¿Hay ...?	ai ...
lift (elevator)	ascensor	as·then·sor
message board	tablón de anuncios	ta·blon de a·noon·thyos
safe	una caja fuerte	oo·na ka·kha fwer·te
swimming pool	piscina	pees·thee·na

Do you ... here?	¿Aquí ...?	a·kee ...
arrange tours	organizan	or·ga·nee·than
	recorridos	re·ko·ree·dos
change money	cambian	kam·byan
	dinero	dee·ne·ro

Can I leave a message for someone?

¿Puedo dejar un mensaje para alguien?	pwe·do de·khar oon men·sa·khe pa·ra al·gyen

Is there a message for me?

¿Tiene un mensaje para mí?	tye·ne oon men·sa·khe pa·ra mee

I'm locked out of my room.

Cerré la puerta y se me olvidaron las llaves dentro.	the·re la pwer·ta y se me ol·vee·da·ron las lya·ves den·tro

The (bathroom) door is locked.

La puerta (del baño) está cerrada.	la pwer·ta (del ba·nyo) es·ta the·ra·da

accommodation

55

complaints

It's too ...	Es demasiado ...	es de·ma·sya·do ...
cold	fría f	free·a
dark	oscura f	os·koo·ra
expensive	cara f	ka·ra
light	clara f	kla·ra
noisy	ruidosa f	rwee·do·sa
small	pequeña f	pe·ke·nya

The ... doesn't work.	No funciona ...	no foon·thyo·na ...
air-conditioning	el aire acondicionado	el ai·re a·kon· dee·thyo·na·do
fan	el ventilador	el ven·tee·la·dor
toilet	el retrete	el re·tre·te
window	la ventana	la ven·ta·na

This ... isn't clean.
Éste/Ésta ... no está   es·te/es·ta ... no es·ta
limpio/a. m/f   leem·pyo/a

a knock at the door

Who is it?	¿Quién es?	kyen es
Just a moment.	Un momento.	oon mo·men·to
Come in.	Adelante.	a·de·lan·te

Can you come back later, please?
¿Puede volver más   pwe·de vol·ver mas
tarde, por favor?   tar·de por fa·vor

checking out

What time is check out?
¿A qué hora hay que dejar libre la habitación?
a ke o·ra ai ke de·*khar* lee·bre la a·bee·ta·*thyon*

How much extra to stay until (6 o'clock)?
¿Cuánto más cuesta quedarse hasta (las seis)?
kwan·to mas kwes·ta ke·*dar*·se *as*·ta (las seys)

Can I have a late check out?
¿Puedo dejar la habitación más tarde?
pwe·do de·*khar* la a·bee·ta·*thyon* mas *tar*·de

Can I leave my bags here?
¿Puedo dejar las maletas aquí?
pwe·do de·*khar* las ma·*le*·tas a·*kee*

There's a mistake in the bill.
Hay un error en la cuenta.
ai oon e·*ror* en la *kwen*·ta

I'm leaving now.
Me voy ahora.
me voy a·*o*·ra

Can you call a taxi for me (for 11 o'clock)?
¿Me puede pedir un taxi (para las once)?
me *pwe*·de pe·*deer* oon *tak*·see (*pa*·ra las *on*·the)

Could I have ..., please?	*¿Me puede dar ..., por favor?*	me *pwe*·de dar ... por fa·*vor*
my deposit	*mi depósito*	mee de·*po*·see·to
my passport	*mi pasaporte*	mee pa·sa·*por*·te
my valuables	*mis objetos de valor*	mees ob·*khe*·tos de va·*lor*
I'll be back ...	*Volveré ...*	vol·ve·*re* ...
in (three) days	*en (tres) días*	en (tres) *dee*·as
on (Tuesday)	*el (martes)*	el (*mar*·tes)

I had a great stay, thank you.
He tenido una estancia muy agradable, gracias.
e te·*nee*·do *oo*·na es·*tan*·thya mooy a·gra·*da*·ble gra·thyas

You've been terrific.
Han sido estupendos.
an *see*·do es·too·*pen*·dos

I'll recommend it to my friends.
Se lo recomendaré a mis amigos.
se lo re·ko·men·da·re a mees a·*mee*·gos

camping

Where's the nearest ...?	*¿Dónde está ...?*	*don·de es·ta ...*
camp site	*el terreno de cámping más cercano*	el te·*re*·no de *kam*·peeng mas ther·*ka*·no
shop	*la tienda más cercana*	la *tyen*·da mas ther·*ka*·na
I'm looking for the nearest ...	*Estoy buscando ...*	es·*toy* boos·*kan*·do ...
showers	*las duchas más cercanas*	las *doo*·chas mas ther·*ka*·nas
toilet block	*los servicios más cercanos*	los ser·*vee*·thyos mas ther·*ka*·nos

Is it coin-operated?
¿Funciona con monedas?
foon·*thyo*·na kon mo·*ne*·das

Is the water drinkable?
¿Se puede beber el agua?
se *pwe*·de *be*·ber el *a*·gwa

Can I ...?	*¿Se puede ...?*	se *pwe*·de ...
camp here	*acampar aquí*	a·kam·*par* a·*kee*
park next to my tent	*aparcar al lado de la tienda*	a·par·*kar* al *la*·do de la *tyen*·da

Do you have ...?	¿Tiene ...?	tye·ne ...
electricity	electricidad	e·lek·tree·thee·da
shower facilities	duchas	doo·chas
a site	un sitio	oon see·tyo
tents for hire	tiendas de	tyen·das de
	campaña para	kam·pa·nya pa·ra
	alquilar	al·kee·lar

How much is it per ...?	¿Cuánto vale por ...?	kwan·to va·le por ...
caravan	caravana	ka·ra·va·na
person	persona	per·so·na
tent	tienda	tyen·da
vehicle	vehículo	ve·ee·koo·lo

Whom do I ask to stay here?

¿Con quién tengo que hablar	kon kyen ten·go ke a·blar
para quedarme aquí?	pa·ra ke·dar·me a·kee

Could I borrow ...?

¿Me puede prestar ...?	me pwe·de pres·tar ...

For cooking utensils, see **self-catering**, page 155.

renting

Do you have a/an ... for rent?	¿Tiene ... para alquilar?	tye·ne ... pa·ra al·kee·lar·
apartment	un piso	oon pee·so
cabin	una cabaña	oo·na ka·ba·nya
house	una casa	oo·na ca·sa
room	una habitación	oo·na a·bee·ta·thyon
villa	un chalet	oon cha·le

furnished	amueblado/a m/f	a·mwe·bla·do/a
partly furnished	semi	se·mee
	amueblado/a m/f	a·mwe·bla·do/a
unfurnished	sin amueblar	seen a·mwe·blar

staying with locals

Can I stay at your place?
¿Me puedo quedar en tu casa?
me *pwe*·do ke·*dar* en too *ka*·sa

Can I help?
¿Puedo ayudar?
pwe·do a·yoo·*dar*

Can I use your telephone?
¿Puedo usar vuestra teléfono?
pwe·do oo·*sar* vwe·*stra* te·*le*·fo·no

Thanks for your hospitality.
Gracias por tu hospitalidad.
gra·thyas por too os·pee·ta·lee·*da*

I have my own ...	*Tengo mi propio ...*	*ten*·go mee *pro*·pyo ...
mattress	*colchón*	kol·*chon*
sleeping bag	*saco de dormir*	*sa*·ko de dor·*meer*

Can I ...?	*¿Puedo ...?*	*pwe*·do ...
bring anything for the meal	*traer algo para la comida*	tra·*er* al·go pa·ra la ko·*mee*·da
do the dishes	*lavar los platos*	la·*var* los *pla*·tos
set/clear the table	*poner/quitar la mesa*	po·*ner*/kee·*tar* la *me*·sa
take out the rubbish	*sacar la basura*	sa·*kar* la ba·*soo*·ra

For compliments to the chef, see **food**, page 147.

signs		
Caballeros	ka·ba·*lye*·ros	**Men**
Caliente	ka·*lyen*·te	**Hot**
Dirección Prohibida	dee·rek·*thyon* pro·hee·*bee*·da	**No Entry**
Frío	*free*·o	**Cold**
Señoras	se·*nyo*·ras	**Women**

Excuse me.
Perdone.
per·*do*·ne

Could you help me, please?
¿Perdone, puede
ayudarme por favor?
per·*do*·ne *pwe*·de
a·yoo·*dar*·me por fa·*vor*

Where's ...?
¿Dónde está ...?
don·de es·ta ...

I'm looking for ...
Busco ...
boos·ko ...

Which way is ...?
¿Por dónde se va a ...?
por *don*·de se va a ...

How can I get there?
¿Cómo se puede ir?
ko·mo se *pwe*·de eer

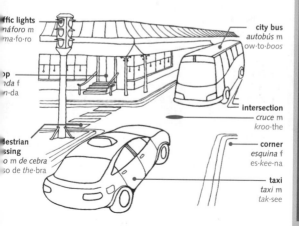

ffic lights
náforo m
ma·fo·ro

op
nda f
n·da

destrian
ssing
o m *de cebra*
so de the·bra

city bus
autobús m
ow·to·*boos*

intersection
cruce m
kroo·the

corner
esquina f
es·*kee*·na

taxi
taxi m
tak·see

directions

61

How far is it?
  ¿A cuánta distancia   a kwan·ta dees·tan·thya
  está?   es·ta

Can you show me (on the map)?
  ¿Me lo puede indicar   me lo pwe·de een·dee·kar
  (en el mapa)?   (en el ma·pa)

It's ...	Está ...	es·ta ...
behind ...	detrás de ...	de·tras de ...
far away	lejos	le·khos
here	aquí	a·kee
in front of ...	enfrente de ...	en·fren·te de ...
left	por la izquierda	por la eeth·kyer·da
near	cerca	ther·ka
next to ...	al lado de ...	al la·do de ...
opposite ...	frente a ...	fren·te a ...
right	por la derecha	por la de·re·cha
straight ahead	todo recto	to·do rek·to
there	ahí	a·ee

Turn ...	Doble ...	do·ble ...
at the corner	en la esquina	en la es·kee·na
at the traffic lights	en el semáforo	en el se·ma·fo·ro
left/right	a la izquierda/	a la eeth·kyer·da/
	derecha	de·re·cha

by bus	por autobús	por ow·to·boos
on foot	a pie	a pye
by taxi	por taxi	por tak·see
by train	por tren	por tren

It's ...	Está ...	es·ta ...
... metres	... metros	... me·tros
... kilometres	... kilómetros	... kee·lo·me·tros
... minutes	... minutos	... mee·noo·tos

For locations and compass directions, see the **dictionary**.

looking for ...

Where's ...?
¿Dónde está ...?   don·de es·ta ...

Where can I buy ...?
¿Dónde puedo comprar ...?   don·de pwe·do kom·prar ...

bank	*banco* m	ban·ko
camping store	*tienda* f *de*	tyen·da de
	provisiones	pro·vee·syo·nes
	de camping	de kam·peeng
supermarket	*supermercado* m	soo·per·mer·ka·do

For more on shops and how to get there, see **directions**, page 61 and the **dictionary**.

making a purchase

How much is this?
¿Cuánto cuesta esto?   kwan·to kwes·ta es·to

I'd like to buy ...
Quisiera comprar ...   kee·sye·ra kom·prar ...

I'm just looking.
Sólo estoy mirando.   so·lo es·toy mee·ran·do

Can I look at it?
¿Puedo verlo?   pwe·do ver·lo

Do you have any others?
¿Tiene otros?   tye·ne o·tros

Do you have something cheaper?
¿Tiene algo más barato?   tye·ne al·go mas ba·ra·to

Do you accept ...?	¿Aceptan ...?	a·thep·tan ...
credit cards	tarjetas de crédito	tar·khe·tas de kre·dee·to
debit cards	tarjetas de débito	tar·khe·tas de de·bee·to
travellers cheques	cheques de viajero	che·kes de vya·khe·ro
Could I have a ... please?	¿Podría darme ... por favor?	po·dree·a dar·me ... por fa·vor
bag	una bolsa	oo·na bol·sa
receipt	un recibo	oon re·thee·bo

Can you write down the price?
¿Puede escribir el precio?
pwe·de es·kree·beer el pre·thyo

Could I have it wrapped?
¿Me lo podría envolver?
me lo po·dree·a en·vol·ver

Does it have a guarantee?
¿Tiene garantía?
tye·ne ga·ran·tee·a

Can I have it sent overseas?
¿Pueden enviarlo por correo a otro país?
pwe·den en·vee·ar·lo por ko·re·o a o·tro pa·ees

Can you order it for me?
¿Me lo puede pedir?   me lo *pwe*·de pe·*deer*

Can I pick it up later?
¿Puedo recogerlo más   *pwe*·do re·ko·*kher*·lo mas
tarde?   *tar*·de

It's faulty.
Es defectuoso.   es de·fek·loo·o·so

I'd like ...,	*Quisiera ...,*	kee·*sye*·ra ...
please.	*por favor.*	por fa·*vor*
my change	*mi cambio*	mee *kam*·byo
my money back	*que me*	ke me
	devuelva	de·*vwel*·va
	el dinero	el dee·*ne*·ro
to return this	*devolver esto*	de·vol·*ver* es·to

local talk

bargain	*ganga* f	*gan*·ga
bargain hunter	*cazador* m *de ofertas*	ka·tha·*dor* de o·*fer*·tas
rip-off	*estafa* f	es·*ta*·fa
sale	*ventas* f pl	*ven*·tas
specials	*rebajas* f pl	re·*ba*·khas

bargaining

el regateo

That's too expensive.
Es muy caro.   es mooy *ka*·ro

Can you lower the price?
¿Podría bajar un   po·*dree*·a ba·*khar* oon
poco el precio?   *po*·ko el *pre*·thyo

I'll give you ...
Te daré ...   te da·*re* ...

shopping

clothes

la ropa

Can I try it on?
¿Me lo puedo probar?   me lo *pwe*·do *pro*·bar

My size is ...
Uso la talla ...   *oo*·so la *ta*·lya ...

It doesn't fit.
No me queda bien.   no me *ke*·da byen

repairs

reparaciones

Can I have my	*¿Puede reparar mi*	*pwe*·de re·pa·*rar* mee
... repaired here?	*... aquí?*	... a·*kee*
backpack	*mochila*	mo·*chee*·la
camera	*cámara*	*ka*·ma·ra
When will my	*¿Cuándo estarán*	*kwan*·do es·ta·*ran*
... be ready?	*listos/as mis ...?* m/f	*lees*·tos/as mees ...
(sun)glasses	*gafas (de sol)* f	*ga*·fas (de sol)
shoes	*zapatos* m	tha·*pa*·tos

For more clothing items, see the **dictionary**.

darn holes

buttons	*botónes* m pl	bo·*to*·nes
needle	*aguja* f	a·*goo*·kha
scissors	*tijeras* f pl	tee·*khe*·ras
thread	*hilo* m	*ee*·lo

hairdressing

I'd like (a) ...	Quisiera ...	kee·sye·ra ...
blow wave	un secado a mano	oon se·ka·do a ma·no
colour	un tinte de pelo	oon teen·te de pe·lo
haircut	un corte de pelo	oon kor·te de pe·lo
highlights	reflejos	re·fle·khos
my beard trimmed	que me recorte la barba	ke me re·kor·te la bar·ba
shave	que me afeite	ke me a·fey·te
trim	que me recorte el pelo	ke me re·kor·te el pe·lo

Don't cut it too short.
No me lo corte demasiado corto.
no me lo kor·te de·ma·sya·do kor·to

Shave it all off!
¡Aféitelo todo!
a·fey·te·lo to·do

Please use a new blade.
Por favor, use una cuchilla nueva.
por fa·vor oo·se oo·na koo·chee·lya nwe·va

---

worth a read

Spanish literature has a long history (dating from the 12th century), resulting in a thriving writing industry today. Look out for authors Ana María Matute, Jorge Luis Borges, Miguel de Unamuno, Carmen Martín Gaite, Juan Goytisolo, Miguel Delibes, Gabriel García Marquez and the 1989 Nobel Prize winner, Camilo José Cela.

books & reading

Is there a/an (English-language) ...?	¿Hay algún/ alguna ... en inglés? m/f	ai al·*goon*/ al·*goo*·na ... en een·*gles*
book by ...	*libro* m de ...	*lee*·bro de ...
bookshop	*librería* m	lee·bre·*ree*·a
entertainment guide	*guía* f *del ocio*	*gee*·a del o·thyo
section	*sección* f	sek·*thyon*

I (don't) like ...
(No) Me gusta/gustan ... sg/pl (no) me *goos*·ta/*goos*·tan ...

Do you have Lonely Planet guidebooks?
¿Tiene libros de Lonely   tye·ne *lee*·bros de *lon*·lee
Planet?   *pla*·net

Do you have a better phrasebook than this?
¿Tiene algún libro de   tye·ne al·*goon* *lee*·bro de
frases mejor que éste?   *fra*·ses me·*khor* ke es·te

For more on books, see **interests**, page 109.

music

I heard a band called ...
Escuché a un grupo   es·koo·*che* a oon *groo*·po
que se llama ...   ke se *lya*·ma ...

I heard a singer called ...
Escuché a un/una   es·koo·*che* a oon/*oo*·na
cantante que se llama ... m/f   kan·*tan*·te ke se *lya*·ma ...

What's their best recording?
¿Cuál es su mejor disco?　　kwal es soo me·*khor dees*·ko

Can I listen to this?
¿Puedo escuchar　　pwe·do es·koo·*char*
este … aquí?　　es·te … a·*kee*

Is this a pirated copy?
¿Es copia pirata?　　es *ko*·pya pee·*ra*·ta

I'd like (a) …　　Quisiera …　　kee·*sye*·ra …
　blank tape　　una cinta　　oo·na *theen*·ta
　　　　virgen　　veer·khen
　CD　　un cómpac　　oon *kom*·pak
　headphones　　unos　　oo·nos
　　　　auriculares　　ow·ree·koo·*la*·res

photography

la fotografía

I need a passport photo taken.
Necesito fotos de　　ne·the·*see*·to *fo*·tos de
pasaporte.　　pa·sa·*por*·te

How much is it to develop this film?
¿Cuánto cuesta revelar　　*kwan*·to *kwes*·ta re·ve·*lar*
este carrete?　　es·te ka·*re*·te

Can you load my film?
¿Puede usted cargar　　*pwe*·de oos·te kar·*gar*
el carrete?　　el ka·*re*·te

I'd like double copies.
Quisiera dos copias.　　kee·*sye*·ra dos *ko*·pyas

shopping

69

When will it be ready?
  ¿Cuándo estará listo?   kwan·do es·ta·ra lees·to

I'm not happy with these photos.
  No estoy contento/a con   no es·toy kon·ten·to/a kon
  estas fotos. m/f   es·tas fo·tos

I don't want to pay the full price.
  No quiero pagar el precio   no kye·ro pa·gar el pre·thyo
  íntegro.   een·te·gro

Do you have slide film?
  ¿Tiene diapositivas?   tye·ne dya·po·see·tee·vas

I need ... film	*Necesito*	ne·the·see·to
for this camera.	*película ... para*	pe·lee·koo·la ... pa·ra
	esta cámara.	es·ta ka·ma·ra
APS	*APS*	a pe e·se
B&W	*en blanco y*	en blan·ko y
	negro	ne·gro
colour	*en color*	en ko·lor
(400) speed	*de sensibilidad*	de sen·see·bee·lee·da
	(cuatrocientos)	(kwa·tro·thyen·tos)

batteries	*pilas* f pl	pee·las
camera	*cámara* f	ka·ma·ra
	(fotográfica)	(fo·to·gra·fee·ka)
disposable	*cámara* f	ka·ma·ra
camera	*desechable*	de·se·cha·ble
flash	*flash* f	flash
underwater	*cámara* f	ka·ma·ra
camera	*submarina*	soob·ma·ree·na

post office

correos

I want to send a ...	*Quisiera enviar ...*	kee·*sye*·ra en·vee·*ar* ...
fax	*un fax*	oon faks
parcel	*un paquete*	oon pa·*ke*·te
postcard	*una postal*	*oo*·na pos·*tal*
I want to buy (an) ...	*Quisiera comprar ...*	kee·*sye*·ra kom·*prar* ...
aerogram	*un aerograma*	oon ae·ro·*gra*·ma
envelope	*un sobre*	oon *so*·bre
stamps	*sellos*	se·*lyos*
airmail	*por vía aérea*	por *vee*·a a·e·re·a
customs declaration	*declaración* f *de aduana*	de·kla·ra·*thyon* de a·*dwa*·na
domestic	*nacional*	na·thyo·*nal*
express mail	*correo* m *urgente*	ko·*re*·o oor·*khen*·te
fragile	*frágil*	*fra*·kheel
glue	*pegamento* m	pe·ga·*men*·to
international	*internacional*	een·ter·na·thyo·*nal*
mail box	*buzón* m	boo·*thon*
postcode	*código* m *postal*	*ko*·dee·go pos·*tal*
registered mail	*correo* m *certificado*	ko·*re*·o ther·tee·fee·*ka*·do
surface mail	*por vía terrestre*	por *vee*·a te·*res*·tre

Please send it by air/surface mail to ...
   Por favor, mándelo por vía aérea/terrestre a ...   por fa·*vor* man·de·lo por *vee*·a a·e·re·a/te·*res*·tre a ...

It contains ...
   Contiene ...   kon·*tye*·ne ...

Where's the poste restante section?

¿Dónde está la lista de correos?   don·de es·ta la lees·ta de ko·re·os

Is there any mail for me?

¿Hay alguna carta para mí?   ai al·goo·na kar·ta pa·ra mee

phone

el teléfono

What's your phone number?

¿Cuál es tu número de teléfono?   kwal es too noo·me·ro de te·le·fo·no

Where's the nearest public phone?

¿Dónde hay una cabina telefónica?   don·de ai oo·na ka·bee·na te·le·fo·nee·ka

I want to make a ... (to Singapore).	Quiero hacer ... (a Singapur).	kye·ro a·ther ... (a seen·ga·poor)
call	una llamada	oo·na lya·ma·da
reverse-charge/ collect call	una llamada a cobro revertido	oo·na lya·ma·da a ko·bro re·ver·tee·do

I want to ...	Quiero ...	kye·ro ...
buy a phone card	comprar una tarjeta telefónica	kom·prar oo·na tar·khe·ta te·le·fo·nee·ka
speak for (three) minutes	hablar por (tres) minutos	ab·lar por (tres) mee·noo·tos

How much does ... cost?	¿Cuánto cuesta ...?	kwan·to kwes·ta...
a (three)- minute call	una llamada de (tres) minutos	oo·na lya·ma·da de (tres) mee·noo·tos
each extra minute	cada minuto extra	ka·da mee·noo·to ek·stra

The number is …
El número es …   el *noo*·me·ro es …

What's the area code for …?
¿Cuál es el prefijo de   kwal es el pre·*fee*·kho de
la zona …?   la *tho*·na …

What's the country code for …?
¿Cuál es el prefijo   kwal es el pre·*fee*·kho
del país …?   del pa·*ees* …

It's engaged.
Está comunicando.   es·*ta* ko·moo·nee·*kan*·do

I've been cut off.
Me han cortado   me an kor·*ta*·do
(la comunicación).   (la ko·moo·nee·ka·*thyon*)

The connection's bad.
Es mala conexión.   es *ma*·la ko·nek·*syon*

Hello. (making a call)   *Hola.*   o·la
Hello? (answering a call)   *¿Diga?*   dee·ga
Can I speak to …?   *¿Está …?*   es·*ta* …
It's …   *Soy …*   soy …

listen for …

de *par*·te de kyen
¿De parte de quién?   **Who's calling?**

kon kyen *kye*·re a·*blar*
¿Con quién quiere   **Who do you want to**
hablar?   **speak to?**

lo *syen*·to *pe*·ro a·o·ra no es·*ta*
Lo siento, pero ahora   **I'm sorry, he's/she's**
no está.   **not here.**

lo *syen*·to *tye*·ne el *noo*·me·ro e·kee·vo·*ka*·do
Lo siento, tiene el   **Sorry, wrong number.**
numero equivocado.

oon mo·*men*·to   *Un momento.*   **One moment.**

see a·*kee* es·*ta*   *Sí, aquí está.*   **Yes, he's/she's here.**

Can I leave a message?
  ¿Puedo dejar un mensaje?   pwe·do de·*khar* oon men·*sa*·khe

Please tell him/her I called.
  Sí, por favor, dile que he llamado.   see por fa·*vor* *dee*·le ke e lya·*ma*·do

I'll call back later.
  Ya llamaré más tarde.   ya lya·ma·*re* mas *tar*·de

mobile/cell phone

el teléfono móvil

I'd like a/an …	*Quisiera …*	kee·*sye*·ra …
adaptor plug	*un adaptador*	oon a·dap·ta·*dor*
charger for my phone	*un cargador para mi teléfono*	oon kar·ga·*dor* pa·ra mee te·*le*·fo·no
mobile/cell phone for hire	*un móvil para alquilar*	oon *mo*·veel pa·ra al·kee·*lar*
prepaid phone	*una tarjeta prepagada*	oo·na tar·*khe*·ta pre·pa·*ga*·da
SIM card for your network	*una tarjeta SIM para su red*	oo·na tar·*khe*·ta seem pa·ra soo red

What are the rates?
  ¿Cuál es la tarifa?   kwal es la ta·*ree*·fa

(30c) per (30) seconds.
  (treinta centavos) por (treinta) segundos   (*treyn*·ta then·*ta*·vos) por (*treyn*·ta) se·*goon*·dos

the internet

Where's the local Internet cafe?
 ¿Dónde hay un cibercafé *don·de ai oon thec ber ka fe*
 cercano? ther·*ka*·no

I'd like to ...	*Quisiera ...*	kee·*sye*·ra ...
check my email	*revisar mi*	re·vee·*sar* mee
	correo	ko·*re*·o
	electrónico	e·lek·*tro*·nee·ko
get Internet	*usar el*	oo·*sar* el
access	*Internet*	een·ter·net
use a printer	*usar una*	oo·*sar* oo·na
	impresora	eem·pre·*so*·ra
use a scanner	*usar un*	oo·*sar* oon
	escáner	es·*ka*·ner

How much	*¿Cuánto cuesta*	*kwan*·to *kwes*·ta
per ...?	*por ...?*	por ...
CD	*cómpact*	*kom*·pakt
hour	*hora*	*o*·ra
(five) minutes	*(cinco)*	(*theen*·ko)
	minutos	mee·*noo*·tos
page	*página*	*pa*·khee·na
Do you have ...?	*¿Tiene ...?*	*tye*·ne ...
Macs	*Apples*	*a*·pels
PCs	*PCs*	pe thes
a Zip drive	*unidad de Zip*	oo·nee·*da* de theep

communications

75

How do I log on?
¿Cómo entro al sistema?   ko·mo en·tro al sees·te·ma

It's crashed.
Se ha quedado colgado.   se a ke·da·do kol·ga·do

I've finished.
He terminado.   e ter·mee·na·do

a spangled web

Nowhere is the rise of 'Spanglish' (anglicised Spanish) more evident than on the Internet. New verbs such as *chatear*, *downloar*, *emailar*, *postear* and *surfear* are beginning to circulate freely in Hispanic cyberspace. In many cases, however, there are Spanish substitutes for common net-related terms. Here are just some of the officially-endorsed alternatives:

chat	charlar	char·lar
cyberspace	ciberespacio	see·ber·e·spa·thyo
download	descargar	des·kar·gar
homepage	página Web inicial	pa·jee·na web ee·nee·thyal
online	en línea	en lee·ne·a
search engine	sistema de búsqueda	sees·te·ma de boos·ke·da
surf	correr tabla por la red	ko·rer ta·bla por la re
username	nombre de usuario	nom·bre de oo·swa·ryo
website	sitio Web	see·tyo web

People usually shoot the breeze for a while before they get down to business.

I'm attending a ...	*Asisto a ...*	a·sees·to a ...
conference	*un congreso*	oon kon·gre·so
course	*un curso*	oon koor·so
meeting	*una reunión*	oo·na re·oo·nyon
trade fair	*una feria de*	oo·na fe·rya de
	muestras	mwes·tras
I'm with ...	*Estoy con ...*	es·toy kon ...
my company	*mi compañía*	mee kom·pa·nyee·a
my colleagues	*mis colegas*	mees ko·le·gas
(two) others	*otros (dos)*	ot·ros (dos)

using your manners

If you're in a formal situation or you want to show respect to someone much older than yourself, you should use the polite form of address (see below). The best approach is to take the lead from how people address you and respond in the same way. It's always a good idea to use the polite form in business, and also with any service providers (be they kiosk attendants or doctors).

you sg	*Usted*	oo·ste
you pl	*Ustedes*	oo·ste·des

What's your name?

¿Cómo se llama	ko·mo se lya·ma
Usted? sg pol	oos·te

For more on polite forms, see **you** in the **a–z phrasebuilder**, page 26.

Where's the ...?   *¿Dónde está ...?*   don·de es·ta ...
  business centre   *el centro*   el then·tro
     financiero   fee·nan·thye·ro
  conference   *el congreso*   el kon·gre·so

Where's the meeting?
  ¿Dónde es a reunión?   don·de es la re·oo·nyon

I'm alone.
  Estoy solo/a. m/f   es·toy so·lo/a

Let me introduce my colleague.
  ¿Puedo presentarle a mi   pwe·do pre·sen·tar·le a mee
  compañero/a? m/f   kom·pa·nye·ro/a

I'm staying at ..., room ...
  Me estoy alojando en ...,   me es·toy a·lo·khan·do en ...,
  la habitación ...   la a·bee·ta·thyon ...

I'm here for ... days/weeks.
  Estoy aquí por ... días/   es·toy a·kee por ... dee·as/
  semanas.   se·ma·nas

Here's my business card.
  Aquí tiene mi tarjeta   a·kee tye·ne mee tar·khe·ta
  de visita.   de vee·see·ta

I have an appointment with ...
  Tengo una cita con ...   ten·go oo·na thee·ta kon ...

That went very well.
  Eso fue muy bien.   e·so fwe mooy byen

Shall we go for a drink/meal?
  ¿Vamos a tomar/   va·mos a to·mar/
  comer algo?   ko·mer al·go

It's on me.
  Invito yo.   een·vee·to yo

bank

el banco

Where can I ...?	¿Dónde puedo ...?	don·de pwe·do ...
I'd like to ...	Me gustaría ...	me goos·ta·ree·a ...
cash a cheque	cambiar un cheque	kam·byar oon che·ke
change money	cambiar dinero	kam·byar dee·ne·ro
change a travellers cheque	cobrar un cheque de viajero	ko·brar oon che·ke de vee·a·khe·ro
get a cash advance	obtener un adelanto	ob·te·ner on a·de·lan·to
withdraw money	sacar dinero	sa·kar dee·ne·ro

What time does the bank open?
¿A qué hora abre el banco?
a ke o·ra a·bre el ban·ko

Can I arrange a transfer?
¿Puedo hacer una transferencia?
pwe·do ha·ther oo·na trans·fe·ren·thya

Where's the nearest foreign exchange office?
¿Dónde está la oficina de cambio más cercano?
don·de es·ta la o·fee·thee·na de kam·byo mas ther·ka·no

The ATM took my card.
El cajero automático se ha tragado mi tarjeta.
el ka·khe·ro ow·to·ma·tee·ko se a tra·ga·do mee tar·khe·ta

I've forgotten my PIN.
Me he olvidado del NPI.
me e ol·vee·da·do del e·ne pe ee

What's the charge for that?
¿Cuánto hay que pagar por eso?
kwan·to ai ke pa·gar por e·so

Can I have smaller notes?
  ¿Me lo puede dar en   me lo *pwe*·de dar en
  billetes más pequeños?   bee·*lye*·tes mas pe·*ke*·nyos

Has my money arrived yet?
  ¿Ya ha llegado mi dinero?   ya a lye·*ga*·do mee dee·*ne*·ro

How long will it take to arrive?
  ¿Cuánto tiempo tardará   *kwan*·to *tyem*·po tar·da·*ra*
  en llegar?   en lye·*gar*

What's the exchange rate?
  ¿Cuál es el tipo de cambio?   kwal es el *tee*·po de *kam*·byo

---

listen for ...

ai oon pro·*ble*·ma kon soo *kwen*·ta
  Hay un problema   **There's a problem with**
  con su cuenta.   **your account.**

no le *ke*·dan *fon*·dos
  No le quedan fondos.   **You have no funds left.**

no po·*de*·mos a·*ther* e·so
  No podemos hacer eso.   **We can't do that.**

por fa·*vor* feer·me a·*kee*
  Por favor firme aquí.   **Please sign here.**

pwe·de es·kree·*beer*·lo
  ¿Puede escribirlo?   **Could you write it down?**

pwe·do ver soo ee·den·tee·fee·ka·*thyon*/
pa·sa·*por*·te por fa·*vor*
  ¿Puedo ver su   **Can I see some ID/your**
  identificación/   **passport, please?**
  pasaporte, por favor?

tye·ne oon des·koo·*byer*·to
  Tiene un descubierto.   **You're overdrawn.**

en ...	*En ...*	In ...
(*kwa*·tro) *dee*·as	*(cuatro) días*	**(four) working**
la·bo·*ra*·bles	*laborables*	**days**
oo·na se·*ma*·na	*una semana*	**one week**

I'd like a/an ...	Quisiera ...	kee·*sye*·ra ...
audio set	un equipo audio	oon e·*kee*·po *ow*·dyo
catalogue	un catálogo	oon ka·*ta*·lo·go
guidebook in English	una guía turística en inglés	*oo*·na *gee*·a too·*rees*·tee·ka en een·*gles*
(local) map	un mapa (de la zona)	oon *ma*·pa (de la *tho*·na)

Do you have information on ... sights?	¿Tiene información sobre los lugares de interés ...?	*tye*·ne een·for·ma·*thyon* *so*·bre los loo·*ga*·res de een·te·*res* ...
cultural	cultural	kool·too·*ral*
local	local	lo·*kal*
religious	religioso	re·lee·*khyo*·so
unique	único	*oo*·nee·ko

Can we hire a guide?
¿Podemos alquilar un guía?
po·*de*·mos al·kee·*lar* oon *gee*·a

I'd like to see ...
Me gustaría ver ...
me goos·ta·*ree*·a ver ...

What's that?
¿Qué es eso?
ke es *e*·so

Who made it?
¿Quién lo hizo?
kyen lo *ee*·tho

How old is it?
　　¿De qué época es?　　　de ke e·po·ka es

Could you take a photograph of me?
　　¿Me puede hacer una foto?　　me *pwe*·de a·*ther* oo·na *fo*·to

Can I take photographs (of you)?
　　¿(Le/Te) Puedo tomar　　(le/te) *pwe*·do to·*mar*
　　fotos? pol/inf　　*fo*·tos

I'll send you the photograph.
　　Le/Te mandaré la foto. pol/inf　le/te man·da·*re* la *fo*·to

getting in

la entrada

What time does it open/close?
　　¿A qué hora abren/cierran?　　a ke *o*·ra ab·ren/*thye*·ran

What's the admission charge?
　　¿Cuánto cuesta la entrada?　　kwan·to *kwes*·ta la en·*tra*·da

It costs ...
　　Cuesta ...　　　　　kwes·ta ...

Is there a discount for ...?	*¿Hay descuentos para ...?*	ai des·*kwen*·tos *pa*·ra ...
children	*niños*	*nee*·nyos
families	*familias*	fa·*mee*·lee·as
groups	*grupos*	*groo*·pos
pensioners	*pensionistas*	pen·syo·*nees*·tas
students	*estudiantes*	es·too·*dyan*·tes

tours

Can you recommend a ...?	¿Puede recomendar algún(a) ...? m/f	pwe·de re·ko·men·dar al·goon/al·goo·na ...
When's the next ...?	¿Cuándo es el/la próximo/a ...? m/f	kwan·do es el/la prok·see·mo/a ...
boat-trip	paseo m en barca	pa·se·o en bar·ka
daytrip	excursión f de un día	eks·koor·syon de oon dee·a
excursion	excursión f	eks·koor·syon

tour	recorrido m	re·ko·ree·do
Do I need to take ... with me?	¿Necesito llevar ...?	ne·the·see·to lye·var ...
Is ... included?	¿Incluye ...?	een·kloo·ye ...
equipment	equipo	e·kee·po
food	comida	ko·mee·da
transport	transporte	trans·por·te

The guide will pay.
El guía va a pagar. el gee·a va a pa·gar

The guide has paid.
El guía ha pagado. el gee·a a pa·ga·do

How long is the tour?
¿Cuánto dura el recorrido? kwan·to doo·ra el re·ko·ree·do

What time should I be back?

Be back here at ...
Vuelva ...   *vwel·va ...*

I'm with them.
Voy con ellos.   voy kon e·lyos

I've lost my group.
He perdido a mi grupo.   e per·dee·do a mee groo·po

the royal lisp

According to a popular legend, one of the Spanish kings
– some say Felipe IV, others Ferdinand I – had a slight
speech impediment. Unable to pronounce the sound s
properly, he lisped his way through conversation. In an
epic act of flattery, the entire court, and eventually all of
Spain, mimicked his lisp. This story provides a colourful
explanation as to why Spaniards pronounce the word
cerveza (beer) as ther·ve·tha, while Latin Americans
continue to pronounce it ser·ve·sa.

It so happens, the story of the lisping king is a myth.
After all, only the letters *c* and *z* are pronounced th (when
they precede an *i* or an *e*), while the letter *s* remains the
same as in English. The reason for this selectiveness is due
to the way Spanish evolved from Latin and has nothing
to do with lisping monarchs at all. In fact, when you hear
someone say *gracias*, *gra·thyas*, they are no more lisping
as when you say 'thank you' in English.

I'm disabled.
Soy minusválido/a. m/f

soy mee·noos·*va*·lee·do/a

What services do you have for disabled people?
¿Qué servicios tienen
para minusválidos/as? m/f

ke ser·*vee*·thyos *tye*·nen
pa·ra mee·noos·va·lee·dos/as

Is there wheelchair access?
¿Hay acceso para la silla
de ruedas?

ai ak·*the*·so *pa*·ra la *see*·lya
de *rwe*·das

Speak more loudly, please.
Hable más alto, por favor.

ab·le mas *al*·to por fa·*vor*

I'm deaf.
Soy sordo/a. m/f

soy *sor*·do/a

Are guide dogs permitted?
¿Se permite la entrada a
los perros lazarillos?

se per·*mee*·te la en·*tra*·da a
los *pe*·ros la·tha·*ree*·lyos

Could you help me cross this street?
¿Me puede ayudar a
cruzar la calle?

me *pwe*·de a·yoo·*dar* a
kroo·*thar* la *ka*·lye

I need assistance.
Necesito asistencia.

ne·the·*see*·to a·sees·*ten*·thya

Braille library	*biblioteca* f *Braille*	bee·blee·o·*te*·ka *brai*·lye
disabled person	*persona* f *minusválida*	per·*so*·na mee·noos·va·lee·da
guide dog	*perro* m *lazarillo*	*pe*·ro la·tha·*ree*·lyo
wheelchair	*silla* f *de ruedas*	*see*·lya de *rwe*·das
ramp	*rampa* f	*ram*·pa
space	*espacio* m	es·*pa*·thyo

signs

Acceso para Sillas de Ruedas	ak·*the*·so pa·ra *thee*·lyas de ru·e·das	**Wheelchair Entrance**
Ascensor	as·then·*sor*	**Elevator/Lift**
Aseos para Minusválidos	a·*the*·os pa·ra mee·nus·va·lee·dos	**Disabled Toilets**
Carros de Minusválidos	*ka*·ros de mee·nus·va·lee·dos	**Disabled Trolleys (in major supermarkets)**

Is there a/an ...?	¿Hay ...?	ai ...
baby change room	una sala en la que cambiarle el pañal al bebé	oo·na sa·la en la ke kam·byar·le el pa·nyal al be·be
(English-speaking) babysitter	canguro (de habla inglésa)	kan·goo·ro (de ab·la een·gle·sa)
child-minding service	servicio de cuidado de niños	ser·vee·thyo de kwee·da·do de nee·nyos
children's menu	menú infantil	me·noo een·fan·teel
family discount	descuento familiar	des·kwen·to fa·mee·lyar
highchair	trona	tro·na

Do you mind if I breastfeed here?
¿Le molesta que dé de pecho aquí?
le mo·les·ta ke de de pe·cho a·kee

Are children allowed?
¿Se admiten niños?
se ad·mee·ten nee·nyos

Is this suitable for ... year old children?
¿Es apto para niños de ... años?
es ap·to pa·ra nee·nyos de ... a·nyos

I need a ...	Necesito un...	ne·the·see·to oon ...
baby seat	asiento m de seguridad para bebés	a·syen·to de se·goo·ree·da pa·ra be·bes
booster seat	asiento m de seguridad para niños	a·syen·to de se·goo·ree·da pa·ra nee·nyos
potty	orinal m de niños	o·ree·nal de nee·nyos
stroller	cochecito m	ko·che·thee·to
creche	guardería f	gwar·de·ree·a
park	parque m	par·ke
playground	parque m infantil	par·ke een·fan·teel
slide	tobogán m	to·bo·gan
swings	columpios m pl	ko·loom·pyos
theme park	parque m de atracciones	par·ke de a·trak·thyo·nes
toyshop	juguetería f	khoo·ge·te·ree·a

bless you!

In Spain, a polite way to respond to someone sneezing is by saying *¡Salud!*, sa·*loo*, (health) or even *¡Jesús!* khe·*soos* (Jesus).

basics

lo básico

Yes.	*Sí.*	see
No.	*No.*	no
Please.	*Por favor.*	por fa·*vor*
Thank you (very much).	*(Muchas) Gracias.*	(*moo*·chas) *gra*·thyas
You're welcome.	*De nada.*	de *na*·da
Excuse me.	*Perdón/*	per·*don*/
	Discúlpeme.	dees·*kool*·pe·me
Sorry.	*Lo siento.*	lo *syen*·to

greetings

los saludos

In Spain people are often quite casual in their interactions. It's fine to use the following expressions in both formal and informal situations.

Hello/Hi.	*Hola.*	o·la
Good morning.	*Buenos días.*	*bwe*·nos *dee*·as
Good afternoon. (until 8pm)	*Buenas tardes.*	*bwe*·nas *tar*·des
Good evening.	*Buenas noches.*	*bwe*·nas *no*·ches
See you later.	*Hasta luego.*	*as*·ta *lwe*·go
Goodbye/Bye.	*Adiós.*	a·*dyos*
How are you?	*¿Qué tal?*	ke tal
Fine, thanks.	*Bien, gracias.*	byen *gra*·thyas

meeting people

89

What's your name?

¿Cómo te llamas? inf		ko·mo te lya·mas
¿Cómo se llama Usted? pol		ko·mo se lya·ma oos·te

My name is ...

Me llamo ...   me lya·mo ...

I'd like to introduce you to ...

Quisiera presentarte a ... inf	kee·sye·ra pre·sen·tar·te a ...
Quisiera presentarle a ... pol	kee·sye·ra pre·sen·tar·le a ...

I'm pleased to meet you.

Mucho gusto.   moo·cho goos·to

titles & addressing people

Señor and *Señora* tend to be used in everyday speech. *Doña*, although rare, is used as a mark of respect towards older women, while *Don* is sometimes used to address men. An elderly neighbour, for example, might be called *Doña Lola*.

Mr	Señor	se·nyor
Sir	Don	don
Miss	Señorita	se·nyo·ree·ta
Ms/Mrs	Señora	se·nyo·ra
Madam	Doña	do·nya

call a friend

You may hear friends calling each other *tío* m, *tee·*o, or *tía* f, *tee·*a, but these words are usually used when talking about others. They're a bit crass (a little like using 'sheila' to describe a girl in Australia). Guys use *colega*, ko·*le·*ga, and *hombre*, om·bre, to address their workmates or male friends. In the south, people call their friends *pixas*, *pee·*chas or *xoxos*, *cho·*chos.

making conversation

Spain is known for its distinct regional areas. A great conversation starter in Spain is to ask someone where they come from. Other good topics are sport, politics, history and travel.

Do you live here?
¿Vives aquí?   vee·ves a·kee

Where are you going?
¿Adónde vas?   a·don·de vas

What are you doing?
¿Qué haces?   ke a·thes

Are you waiting (for a city bus)?
¿Estás esperando   es·tas es·pe·ran·do
(un autobús)?   (oon ow·to·boos)

Can I have a light, please?
¿Tienes fuego, por favor? tye·nes fwe·go por fa·vor

Do you like this?
¿Te gusta esto?   te goos·ta es·to

I love this.
Me encanta esto.   me en·kan·ta es·to

I'm here ...	*Estoy aquí ...*	es·toy a·kee ...
for a holiday	*de vacaciones*	de va·ka·thyo·nes
on business	*en viaje de*	en vya·khe de
	negocios	ne·go·thyos
to study	*estudiando*	es·tu·dyan·do
with my family	*con mi familia*	kon mee fa·mee·lya
with my partner	*con mi pareja* m&f	kon mee pa·re·kha

listen for ...

es·tas a·kee de va·ka·thyo·nes
¿Estás aquí de   **Are you here on**
vacaciones?   **holiday?**

What's this called?
  ¿Cómo se llama esto? ko·mo se lya·ma es·to

What do you think (about ...)?
  ¿Qué piensas (de ...)? ke pyen·sas (de ...)

What a gorgeous baby!
  ¡Qué niño/a más ke nee·nyo/a mas
  precioso/a! m/f pre·thyo·so/a

Can I take a photo?
  ¿Puedo hacer una foto? pwe·do a·ther oo·na fo·to

That's (beautiful), isn't it?
  ¿Es (precioso), no? es (pre·thyo·so) no

How long are you here for?
  ¿Cuánto tiempo te vas kwan·to tyem·po te vas
  a quedar? a ke·dar

I'm here for ... weeks/days.
  Estoy aquí por ... es·toy a·kee por ...
  semanas/días. se·ma·nas/dee·as

This is my ...	*Éste/a es mi ...* m/f	es·te/a es mee ...
child	*hijo/a* m/f	ee·kho/a
colleague	*colega* m&f	ko·le·ga
friend	*amigo/a* m/f	a·mee·go/a
husband	*marido*	ma·ree·do
partner	*pareja* m&f	pa·re·kha
wife	*esposa*	es·po·sa

local talk

Drop a few casual expressions into your Spanish and see the difference it makes in interacting with locals:

Great!	*¡Cojonudo!*	ko·kho·noo·do
How cool!	*¡Qué guay!*	ke gwai
How interesting!	*¡Qué interesante!*	ke een·te·re·san·te
Really?	*¿De veras?*	de ve·ras
That's fantastic!	*¡Estupendo!*	es·too·pen·do
What's up?	*¿Qué hay?*	ke ai
You don't say!	*¡No me digas!*	no me dee·gas

nationalities

You'll find that many country names are similar to English. If you're not sure, try to say the name of your country with a Spanish flavour and it's more than likely you'll be understood.

Where are you from?
   ¿De dónde eres?   de *don*·de e·res

I'm from ...	*Soy de ...*	soy de ...
Australia	*Australia*	ow·*stra*·lya
Canada	*Canadá*	ka·na·*da*
Sweden	*Suecia*	swe·thya

For more countries, see the **dictionary**.

age

How old ...?	*¿Cuántos años ...?*	*kwan*·tos a·nyos ...
are you	*tienes*	*tye*·nes
is your son/ daughter	*tiene tu hijo/a* m/f	*tye*·ne too ee·kho/a

I'm ... years old.
   Tengo ... años.   *ten*·go ... a·nyos

He's/She's ... years old.
   Tiene ... años.   *tye*·ne ... a·nyos

I'm younger than I look.
   Soy más joven de lo   soy mas *kho*·ven de lo
   que parezco.   ke pa·*reth*·ko

Too old!
   ¡Demasiado viejo!   de·ma·sya·do *vye*·kho

For your age, see **numbers**, page 29.

occupations & study

What do you do?
¿A qué te dedicas? a ke te de·*dee*·kas

What are you studying?
¿Qué estudias? ke es·*too*·dyas

I'm self-employed.
Soy trabajador/ soy tra·ba·kha·*dor*/
trabajadora tra·ba·kha·*do*·ra
autónomo/a. m/f ow·*to*·no·mo/a

I'm a/an ...	*Soy ...*	soy ...
architect	*arquitecto/a* m/f	ar·kee·*tek*·to/a
mechanic	*mecánico/a* m/f	me·*ka*·nee·ko/a
writer	*escritor/*	es·kree·*tor*/
	escritora m/f	es·kree·*to*·ra
I work in ...	*Trabajo en ...*	tra·*ba*·kho en ...
education	*enseñanza*	en·se·*nyan*·tha
hospitality	*hostelería*	os·te·le·*ree*·a
I'm ...	*Estoy ...*	es·*toy* ...
retired	*jubilado/a* m/f	khoo·bee·*la*·do/a
unemployed	*en el paro*	en el *pa*·ro
I'm studying ...	*Estudio ...*	es·*too*·dyo ...
business	*comercio*	ko·*mer*·thyo
languages	*idiomas*	ee·*dyo*·mas
science	*ciencias*	*thyen*·thyas

SOCIAL

94

I'm studying at ...	*Estudio en ...*	es·*too*·dyo en ...
college	*el instituto*	el eens·tee·*too*·to
school	*el colegio*	el ko·*le*·khyo
trade school	*el instituto de*	el eens·tee·*too*·to de
	formación	for·ma·*thyon*
	profesional	pro·fe·syo·*nal*
university	*la universidad*	la oo·nee·ver·see·*da*

For more occupations and studies, see the **dictionary**.

family

la familia

Do you have a ...?	*¿Tienes ...?*	*tye*·nes ...
I (don't) have a ...	*(No) Tengo ...*	(no) *ten*·go ...
brother	*un hermano*	oon er·*ma*·no
family	*una familia*	oo·na fa·*mee*·lya
partner	*una pareja* m&f	oo·na pa·*re*·kha

Do you live with your ...?
¿Vives con tu ...?　　　　vee·ves kon too ...

I live with my ...
Vivo con mi ...　　　　vee·vo kon mee ...

This is my ...
Éste/a es mi ... m/f　　　　es·te/a es mee ...

Are you married?
¿Estás casado/a? m/f　　　　es·*tas* ka·sa·do/a

I'm ...	*Estoy ...*	es·*toy* ...
married	*casado/a* m/f	ka·*sa*·do/a
separated	*separado/a* m/f	se·pa·*ra*·do/a

I'm single.
Soy soltero/a. m/f　　　　soy sol·*te*·ro/a

I live with someone.
Vivo con alguien.　　　　vee·vo kon *al*·gyen

children

When's your birthday?
   ¿Cuándo es tu   *kwan·*do es too
   cumpleaños?   koom·ple·*a·*nyos

Do you go to school or kindergarten?
   ¿Vas al colegio o a la   vas al ko·*le·*khyo o a la
   guardería?   gwar·de·*ree·*a

What grade are you in?
   ¿En qué curso estás?   en ke *koor·*so es·*tas*

Do you like ...?	*¿Te gusta ...?*	te *goos·*ta ...
school	*el colegio*	el ko·*le·*khyo
sport	*el deporte*	el de·*por·*te
your teacher	*tu profesor/*	too pro·fe·*sor/*
	profesora m/f	pro·fe·*so·*ra

What do you do after school?
   ¿Qué haces después del   ke *a·*thes des·*pwes* del
   colegio?   ko·*le·*khyo

Do you learn English?
   ¿Aprendes inglés?   a·*pren·*des een·*gles*

I come from very far away.
   Vengo de muy lejos.   *ven·*go de mooy *le·*khos

Are you lost?
   ¿Estás perdido/a? m/f   es·*tas* per·*dee·*do/a

Show me how to play.
   Dime cómo se juega.   *dee·*me *ko·*mo se *khwe·*ga

Well done!
   ¡Muy bien!   mooy byen

farewells

Tomorrow is my last day here.
> *Mañana es mi último*
> *día aquí.*

ma·*nya*·na es *mee ool*·lee·mo
dee·a a·*kee*

It's been great meeting you.
> *Me ha encantado*
> *conocerte.*

me a en·kan·*ta*·do
ko·no·*ther*·te

Keep in touch!
> *¡Nos mantendremos en*
> *contacto!*

nos man·ten·*dre*·mos en
kon·*tak*·to

I'll send you copies of the photos.
> *Te enviaré copias de*
> *las fotos.*

te en·*vee*·a·re ko·pyas de
las *fo*·tos

spanish grannies

Even idioms translate across languages. Here are a few
golden oldies:

It's like casting pearls before swine.
> *Es como echar*
> *margaritas a los*
> *cerdos.*

es *ko*·mo e·*char*
ma·ga·*ree*·tas a los
ther·dos

(lit: it's like feeding daisies to the pigs)

It doesn't rain, it pours.
> *Éramos pocos y*
> *parió la abuela.*

e·ra·mos *po*·kos y
pa·ree·o la a·*bwe*·la

(lit: there were a few of us and then granny gave birth)

This is like watching grass grow.
> *Es más largo que un*
> *día sin pan.*

es mas *lar*·go ke oon
dee·a seen pan

(lit: it's longer than a day without bread)

If you ever visit (Scotland) you can ...	Si algún día visitas (Escocia) ...	see al·*goon dee*·a vee·*see*·tas (es·*ko*·thya) ...
come and visit	ven a visitarnos	ven a vee·see·*tar*·nos
stay with me	te puedes quedar conmigo	te *pwe*·des ke·*dar* kon·*mee*·go

Here's my ...	Ésta es mi ...	*es*·ta es mee ...
What's your ...?	¿Cuál es tu ...?	kwal es too ...
address	dirección	dee·rek·*thyon*
email address	dirección de email	dee·rek·*thyon* de ee·mayl
fax number	número de fax	*noo*·me·ro de faks
mobile number	número de móvil	*noo*·me·ro de *mo*·veel
work number	número de teléfono en el trabajo	*noo*·me·ro de te·*le*·fo·no en el tra·*ba*·kho

For more on addresses, see **directions**, page 61.

brave new world

With Columbus' discovery of the New World in 1492 began an era of Spanish expansion in America, which is reflected in the language. *Patata*, *tomate*, *cacao* and *chocolate* are a few examples of words taken from the indigenous American languages. Bear in mind that Spanish has evolved differently and it's a good idea to take the *Latin American Spanish phrasebook* with you, rather than this one, if you're travelling there.

writing to people

If you want to impress your new friends by writing to them in Spanish when you get back home, here are some useful words and phrases:

Dear ...
Querido/a ... m/f

I'm sorry it's taken me so long to write.
Siento haber tardado tanto en escribir.

It was great to meet you.
Me encantó conocerte.

Thank you so much for your hospitality.
Muchísimas gracias por tu hospitalidad.

I miss you a lot.
Te echo mucho de menos.

I had a fantastic time in ...
Me lo pasé genial en ...

My favourite place was ...
Mi lugar preferido fue ...

I hope to visit ... again.
Espero visitar otra vez ...

Say 'hi' to ... (and ...) for me.
Saluda a ... (y a ...) de mi parte.

I'd love to see you again.
Tengo ganas de verte otra vez.

Write soon!
¡Escríbeme pronto!

With love,
Un beso,

Regards,
Saludos,

basque

Basque, or *Euskara*, is spoken at the western end of the Pyrenees and along the Bay of Biscay – from Bayonne in France to Bilbao in Spain, and then inland, almost to Pamplona.

No one quite knows its origin. Some have related it to the Sioux language, to Japanese, and even to the language of the Atlanteans. To complicate matters, dialects are also spoken in the Basque country, including Bizkaian, Gipuzkoan, High Navarrese, Aezkoan, Salazarese, Lapurdian, Low Navarrese and Suberoan. The most likely theory is that Basque is the lone survivor of a language family which once extended across Europe, and was wiped out by the languages of the Celts, the Germanic tribes and the Romans. It's amazing that Basque has survived so close to its original form.

Speaking Spanish in the Basque-speaking towns might be expected from a foreigner, but is not as warmly received as an attempt at one of the most ancient languages of Europe.

> greetings & civilities

Hi!	*Kaixo!*	kai·sho
Good morning.	*Egun on.*	e·goo *non*
Good afternoon/ evening.	*Arratsalde on.*	a·ra·chyal·de *on*
Goodbye.	*Agur.*	a·*goor*
Take care.	*Ondo ibili.*	on·do ee·*beel*·ee
How are you?	*Zer moduz?*	ser mo·*doos*
Fine, thank you.	*Ongi, eskerrik asko.*	on·gee e·*ske*·reek as·ko
Excuse me.	*Barkatu.*	bar·*ka*·too
Please.	*Mesedez.*	me·*se*·des
Thank you.	*Eskerrik asko.*	es·*ke*·reek *kas*·ko
You're welcome.	*Ez horregatik.*	es o·re·ga·teek

> language difficulties

Do you speak English?
Ingelesez ba al
dakizu?

een·ge·le·ses ba al
da·kee·soo

I know a little Basque.
Euskara apur bat
badakit.

e·oos·ka·ra a·poor bat
ba·da·keet

I don't understand.
Ez dut ulertzen.

es toot oo·ler·tzen

Could you speak in Castillian please?
Erdaraz egingo al
didazu, mesedez?

er·da·ras e·geen·go al
dee·da·soo me·se·des

How do you say that in Basque?
Nola esaten da hori
euskaraz?

no·la e·sa·ten da o·ree
e·oo·ska·ras

---

local talk

Hurray for us!
Gora gu 'ta gutarrak!

go·ra goo ta goo·ta·rak

The Basque Country's always partying!
Euskal Herrian
beti jai!

e·oos·kal e·ree·an
be·tee yai

catalan

Catalan is spoken by up to 10 million people in the north-east of Spain, a territory that comprises Catalonia, coastal Valencia and the Balearic Islands (Majorca, Minorca and Ibiza). Outside Spain, Catalan is also spoken in Andorra, the south of France and the town of Alguer in Sardinia.

Many famous creative types have been Catalan speakers: painters like Dalí, Miró and Picasso, architects like Gaudí and writers like Mercé Rodoreda.

Despite the fact that almost all Catalan speakers from Spain are bilingual, they appreciate it when visitors attempt to communicate, if even in the simplest way, in Catalan.

> greetings & civilities

Hello!	*Hola!*	o·la
Good morning.	*Bon dia.*	bon *dee*·a
Good afternoon.	*Bona tarda.*	*bo*·na *tar*·da
Good evening.	*Bon vespre.*	bon *bes*·pra
Goodbye.	*Adéu.*	a·*the*·oo
How are you?	*Com estàs?*	kom as·*tas*
(Very) Well.	*(Molt) Bé.*	(mol) be
Excuse me.	*Perdoni.*	par·*tho*·nee
Sorry.	*Ho sento.*	oo *sen*·to
Please.	*Sisplau.*	sees·*pla*·oo
Thank you.	*Gràcies.*	*gra*·see·as
Yes/No.	*Sí/No.*	see/no

> language difficulties

Do you speak English?
Parla anglès? — par·la an·*gles*

Could you speak in Castilian please?
Pot parlar castellà sisplau? — pot par·la kas·la·*lya* sees·*pla*·oo

I (don't) understand.
(No) Ho entenc. — (no) oo an·teng

How do you say ...?
Com es diu ...? — kom az *dee*·oo

---

local talk

No problem!
Això rai! — a·*sho* ra·ee

What a laugh!
Quin tip de riure! — kin tip da ri·a·oo·ra

galician

Galician, or *Galego*, is an official language of the Autonomous Community of Galicias and is also widely understood in neighbouring regions Asturias and Castilla-Léon. It's very similar to Portuguese, as the two languages have roots in Vulgar Latin.

Galicians are likely to revert to Spanish when addressing a stranger, especially a foreigner, but making a small effort to communicate in Galician will always be welcomed.

> greetings & civilities

Hello!	Ola!	o·la
Good day.	Bon dia.	bon dee·a
Good afternoon/ evening.	Boa tarde.	bo·a tar·de
Goodbye.	Adeus.	a·de·oos
	Até logo.	a·te lo·go
Excuse me.	Perdón.	per·don
Please.	Por favor.	por fa·vor
Thank you.	Grácias.	gra·see·as
Many thanks.	Moitas grácias.	moy·tas gra·see·as
That's fine.	De nada.	de na·da
Yes/No.	Si/Non.	see/non

> language difficulties

Do you speak English?
   Fala inglés? fa·la een·gles

Could you speak in Castilian please?
   Pode falar en español, po·de fa·la en e·spa·nyol
   por favor? por fa·bor

I (don't) understand.
   (Non) Entendo. (non) en·ten·do

What's this called in Galician?
   Como se chama iso en ko·mo se cha·ma ee·so en
   galego? ga·le·go

common interests

los intereses en común

What do you do in your spare time?
¿Qué te gusta hacer en tu tiempo libre?
ke te goos·ta a·ther en too tyem·po lee·bre

Do you like (travelling)?
¿Te gusta (viajar)?
te goos·ta (vya·khar)

I (don't) like ...	*(No) Me gusta ...*	(no) me goos·ta ...
cooking	*cocinar*	ko·thee·nar
dancing	*ir a bailar*	eer a bai·lar
films	*el cine*	el thee·ne
gardening	*jardinería*	kha·dee·ne·ree·a
hiking	*el excursionismo*	el eks·koor·syo·nees·mo
music	*la música*	la moo·see·ka
painting	*la pintura*	la peen·too·ra
photography	*la fotografía*	la fo·to·gra·fee·a
pub crawls	*ir de bar en bar*	eer de bar en bar
reading	*leer*	le·er
shopping	*ir de compras*	eer de kom·pras
socialising	*salir*	sa·leer
sport	*el deporte*	el de·por·te

For sporting activities, see **sport**, page 129.

music

Do you like to ...?	¿Te gusta ...?	te goos·ta ...
go to concerts	ir a conciertos	eer a kon·thyer·tos
listen to music	escuchar	es·koo·char
	música	moo·see·ka
play an	tocar algún	to·kar al·goon
instrument	instrumento	eens·troo·men·to
sing	cantar	kan·tar
What ... do you like?	¿Qué ... te gusta/ gustan? sg/pl	ke ... te goos·ta/ goos·tan
music	música sg	moo·see·ka
bands	grupos pl	groo·pos
classical music	música f clásica	moo·see·ka kla·see·ka
electronic music	música f electrónica	moo·see·ka e·lek·tro·nee·ka
jazz	jazz m	khath
metal	metal m	me·tal
pop	música f pop	moo·see·ka pop
punk	música f punk	moo·see·ka poonk
rock	música f rock	moo·see·ka rok
R&B	rhythm and blues m	ree·dem and bloos
traditional music	música f popular	moo·see·ka po·pu·lar
world music	música f étnica	moo·see·ka et·nee·ka

art

When's the gallery open?
  ¿A qué hora abre la galería? a ke o·ra a·bre la ga·le·ree·a

What's in the collection?
  ¿Qué hay en la colección? ke ai en la ko·lek·thyon

What kind of art are you interested in?
¿Qué tipo de arte te interesa?
ke *tee*·po de *ar*·te te een·te·*re*·sa

I'm interested in ...
Me interesa/ interesan ... sg/pl
me een·te·*re*·sa/ een·te·*re*·san ...

What do you think of ...?
¿Qué piensas de ...?
ke *pyen*·sas de ...

It's a/an ... exhibition.
Es una exposición de ...
es *oo*·na eks·po·see·*thyon* de ...

I like the works of ...
Me gustan las obras de ...
me *goos*·tan las *o*·bras de ...

It reminds me of ...
Me recuerda a ...
me re·*kwer*·da a ...

... art	*arte* m ...	*ar*·te ...
graphic	*gráfico*	*gra*·fee·ko
impressionist	*impresionista*	eem·pre·syo·*nees*·ta
modernist	*modernista*	mo·der·*nees*·ta
Renaissance	*renacentista*	re·na·then·*tees*·ta

cinema & theatre

el cine & el teatro

I feel like going to (a comedy).
*Tengo ganas de ir
a (una comedia).*
ten·go ga·nas de eer
a (oo·na ko·me·dya)

What's showing at the cinema (tonight)?
*¿Qué película dan en el
cine (esta noche)?*
ke pe·lee·koo·la dan en el
thee·ne (es·ta no·che)

Is it in English?
¿Es en inglés?
es en een·gles

Does it have (English) subtitles?
*¿Tiene subtítulos
(en inglés)?*
tye·ne soob·tee·too·los
(en een·gles)

I want to sell this ticket.
Quiero vender esta entrada.
kye·ro ven·der es·ta en·tra·da

Are those seats taken?
*¿Están ocupados estos
asientos?*
es·tan o·koo·pa·dos es·tos
a·syen·tos

Have you seen ...?
¿Has visto ...?
as vees·to ...

Who's in it?
¿Quién actúa?
kyen ak·too·a

It stars ...
Actúa ...
ak·too·a ...

Did you like the ...? *¿Te gustó el ...?* te goos·to el ...
    ballet   *ballet*   ba·le
    film   *cine*   thee·ne
    play   *teatro*   te·a·tro

I (don't) like ...
(No) me gusta/gustan ... sg/pl (no) me goos·ta/goos·tan ...

I thought it was ... *Pienso que fue ...* pyen·so ke fwe ...
  excellent *excelente* eks·the·*len*·te
  long *largo* *lar*·go
  OK *regular* re·goo·*lar*

animated films	*películas* f pl *de*	pe·*lee*·koo·las de
	dibujos	dee·*boo*·khos
	animados	a·nee·*ma*·dos
comedy	*comedia* f	ko·*me*·dya
documentary	*documentales* m pl	do·koo·men·*ta*·les
drama	*drama* m	*dra*·ma
film noir	*cine* m *negro*	*thee*·ne ne·gro
(Spanish) cinema	*cine* m *(español)*	*thee*·ne (es·pa·*nyol*)
horror movies	*cine* m *de terror*	*thee*·ne de te·*ror*
sci-fi	*cine* m *de*	*thee*·ne de
	ciencia ficción	*thyen*·thya feek·*thyon*
short films	*cortos* m pl	*kor*·tos
thrillers	*cine* m *de*	*thee*·ne de
	suspenso	soos·*pen*·so

reading

What kind of books do you read?
  ¿Qué tipo de libros lees? ke *tee*·po de *lee*·bros *le*·es

**Which (Spanish) author do
you recommend?**
  ¿Qué autor (español) ke ow·*tor* (es·pa·*nyol*)
  recomiendas? re·ko·*myen*·das

Have you read ...?
¿Has leído ...?   as le·*ee*·do ...

On this trip I'm reading ...
En este viaje estoy   en *es*·te vya·khe es·*toy*
leyendo ...   le·*yen*·do ...

I'd recommend ...
Recomiendo a ...   re·ko·*myen*·do a ...

Where can I exchange books?
¿Dónde puedo cambiar   *don*·de *pwe*·do kam·*byar*
libros?   lee·bros

For more on books, see **shopping**, page 68.

---

dog in the manger

Proverbs are big in Spain. The Marques de Santilllana compiled a national collection in the second half of the 15th century, and one of the characters in *Don Qixote*, Sancho Panza, speaks almost entirely in proverbs.

The author Cervantes described these popular sayings as 'short sentences based on long experience', or is that long-windedness?

ser como el perro del hortelano, que ni come las berzas, ni las deja comer al amo

(lit: to be like the market gardener's dog who doesn't eat the cabbages and won't let his master eat them either)

feelings

los sentimientos

Feelings are described with either nouns or adjectives: the nouns use 'have' in Spanish (eg, 'I have hunger') and the adjectives use 'be' (like in English).

I'm (not) ...	(No) Tengo ...	(no) ten·go ...
Are you ...?	¿Tienes ...?	tye·nes ...
cold	frío	free·o
hot	calor	ka·lor
hungry	hambre	am·bre
in a hurry	prisa	pree·sa
thirsty	sed	se

I'm (not) ...	(No) Estoy ...	(no) es·toy ...
Are you ...?	¿Estás ...?	es·tas ...
annoyed	fastidiado/a m/f	fas·tee·dya·do/a
embarrassed	avergonzado/a m/f	a·ver·gon·tha·do/a
horny	cachondo/a m/f	ka·chon·do/a
tired	cansado/a m/f	kan·sa·do/a
well	bien	byen

For health-related feelings, see **health**, page 182.

opinions

las opiniones

Did you like it?
  ¿Te gustó? te goos·to

What did you think of it?
  ¿Qué pensaste de eso? ke pen·sas·te de e·so

I thought it was ...	Pienso que fue ...	pyen·so ke fwe ...
It's ...	Es ...	es ...
beautiful	bonito/a m/f	bo·nee·to/a
bizarre	raro/a m/f	ra·ro/a
crap	un coñazo/a m/f	oon ko·nya·tho/a
crazy	loco/a m/f	lo·ko/a
entertaining	entretenido/a m/f	en·tre·te·nee·do/a
excellent	fantástico/a m/f	fan·tas·tee·ko/a
full on	heavy	khe·vee
horrible	horrible	o·ree·ble

by degrees

a little	un poco	oon po·ko
I'm a little sad.	Estoy un poco triste.	es·toy oon po·ko trees·te
quite	bastante	bas·tan·te
I'm quite disappointed.	Estoy bastante decepcionado/a. m/f	es·toy bas·tan·te de·thep·thyo·na·do/a
very	muy	mooy
I feel very lucky.	Me siento muy afortunado/a. m/f	me syen·to mooy a·for·too·na·do/a

politics & social issues

la política & los temas sociales

Who do you vote for?
¿A quién votas?
a kyen vo·tas

I support the ... party.
Apoyo al partido ...
a·po·yo al par·tee·do ...

Did you hear about ...?
¿Has oído que ...? as o·ee·do ke ...

Are you in favour of ...?
¿Estás a favor de ...? es·tas a fa·vor de ...

How do people feel about ...?
¿Cómo se siente la ko·mo se syen·te la
gente de ...? khen·te de ...

drugs	*drogas* f pl	*dro·gas*
the economy	*economía* f	*e·ko·no·mee·a*
immigration	*inmigración* f	*een·mee·gra·thyon*
racism	*racismo* m	*ra·thees·mo*
unemployment	*desempleo* m	*de·sem·ple·o*

---

octopus in the garage

Keeping the attention of your audience can be a challenge in a foreign language. Try emphasising your opinion with some of these colourful expressions:

He's/She's the best.
Es un trozo de pan. es oon tro·tho de pan
(lit: he's/she's a piece of bread)

You can't make a silk purse out of a sow's ear.
Aunque el mono se a·oon·ke el mo·no se
vista de seda, vees·ta de se·da
mono se queda. mo·no se ke·da
(lit: though the monkey may wear silk, it's still a monkey)

He's/She's a fish out of water.
Se encuentra se en·koo·en·tra
como un pulpo en ko·mo oon pool·po en
un garaje. oon ga·ra·khe
(lit: he's/she's like an octopus in a garage)

the environment

Is there an environmental problem here?

¿Aquí hay un problema	a·*kee* ai oon pro·*ble*·ma
con el medio ambiente?	kon el *me*·dyo am·*byen*·te

Is this (forest) protected?

¿Está este (bosque)	es·*ta* es·te (*bos*·ke)
protegido?	pro·te·*khee*·do

biodegradable	*biodegradable*	bee·o·de·gra·*da*·ble
deforestation	*deforestación* f	de·fo·res·ta·*thyon*
hunting	*caza* f	*ka*·tha
oil spill	*fuga* f *de petróleo*	*foo*·ga de pe·*tro*·le·o
pollution	*contaminación* f	kon·ta·mee·na·*thyon*

perhaps, perhaps, perhaps

Don't feel you're limited to a plain 'yes' or 'no'.

Maybe.	*Quizás.*	kee·*thas*
OK.	*Vale.*	*va*·le
No way!	*¡De ningún modo!*	de neen·*goon mo*·do
It's/I'm OK.	*Está/Estoy bien.*	es·*ta*/es·*toy* byen
Just a minute.	*Un momento.*	oon mo·*men*·to
No problem.	*Sin problema.*	seen pro·*ble*·ma
Of course!	*¡Claro (que sí)!*	*kla*·ro (ke see)
Sure.	*Claro.*	*kla*·ro
You bet!	*¡Ya lo creo!*	ya lo *kre*·o
Just joking.	*Era broma.*	e·ra *bro*·ma

where to go

adónde ir

What's there to do in the evenings?
¿Qué se puede hacer   ke se *pwe*·de a·*ther*
por las noches?   por las *no*·ches

What's on …?	*¿Qué hay …?*	ke ai …
locally	*en la zona*	en la *tho*·na
this weekend	*este fin de*	*es*·te feen de
	semana	se·*ma*·na
today	*hoy*	oy
tonight	*esta noche*	*es*·ta *no*·che

Where are …?	*¿Dónde hay …?*	*don*·de ai …
gay venues	*lugares gay*	loo·*ga*·res gai
places to eat	*lugares para*	loo·*ga*·res *pa*·ra
	comer	ko·*mer*
pubs	*pubs*	poobs

Is there a local … guide?	*¿Hay una guía …* *de la zona?*	ai oo·na gee·a … de la *tho*·na
entertainment	*del ocio*	del o·thyo
film	*de cine*	de *thee*·ne
gay	*de lugares gay*	de loo·*ga*·res gai
music	*de música*	de *moo*·see·ka

read my lips

Foreign movies are usually dubbed into Spanish, but in bigger cities you'll find some films have Spanish subtitles. Look for *v.o.* (*version original*, 'original version') or *v.o.s.* (*version original subtitulada*, 'original version with subtitles') in listings.

I feel like going to a/the ...	Tengo ganas de ir ...	ten·go ga·nas de eer ...
ballet	al ballet	al ba·le
bar	a un bar	a oon bar
cafe	a un café	a oon ka·fe
concert	a un concierto	a oon kon·thyer·to
karaoke bar	a un bar de karaoke	a oon bar de ka·ra·o·ke
movies	al cine	al thee·ne
nightclub	a una discoteca	a oo·na dees·ko·te·ka
party	a una fiesta	a oo·na fyes·ta
restaurant	a un restaurante	a oon res·tow·ran·te
theatre	al teatro	al te·a·tro

invitations

What are you doing this evening?
¿Qué haces esta noche?   ke a·thes es·ta no·che

What are you up to (right now)?
¿Qué haces (ahora)?   ke a·thes (a·o·ra)

Would you like to go for a ...?	¿Quieres que vayamos a ...?	kye·res ke va·ya·mos a ...
coffee	tomar un café	to·mar oon ka·fe
drink	tomar algo	to·mar al·go
meal	comer	ko·mer
walk	pasear	pa·se·ar

I feel like going ...	Me apetece ir a ...	me a·pe·te·the eer a ...
dancing	bailar	bai·lar
out somewhere	salir	sa·leer

My round.
Invito yo.   een·vee·to yo

Do you know a good restaurant?
¿Conoces algún buen   ko·no·thes al·goon bwen
restaurante?   res·tow·ran·te

Do you want to come to the
(...) concert with me?
¿Quieres venir conmigo   kye·res ve·neer kon·mee·go
al concierto (de ...)?   al kon·thyer·to (de ...)

We're having a party.
Vamos a dar una fiesta.   va·mos a dar oo·na fyes·ta

Do you want to come?
¿Por qué no vienes?   por ke no vye·nes

Are you ready?
¿Estás listo/a? m/f   es·tas lees·to/a

are you my type?

If jobs, age and nationality don't really cut it when trying
to describe yourself (and others), see if these words help:

activist	*activista* m&f	ak·tee·vees·ta
alcoholic	*alcohólico/a* m/f	al·ko·o·lee·ko/a
artistic	*artísticó/a* m/f	ar·tees·tee·ko/a
creative	*creador/*	kre·a·dor/
	creadora m/f	kre·a·do·ra
daggy/dorky	*hortera* m&f	or·te·ra
goth	*siniestra* m&f	see·nye·stra
heavy	*heavy* m&f	khe·vee
intellectual	*intelectual* m&f	een·te·lek·twal
progressive	*progre* m&f	pro·gre
sporty	*deportivo/a* m/f	de·por·tee·vo/a
trendy/stylish	*moderno/a* m/f	mo·der·no/a
workaholic	*adícto/a* m/f	a·deek·to/a
	al trabajo	al tra·ba·kho
yuppie	*yupi* m&f	yoo·pee

responding to invitations

Sure!
¡Por supuesto!   por soo·*pwes*·to

Yes, I'd love to.
Me encantaría.   me en·kan·ta·*ree*·a

Where will we go?
¿A dónde vamos?   a *don*·de va·*mos*

That's very kind of you.
Es muy amable por   es mooy a·*ma*·ble por
tu parte.   too *par*·te

No, I'm afraid I can't.
Lo siento pero no puedo.   lo *syen*·to *pe*·ro no *pwe*·do

Sorry, I can't sing/dance.
Lo siento, no sé cantar/bailar.   lo *syen*·to no se kan·*tar*/bai·*lar*

What about tomorrow?
¿Qué tal mañana?   ke tal ma·*nya*·na

arranging to meet

What time shall we meet?
¿A qué hora quedamos?   a ke *o*·ra ke·*da*·mos

Where will we meet?
¿Dónde quedamos?   *don*·de ke·*da*·mos

Let's meet ...	*Quedamos ...*	ke·*da*·mos ...
at (eight) o'clock	a *(las ocho)*	a (las *o*·cho)
at the (entrance)	en *(la entrada)*	en (la en·*tra*·da)

I'll pick you up.
Paso a recogerte.   pa·so a re·ko·*kher*·te

I'll be coming later.
Iré más tarde.   ee·*re* mas *tar*·de

Where will you be?
¿Dónde estarás?   don·de es·ta·*ras*

If I'm not there by (nine), don't wait for me.
Si no estoy a (las nueve),   see no es·*toy* a (las *nwe*·ve)
no me esperes/esperéis. sg/pl   no me es·*pe*·res/es·pe·*reys*

OK!
¡Hecho!   e·cho

I'll see you then.
Nos vemos.   nos *ve*·mos

See you later/tomorrow.
Hasta luego/mañana.   as·ta *lwe*·go/ma·*nya*·na

I'm looking forward to it.
Tengo muchas ganas
de ir.   *ten*·go moo·chas ga·nas
de eer

Sorry I'm late.
Siento llegar tarde.   syen·to lye·*gar tar*·de

Never mind.
No pasa nada.   no *pa*·sa *na*·da

attention-getter

Hey!	*¡Eh, tú!*	e too
Look!	*¡Mira!*	*mee*·ra
Listen (to this)!	*¡Escucha (esto)!*	es·*koo*·cha (es·to)

nightclubs & bars

Where can we go (salsa) dancing?
    ¿Dónde podemos ir a   don·de po·de·mos eer a
    bailar (la salsa)?   bai·lar (la sal·sa)

How do I get there?
    ¿Cómo se llega?   ko·mo se lye·ga

What type of music do you like?
    ¿Qué tipo de música   ke tee·po de moo·see·ka
    prefieres?   pre·fye·res

I really like (reggae).
    Me encanta (el reggae).   me en·kan·ta (el re·gai)

Come on!
    ¡Vamos!   va·mos

This place is great!
    ¡Este lugar me encanta!   es·te loo·gar me en·kan·ta

drugs

I don't take drugs.
    No consumo ningún   no kon·soo·mo neen·goon
    tipo de drogas.   tee·po de dro·gas

I take ... occasionally.
    Tomo ... de vez en cuando.   to·mo ... de veth en kwan·do

Do you want to have a smoke?
    ¿Nos fumamos un porro?   nos foo·ma·mos oon po·ro

I'm high.
    Estoy colocado/a. m/f   es·toy ko·lo·ka·do/a

For more on bars, drinks and partying, see **eating out**, page 150.

asking someone out

saliendo con alguien

Don't be surprised if invitations come late in the day. Social life in Spain continues well into the night: sometimes people begin to eat dinner at 10pm and many clubs open at midnight.

Would you like to do something (tonight)?
¿Quieres hacer algo   kye·res a·ther al·go
(esta noche)?   (es·ta no·che)

Yes, I'd love to.
Me encantaría.   me en·kan·ta·ree·a

I'm busy.
Estoy ocupado/a. m/f   es·toy o·koo·pa·do/a

local talk

He's/She's hot.
Él/Ella es   el/e·lya es
cachondo/a. m/f   ka·chon·do/a

What a babe.
Vaya hembra.   va·ya em·bra

He/She gets around.
Se va a la cama con   se va a la ka·ma kon
cualquiera.   kwal·kye·ra

pick-up lines

frases para ligar

Would you like a drink?
¿Te apetece una copa?   te a·pe·te·the oo·na ko·pa

Do you have a light?
¿Tienes fuego?   tye·nes fwe·go

You're great.
Eres estupendo/a. m/f   e·res es·too·pen·do/a

You mustn't come here much, because
I would have noticed you sooner.
No debes venir mucho   no de·bes ve·neer moo·cho
por aquí porque me habría   por a·kee por·ke me a·bree·a
fijado en ti antes.   fee·kha·do en tee an·tes

I've been watching you for a while, and
you're (the best-looking girl) here.
Hace rato que te observo y   a·the ra·to ke te ob·ser·vo ee
eres (la chica mas guapa)   e·res (la chee·ka mas gwa·pa)
aqui.   a·kee

rejections

I'm here with my boyfriend/girlfriend.
Estoy aquí con mi   es·toy a·kee kon mee
novio/a. m/f   no·vyo/a

Excuse me, I have to go now.
Lo siento, pero me tengo   lo syen·to pe·ro me ten·go
que ir.   ke eer

Leave me alone!
Déjame en paz.   de·kha·me en path

Hey, I'm not interested in talking to you.
Mira tío/a, es que no me   mee·ra tee·o/a es ke no me
interesa hablar   een·te·re·sa ab·lar
contigo. m/f   kon·tee·go

Listen, why don't you go and get fucked.
Oye rico/a, por qué no   o·ye ree·ko/a por ke no
te vas a tomar por   te vas a to·mar por
el culo. m/f   el koo·lo

getting closer

Can I kiss you?
  ¿Te puedo besar?   te pwe·do be·sar

Do you want to come inside for a drink?
  ¿Quieres entrar a   kye·res en·trar a
  tomar algo?   to·mar al·go

Do you want a massage?
  ¿Quieres un masaje?   kye·res oon ma·sa·khe

Let's go to bed!
  ¡Vámonos a la cama!   va·mo·nos a la ka·ma

sex

el sexo

Kiss me!
  ¡Dame un beso!   da·me oon be·so

I want you.
  Te deseo.   te de·se·o

I want to make love to you.
Quiero hacerte el amor.   kye·ro a·ther·te el a·mor

Do you have a condom?
¿Tienes un condón?   tye·nes oon kon·don

Touch me here.
Tócame aquí.   to·ka·me a·kee

Do you like this?
¿Esto te gusta?   es·to te goos·ta

I (don't) like that.
Eso (no) me gusta.   e·so (no) me goos·ta

I think we should stop now.
Pienso que deberíamos parar.   pyen·so ke de·be·ree·a·mos pa·rar

Oh yeah!
¡Así!   a·see

faster	*rápido*	ra·pee·do
harder	*fuerte*	fwer·te
slower	*despacio*	des·pa·thyo
softer	*suave*	swa·ve

I can't get it up, sorry.
Lo siento, no puedo levantarla.   lo syen·to no pwe·do le·van·tar·la

Don't worry, I'll do it myself.
No te preocupes, lo hago yo.   no te pre·o·koo·pes lo a·go yo

---

endearments

heart	*corazon* m&f	ko·ro·thon
little love	*amorcito/a* m/f	a·mor·thee·to/a
my life	*mi vida* m&f	mee vee·da
my love	*mi amor* m&f	mee a·mor
sky	*cielo* m&f	thye·lo
treasure	*tesoro* m&f	te·so·ro

That was amazing.
   Eso fue increíble.   e·so fwe een·kre·ee·ble

Are you sleepy?
   ¿Tienes sueño?   tye·nes swe·nyo

Can I stay over?
   ¿Puedo quedarme?   pwe·do ke·*dar*·me

I love you.
   Te quiero.   te *kye*·ro

I think we're good together.
   Creo que estamos   kre·o ke es·*ta*·mos
   muy bien juntos.   mooy byen *khoon*·tos

problems

los problemas

Are you seeing someone else?
   ¿Me estás engañando   me es·*tas* en·ga·*nyan*·do
   con alguien?   kon al·gyen

I never want to see you again.
   No quiero volver a verte.   no *kye*·ro vol·*ver* a *ver*·te

He's just a friend.
   Es un amigo   es oon a·*mee*·go
   nada más.   *na*·da mas

She's just a friend.
   Es una amiga   es *oo*·na a·*mee*·ga
   nada más.   *na*·da mas

I want to stay friends.
Me gustaría que
quedáramos como
amigos.

me goos·ta·*ree*·a ke
ke·*da*·ra·mos *ko*·mo
a·*mee*·gos

We'll work it out.
Lo resolveremos.

lo re·sol·ve·*re*·mos

passionate language

That's not true!	*¡Eso no es verdad!*	*e*·so no es ver·*da*
In your dreams!	*¡En sueños!*	en *swe*·nyos
Come off it!	*¡No me jodas!*	no me *kho*·das
Damn!	*¡Hostia!*	*os*·tya
Fuck!	*¡Joder!*	kho·*der*
Shit!	*¡Mierda!*	*myer*·da

beliefs & cultural differences
creencias & diferencias culturales

religion

What's your religion?
¿Cuál es tu religión?   kwal es too re·lee·khyon

Can I pray here?
¿Puedo rezar aquí?   pwe·do re·thar a·kee

I'm (not) ...	*(No) Soy ...*	(no) soy ...
agnostic	*agnóstico/a* m/f	ag·nos·tee·ko/a
Buddhist	*budista*	boo·dees·ta
Catholic	*católico/a* m/f	ka·to·lee·ko/a
Christian	*cristiano/a* m/f	krees·tya·no/a
Hindu	*hindú*	een·doo
Jewish	*judío/a* m/f	khoo·dee·o/a
Muslim	*musulmán/*	moo·sool·man/
	musulmána m/f	moo·sool·ma·na
practising	*practicante*	prak·tee·kan·te
religious	*religioso/a* m/f	re·lee·khyo·so/a

I (don't) believe in ...	*(No) Creo en ...*	(no) kre·o en ...
God	*Dios*	dyos
destiny/fate	*el destino*	el des·tee·no

cultural differences

las diferencias culturales

Is this a local or national custom?
¿Esto es una costumbre   es·to es oo·na kos·toom·bre
local o nacional?   lo·kal o na·thyo·nal

I'm not used to this.
No estoy acostumbrado/a   no es·toy a·kos·toom·bra·do/a
a esto. m/f   a es·to

This is (very) ...	Esto es (muy) ...	es·to es (mooy) ...
fun	*divertido*	dee·ver·*tee*·do
interesting	*interesante*	een·te·re·*san*·te
different	*diferente*	dee·fe·*ren*·te

I'm sorry, it's against my beliefs.
  Lo siento, eso va en   lo *syen*·to e·so va en
  contra de mis creencias.   *kon*·tra de mees kre·*en*·thyas

I don't mind watching, but I'd rather not join in.
  No me importa mirar,   no me eem·*por*·ta mee·*rar*
  pero prefiero no   *pe*·ro pre·*fye*·ro no
  participar.   par·tee·thee·*par*

I'll try it.
  Lo probaré.   lo pro·ba·*re*

Sorry, I didn't mean to do something wrong.
  Lo siento, lo hice   lo *syen*·to lo *ee*·the
  sin querer.   seen ke·*rer*

sporting interests

los intereses deportivos

What sport do you play?
¿Qué deporte practicas? ke de·*por*·te prak·*tee*·kas

What sport do you follow?
¿A qué deporte eres a ke de·*por*·te e·res
aficionado/a? m/f a·fee·thyo·*na*·do/a

I play/do ...
Practico ... prak·*tee*·ko ...

I follow ...
Soy aficionado/a al ... m/f soy a·fee·thyo·*na*·do/a al ...

basketball	*baloncesto* m	ba·lon·*thes*·to
cycling	*ciclismo* m	thee·*klees*·mo
football (soccer)	*fútbol* m	*foot*·bol
tennis	*tenis* m	*te*·nis
volleyball	*voleibol* m	bo·*lei*·bol

Do you like sport?
¿Te gustan los deportes? te *goos*·tan los de·*por*·tes

Yes, very much.
Me encantan. me en·*kan*·tan

Not really.
En realidad, no mucho. en re·a·lee·*da* no *moo*·cho

I like watching it.
Me gusta mirar. me *goos*·ta mee·*rar*

Who's your favourite sportsperson?

¿Quién es tu deportista favorito/a? m/f		kyen es too de·por·*tees*·ta fa·vo·*ree*·to/a

What's your favourite team?

¿Cuál es tu equipo favorito?		kwal es too e·*kee*·po fa·vo·*ree*·to

going to a game

ir al partido

Would you like to go to a (basketball) game?

¿Te gustaría ir a un partido de (baloncesto)?		te goos·ta·*ree*·a eer a oon par·*tee*·do de (ba·lon·*thes*·to)

Who are you supporting?

¿Con qué equipo vas?		kon ke e·*kee*·po vas

scoring

What's the score?	¿Cómo van?	*ko*·mo van
draw/even	empatados	em·pa·*ta*·dos
love (zero)	cero	*the*·ro
match-point	match point	mach poyn
nil (zero)	cero	*the*·ro

How much time is left?

¿Cuánto tiempo queda de partido?		*kwan*·to *tyem*·po *ke*·da de par·*tee*·do

Who's ...?	¿Quién ...?	kyen ...
playing	juega	*khwe*·ga
winning	va ganando	va ga·*nan*·do

That was a ... game!	¡Ese partido fue ...!	*e*·se par·*tee*·do fwe ...
boring	aburrido	a·boo·*ree*·do
great	cojonudo	ko·kho·*noo*·do

playing sport

practicando deportes

Do you want to play?
¿Quieres jugar?
kye·res khoo·gar

Can I join in?
¿Puedo jugar?
pwe·do khoo·gar

Yeah, that'd be great.
Sí, me encantaría.
see me en·kan·ta·ree·a

Not at the moment, thanks.
Ahora mismo no, gracias.
a·o·ra mees·mo no gra·thyas

I have an injury.
Tengo una lesión.
ten·go oo·na le·syon

Where's the best place to run around here?
¿Cuál es el mejor sitio
para hacer footing por
aquí cerca?
kwal es el me·khor see·tyo
pa·ra a·ther foo·teen por
a·kee ther·ka

Do I have to be a member to attend?
¿Hay que ser socio/a
para entrar? m/f
ai ke ser so·thyo/a
pa·ra en·trar

Is there a women-only pool?
¿Hay alguna piscina
sólo para mujeres?
ai al·goo·na pees·thee·na
so·lo pa·ra moo·khe·res

Where are the change rooms?
¿Dónde están los
vestuarios?
don·de es·tan los
ves·twa·ryos

Can I have a locker?
¿Puedo usar una
taquilla?
pwe·do oo·sar oo·na
ta·kee·lya

Where's the	*¿Dónde está …*	don·de es·ta …
nearest …?	*más cercano/a?* m/f	mas ther·ka·no/a
gym	*el gimnasio* m	el kheem·na·syo
swimming pool	*la piscina* f	la pees·thee·na
tennis court	*la pista* f *de tenis*	la pees·ta de te·nees

What's the charge per ...?	¿Cúanto cobran por ...?	kwan·to ko·bran por ...
day	día	dee·a
game	partida	par·tee·da
hour	hora	o·ra
visit	visita	vee·see·ta

Can I hire a ...?	¿Es posible alquilar una ...?	es po·see·ble al·kee·lar oo·na ...
ball	pelota	pe·lo·ta
bicycle	bicicleta	bee·thee·kle·ta
court	cancha	kan·cha
racquet	raqueta	ra·ke·ta

fair play?

I disagree!	No estoy de acuerdo!	no es·toy de a·kwer·do
Yeah, sure!	Sí hombre!	see om·bre
Yes, but ...	Sí pero ...	see pe·ro ...
Whatever.	Lo que sea.	lo ke se·a

diving

el buceo

I'd like to (go) ...	Me gustaría ...	me goos·ta·ree·a ...
explore wrecks	explorar naufragios	eks·plo·rar now·fra·khyos
learn to dive	aprender a bucear	a·pren·der a boo·the·ar
scuba diving	hacer submarinismo	a·ther soob·ma·ree·nees·mo
snorkelling	bucear con tubo	boo·the·ar kon too·bo

Where are some good diving sites?

¿Dónde hay buenos lugares	don·de ai bwe·nos loo·ga·res	
para bucear?	pa·ra boo·the·ar	

Are there jellyfish?

¿Hay medusas?   ai me·doo·sas

Where can we hire ...?

¿Dónde se puede alquilar ...?   don·de se pwe·de al·kee·lar ...

diving course	curso m de buceo	koor·so de boo·the·o
diving equipment	equipo m de buceo	e·kee·po de boo·the·o
flippers	aletas f pl	a·le·tas
mask	gafas f pl	ga·fas
wetsuits	trajes m pl	tra·khes
	isotérmicos	ee·so·ter·mee·kos

extreme sports

los deportes extremos

Are you sure this is safe?

¿De verdad que esto es	de ver·da ke es·to es
seguro?	se·goo·ro

Is the equipment secure?

¿Está seguro el equipo?   es·ta se·goo·ro el e·kee·po

This is insane!

¡Esto es una locura!   es·to es oo·na lo·koo·ra

abseiling	rappel m	ra·pel
bungy-jumping	puenting m	pwen·teen
caving	espeleología f	es·pe·le·o·lo·khee·a
game fishing	pesca f deportiva	pes·ka de·por·tee·va
mountain biking	ciclismo m de	thee·klees·mo de
	montaña	mon·ta·nya
rock-climbing	escalada f	es·ka·la·da

soccer

Who plays for (Real Madrid)?
  ¿Quién juega en el   kyen *khwe*·ga en el
  (Real Madrid)?   (re·*al* ma·*dree*)

What a terrible team!
  ¡Qué equipo más espantoso!   ke e·*kee*·po mas es·pan·*to*·so

He's a great player.
  Es un gran jugador.   es oon gran khoo·ga·*dor*

He played brilliantly in the match against (Italy).
  Jugó de fenomenal   khoo·*go* de fe·no·me·*nal*
  en el partido contra   en el par·*tee*·do *kon*·tra
  (Italia).   (ee·*ta*·lya)

Which team is at the top of the league?
  ¿Qué equipo está en   ke e·*kee*·po es·*ta* en
  primera posición en   pree·*me*·ra po·see·*thyon* en
  la liga?   la *lee*·ga

corner	saque m de esquina	sa·ke de es·kee·na
free kick	tiro m libre	tee·ro lee·bre
goalkeeper	portero m	por·te·ro
offside	fuera de juego	fwe·ra de khwe·go
penalty	penalty m	pe·nal·tee

sports talk

What a ...!	¡Qué ...!	ke ...
goal	gol	gol
pass	pase	pa·se

Your/My point.
Tu/Mi punto. — too/mee *poon*·to

Kick it to me!
¡Pásamelo! — pa·sa·me·lo

You're a good player.
Juegas bien. — khwe·gas byen

Thanks for the game.
Gracias por el partido. — gra·thyas por el par·tee·do

tennis

el tenis

Would you like to play tennis?
¿Quieres jugar al tenis? — kye·res khoo·gar al te·nees

Can we play at night?
¿Se puede jugar de noche? — se pwe·de khoo·gar de no·che

Game, Set, Match.
Juego, set y partido. — khwe·go set ee par·tee·do

ace	ace m	eys
advantage	ventaja f	ven·ta·kha
fault	falta f	fal·ta
play doubles	jugar dobles	khoo·gar do·bles
(against)	(contra)	(kon·tra)
serve	saque m	sa·ke

walking & mountaineering

For language on hiking, see **outdoors**, page 137.

water sports

los deportes acuáticos

Can I book a lesson?
¿Puedo reservar una clase?   pwe·do re·ser·var oo·na kla·se

Is safety gear provided?
¿Proporcionan el equipo   pro·por·thyo·nan el e·kee·po
de seguridad?   de se·goo·ree·da

Are there any ...?	*¿Hay ...?*	ai ...
reefs	*arrecifes*	a·re·thee·fes
rips	*corrientes*	ko·ryen·tes
water hazards	*peligros en*	pe·lee·gros en
	el agua	el a·gwa

motorboat	*lancha* f *motora*	lan·cha mo·to·ra
sail	*vela* f	ve·la
surfboard	*tabla* f *de surf*	ta·bla de soorf
surfing	*surf* m	soorf
water-skis	*esquís* m pl *acuáticos*	es·kees a·kwa·tee·kos
wave	*ola* f	o·la

local sports

If you hear the sounds of bat, ball and exertion, it may be *pelotari*, pelota players, enjoying the traditional game of *pelota vasca*, a type of handball. It's also known as *jai-alai* in Basque.

ball	*pelota* f	pe·lo·ta
striker	*delantero/a* m/f	de·lan·te·ro/a
wall	*frontón* m	fron·ton

hiking

el excursionismo

There's plenty of walking, hiking and mountaineering to do in Spain. A recognised cross-country walking trail is known as *Gran Recorrido* (GR), gran re·ko·*ree*·do, while the shorter walking paths scattered throughout the country are called *Pequeños Recorridos* (PR), pe·*ke*·nyos re·ko·*ree*·dos.

Where can I ...?	¿Dónde puedo ...?	don·de pwe·do ...
buy supplies	comprar viveres	kom·*prar* vee·ver·es
find someone who knows this area	encontrar a alguien que conozca el área	en·kon·*trar* a *al*·gyen ke ko·*noth*·ka el a·re·a
get a map	obtener un mapa	ob·te·*ner* oon *ma*·pa
hire hiking gear	alquilar un equipo para ir de excursion	al·kee·*lar* oon e·*kee*·po *pa*·ra eer de eks·koor·*syon*

outdoors

Where can I find out about hiking trails?

¿Dónde hay información sobre caminos rurales de la zona?	don·de ai een·for·ma·thyon so·bre ka·mee·nos roo·ra·les de la tho·na

How long is the trail?

¿Cuántos kilómetros tiene el camino?	kwan·tos kee·lo·me·tros tye·ne el ka·mee·no

How high is the climb?

¿A qué altura se escala?	a ke al·too·ra se es·ka·la

Do we need a guide?

¿Se necesita un guía?	se ne·the·see·ta oon gee·a

Are there guided treks?

¿Se organizan excursiones guiadas?	se or·ga·nee·than eks·koor·syo·nes gee·a·das

Do we need to take ...?	¿Se necesita llevar ...?	se ne·the·see·ta lye·var ...
bedding	algo en que dormir	al·go en ke dor·meer
food	comida	ko·mee·da
water	agua	a·gwa

Is the track ...?	¿Es ... el sendero?	es ... el sen·de·ro
(well-)marked	(bien) marcado	(byen) mar·ka·do
open	abierto	a·byer·to
scenic	pintoresco	peen·to·res·ko

Which is the ... route?	¿Cuál es el camino más ...?	kwal es el ka·mee·no mas ...
easiest	fácil	fa·theel
shortest	corto	kor·to

Where's a ...?	¿Dónde hay ...?	*don*·de ai ...
camping site	*un cámping*	oon *kam*·peen
village	*un pueblo*	oon *pwe*·blo
Where are the ...?	¿Dónde hay ...?	*don*·de ai ...
showers	*duchas*	*doo*·chas
toilets	*servicios*	ser·*vee*·thyos

Where have you come from?
¿De dónde vienes?   de *don*·de vye·nes

How long did it take?
¿Cuánto ha tardado?   kwan·to a tar·*da*·do

Does this path go to ...?
¿Este camino va a ...?   es·te ka·*mee*·no va a ...

Can we go through here?
¿Se puede pasar por aquí?   se *pwe*·de pa·*sar* por a·*kee*

Is the water OK to drink?
¿Se puede beber el agua?   se *pwe*·de be·*ber* el a·gwa

I'm lost.
Estoy perdido/a. m/f   es·*toy* per·*dee*·do/a

Is it safe?
¿Es seguro?   es se·*goo*·ro

Is there a hut there?
¿Hay una cabaña allí?   ai *oo*·na ka·*ba*·nya a·*lyee*

When does it get dark?
¿A qué hora oscurece?   a ke o·ra os·koo·*re*·the

signs

¡Prohibido	pro·ee·*bee*·do	**No Swimming!**
Nadar!	na·*dar*	

at the beach

Where's the ... beach?	¿Dónde está la playa ...?	don·de es·ta la pla·ya ...
best	mejor	me·khor
nearest	más cercana	mas ther·ka·na
nudist	nudista	noo·dees·ta

Is it safe to dive/swim here?
¿Es seguro bucear/ nadar aquí?   es se·goo·ro boo·the·ar/ na·dar a·kee

What time is high/low tide?
¿A qué hora es la marea alta/baja?   a ke o·ra es la ma·re·a al·ta/ba·kha

Do we have to pay?
¿Hay que pagar?   ai ke pa·gar

How much to rent ...?	¿Cuánto por alquilar ... ?	kwan·to por al·kee·lar ...
a chair	una silla	oo·na see·lya
a hut	una cabaña	oo·na ka·ba·nya
an umbrella	un parasol	oon pa·ra·sol

listen for ...

kwee·da·do kon la re·sa·ka
Cuidado con la resaca.   Be careful of the undertow.

es pe·lee·gro·so
¡Es peligroso!   It's dangerous!

e·res mo·de·lo
¿Eres modelo?   Are you a model?

weather

el tiempo

What's the weather like?
¿Qué tiempo hace? ke tyem·po a tho

Today it's ...	*Hoy hace ...*	oy a·the ...
Will it be ...	*Mañana*	ma·nya·na
tomorrow?	*hará ...?*	a·ra ...
cold	*frío*	free·o
freezing	*un frío*	oon free·o
	que pela	ke pe·la
hot	*calor*	ka·lor
sunny	*sol*	sol
warm	*calor*	ka·lor
windy	*viento*	vyen·to

(Today) It's raining.
(Hoy) Está lloviendo. (oy) es·ta lyo·vyen·do

(Tomorrow) It will be raining.
(Mañana) Lloverá. (ma·nya·na) lyo·ve·ra

Where can I	*¿Dónde puedo*	don·de pwe·do
buy ...?	*comprar ...?*	kom·prar ...
a rain	*un*	oon
jacket	*impermeable*	eem·per·me·a·ble
sunblock	*crema solar*	kre·ma so·lar
an umbrella	*un paraguas*	oon pa·ra·gwas
hail	*granizo* m	gra·nee·tho
storm	*tormenta* f	tor·men·ta
sun	*sol* m	sol

flora & fauna

What ... is that?	¿Qué ... es ése/ésa? m/f	ke ... es e·se/e·sa
animal	animal m	a·nee·mal
flower	flor f	flor
plant	planta f	plan·ta
tree	árbol m	ar·bol

What's it used for?
¿Para qué se usa?   pa·ra ke se oo·sa

Can you eat the fruit?
¿Se puede comer la fruta?   se pwe·de ko·mer la froo·ta

Is it endangered?
¿Está en peligro   es·ta en pe·lee·gro
de extinción?   de eks·teen·thyon

Is it ...?	¿Es ...?	es ...
common	común	ko·moon
dangerous	peligroso/a m/f	pe·lee·gro·so/a
protected	protegido/a m/f	pro·te·khee·do/a

For geographical and agricultural terms, and names of animals and plants, see the **dictionary**.

key language

lenguaje clave

The main meal in Spain, 'lunchtime' is called *la hora de comer*, la o·ra de ko·mer. It's served between 1.30pm and 4.30pm.

breakfast	*desayuno* m	de·sa·yoo·no
lunch	*comida* f	ko·mee·da
dinner	*cena* f	the·na
snack	*tentempié* m	ten·tem·pye
eat	*comer*	ko·mer
drink	*beber*	be·ber
Please.	*Por favor.*	por fa·vor
Thank you.	*Gracias.*	gra·thyas
I'd like ...	*Quisiera ...*	kee·sye·ra ...
I'm starving!	*¡Estoy hambriento/a!* m/f	es·toy am·bryen·to/a

finding a place to eat

buscando un lugar para comer

Can you recommend a ...?	*¿Puede recomendar un/una ...?* m/f	pwe·de re·ko·men·dar oon/oo·na ...
bar	*bar* m	bar
cafe	*café* m	ka·fe
coffee bar	*cafetería* f	ka·fe·te·ree·a
restaurant	*restaurante* m	res·tow·ran·te

Are you still serving food?

¿Siguen sirviendo comida?   see·gen seer·vyen·do ko·mee·da

How long is the wait?
¿Cuánto hay que esperar?   kwan·to ai ke es·pe·rar

Where would you go for (a) ...?	*¿Adónde se va para ...?*	a·don·de se va pa·ra ...
celebration	*celebrar*	sel·e·brar
cheap meal	*comer barato*	ko·mer ba·ra·to
local specialities	*comer comida típica*	ko·mer ko·mee·da tee·pee·ka

I'd like to reserve a table for ...	*Quisiera reservar una mesa para ...*	kee·sye·ra re·ser·var oo·na me·sa pa·ra ...
(two) people	*(dos) personas*	(dos) per·so·nas
(eight) o'clock	*las (ocho)*	las (o·cho)

---

listen for ...

lo syen·to e·mos the·ra·do	
Lo siento, hemos cerrado.	**Sorry, we're closed.**
no te·ne·mos me·sa	
No tenemos mesa.	**We have no tables.**
oon mo·men·to	
Un momento.	**One moment.**

I'd like ..., please.	*Quisiera ..., por favor.*	kee·sye·ra ... por fa·vor
a table for (five)	*una mesa para (cinco)*	oo·na me·sa pa·ra (theen·ko)
the (non-) smoking section	*(no) fumadores*	(no) foo·ma·do·res
the drink list	*la lista de bebidas*	la lees·ta de be·bee·das
the menu	*el menú*	el me·noo

Do you have ... ?	*¿Tienen ... ?*	tye·nen ...
children's meals	*comidas para niños*	ko·mee·das pa·ra nee·nyos
a menu in English	*un menú en inglés*	oon me·noo en een·gles

at the restaurant

Is it self-serve?
¿Es de autoservicio? es de ow·to·ser·vee·thyo

Is service included in the bill?
¿La cuenta incluye la kwen·ta een·kloo·ye
servicio? ser·vee·thyo

What would you recommend?
¿Qué recomienda? ke re·ko·myen·da

I'll have what they're having.
Tomaré lo mismo que ellos. to·ma·re lo mees·mo ke e·lyos

Does it take long to prepare?
¿Tarda mucho en tar·da moo·cho en
prepararse? pre·pa·rar·se

What's in that dish?
¿Que lleva ese plato? ke lye·va e·se pla·to

For more on special diets, see **vegetarian & special meals**, page 159, and **health**, page 184.

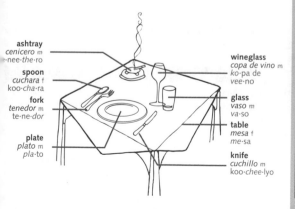

ashtray
cenicero m
·nee·the·ro

spoon
cuchara f
koo·cha·ra

fork
tenedor m
te·ne·dor

plate
plato m
pla·to

wineglass
copa de vino m
ko·pa de
vee·no

glass
vaso m
va·so

table
mesa f
me·sa

knife
cuchillo m
koo·chee·lyo

eating out

145

Are these complimentary?
  ¿Éstos son gratis?   es·tos son gra·tees

We're just having drinks.
  Sólo queremos tomar algo.   so·lo ke·re·mos to·mar al·go

I'd like a local speciality.
  Quisiera un plato   kee·sye·ra oon pla·to
  típico.   tee·pee·ko

at the table

a la mesa

Please bring ...	Por favor nos trae ...	por fa·vor nos tra·e ...
the bill	la cuenta	la kwen·ta
a glass	un vaso	oon va·so
a serviette	una servilleta	oo·na ser·vee·lye·ta
a wineglass	una copa	oo·na ko·pa
	de vino	de vee·no

For more words you might find on a menu, see the **culinary reader**, page 161.

For more words you might find on a menu, see the **culinary reader**, page 161.

listen for ...

le goos·ta ...
  ¿Le gusta ...?   **Do you like ...?**

re·ko·myen·do ...
  Recomiendo ...   **I suggest the ...**

ko·mo lo kye·re pre·pa·ra·do
  ¿Cómo lo quiere   **How would you like**
  preparado?   **that cooked?**

Aperitivos	a·pe·ree·*tee*·vos	Appetisers
Caldos	*kal*·dos	Soups
Cervezas	ther·*ve*·thas	Beers
De Entrada	de en·*tra*·da	Entrees
Digestivos	dee·khes·*tee*·vos	Digestifs
Ensaladas	en·sa·*la*·das	Salads
Licores	lee·*ko*·res	Spirits
Postres	*pos*·tres	Desserts
Refrescos	re·*fres*·kos	Soft Drinks
Segundos Platos	se·*goon*·dos *pla*·tos	Main Courses
Vinos Blancos	vee·nos *blan*·kos	White Wines
Vinos Dulces	vee·no *dool*·thes	Dessert Wines
Vinos Espumosos	vee·nos es·poo·*mo*·sos	Sparkling Wines
Vinos Tintos	vee·nos *teen*·tos	Red Wines

talking food

hablando de comida

I love this dish.
Me encanta este plato.
me en·*kan*·ta es·te *pla*·to

We love the local cuisine.
Nos encanta la comida típica de la zona.
nos en·*kan*·ta la ko·*mee*·da *tee*·pee·ka de la *tho*·na

That was delicious!
¡Estaba buenísimo!
es·*ta*·ba bwe·*nee*·see·mo

My compliments to the chef.
Mi enhorabuena al cocinero.
mee en·o·ra·*bwe*·na al ko·thee·*ne*·ro

I'm full.
Estoy lleno/a. m/f
es·toy lye·no/a

This is ...	*Esto está ...*	es·to es·ta ...
burnt	*quemado*	ke·*ma*·do
(too) cold	*(muy) frío*	(mooy) *free*·o
superb	*exquisito*	eks·kee·*see*·to

meals

> breakfast

What's a typical Spanish (breakfast)?

¿Cómo es un típico (desayuno) español?		*ko·mo es oon tee·pee·ko (de·sa·yoo·no) es·pa·nyol?*

omelette	*tortilla*	tor·tee·lya
muesli	*muesli*	mwes·lee
toast	*tostadas*	tos·ta·das

For typical dishes, see the **culinary reader**, page 161, and for other food items see the **dictionary**.

> light meals

What's that called?	*¿Cómo se llama eso?*	ko·mo se lya·ma e·so
I'd like ..., please.	*Quisiera ..., por favor.*	kee·sye·ra ... por fa·vor
a piece	*un trozo*	oon tro·tho
a sandwich	*un sándwich*	oon san·weech
one slice	*una loncha*	oo·na lon·cha
that one	*ése/a* m/f	e·se/a
two	*dos*	dos

Is there any ...?	¿Hay ...?	ai ...
chilli sauce	salsa f de guindilla	sal·sa de geen·dee·lya
pepper	pimienta f	pee·myen·ta
salt	sal f	sal
tomato sauce/ ketchup	salsa f de tomate	sal·sa de to·ma·te
vinegar	vinagre m	vee·na·gre

methods of preparation

los métodos de cocción

I'd like it ...	Lo quiero ...	lo kye·ro ...
I don't want it ...	No lo quiero ...	no lo kye·ro ...
deep-fried	frito en aceite abundante	free·to en a·they·te a·boon·dan·te
medium	no muy hecho	no mooy e·cho
rare	vuelta y vuelta	vwel·ta ee vwel·ta
re-heated	recalentado	re·ka·len·ta·do
steamed	al vapor	al va·por
well-done	muy hecho	mooy e·cho
with the dressing on the side	con el aliño aparte	kon el a·lee·nyo a·par·te
without ...	sin ...	seen ...

in the bar

Excuse me!	*¡Oiga!*	*oy·ga*
I'm next.	*Ahora voy yo.*	*a·o·ra voy yo*
I'll have ...	*Para mí …*	*pa·ra mee ...*

Same again, please.
Otra de lo mismo.　　　　o·tra de lo *mees*·mo

No ice, thanks.
Sin hielo, gracias.　　　　seen *ye*·lo *gra*·thyas

I'll buy you a drink.
Te invito a una copa.　　　te een·*vee*·to a *oo*·na *ko*·pa

What would you like?
¿Qué quieres tomar?　　　ke *kye*·res to·*mar*

It's my round.
Es mi ronda.　　　　　　　es mee *ron*·da

You can get the next one.
La próxima la pagas tú.　　la *prok*·see·ma la *pa*·gas too

How much is that?
¿Cuánto es eso?　　　　　*kwan*·to es e·so

Do you serve meals here?
¿Sirven comidas aquí?　　*seer*·ven ko·*mee*·das a·*kee*

listen for ...

a·kee tye·ne *¡Aquí tiene!*	**Here you go!**
don·de le gus·ta·ree·a sen·tar·se *¿Dónde le gustaría sentarse?*	**Where would you like to sit?**
en ke le pwe·do ser·veer *¿En qué le puedo servir?*	**What can I get for you?**
kye·re to·mar al·go myen·tras es·pe·ra *¿Quiere tomar algo mientras espera?*	**Would you like a drink while you wait?**

FOOD

150

tapas

Tapas are scrumptious cooked bar snacks, available pretty much around the clock at bars and some clubs. You'll find they're free in some places, laid out in the bar for you to choose from. This follows village tradition at the turn of the century in the whole of Andalusia, as well as in Extremadura, Low Castile, Murcia and the working-class districts of Madrid and Barcelona.

Other places will rotate the dishes. Listen for ...

da·me oo·na pree·*me*·ra
¡Dame una primera!   **Give me a starter!**

oo·na se·*goon*·da
¡Una segunda!   **Give me a main dish!**

... as the bar attendant orders a different speciality each time from the cook. See if you can stay on your stool long enough to get back to number one again.

• how hungry are you?

banderilla/	ban·de·ree·lya/	small tapa serving
moruno/	mo·*roo*·no/	on bread or a
pinchito	peen·*chee*·to	toothpick
ración	ra·*thyon*	large tapa serving

• common tapas:

montadito	mon·ta·*deet*·o	bread-topped tapa
pan tumaca	pan too·*ma*·ka	tapa of toasted bread rubbed with tomatoes & garlic, served with oil
queso en	*ke*·soh en	cheese in olive oil,
aceite	a·*say*·tay	served as a tapa

• regional tapas:

naveganta	na·ve·gan·ta	in Burgos
pintxo	*peen*·cho	in Basque Country

eating out

151

nonalcoholic drinks

I don't drink alcohol.
No bebo alcohol. no *be*·bo al·ko·*hol*

(cup of) coffee ...	*(taza de) café* m ...	(*ta*·tha de) ka·*fe* ...
(cup of) tea ...	*(taza de) té* m ...	(*ta*·tha de) te ...
with milk	*con leche*	kon *le*·che
without sugar	*sin azúcar*	seen a·*thoo*·kar
soft drink	*refrescos* m	re·*fres*·ko
... water	*agua* f ...	*a*·gwa ...
boiled	*hervida*	er·vee·da
mineral	*mineral*	mee·ne·*ral*
(sparkling)	*(con gas)*	(kon gas)

alcoholic drinks

beer	*cerveza* f	ther·*ve*·tha
brandy	*coñac* m	ko·*nyak*
champagne	*champán* m	cham·*pan*
cocktail	*combinado* m	kom·bee·*na*·do
sangria (red-wine punch)	*sangría* f	san·*gree*·a
a shot of ...	*un chupito* m *de* ...	oon choo·*pee*·to de ...
gin	*ginebra* f	khee·*ne*·bra
rum	*ron* m	ron
tequila	*tequila* m	te·*kee*·la
vodka	*vodka* m	*vod*·ka
whisky	*güisqui* m	*gwees*·kee

a big fan of the mini

Many Spanish bars provide massive plastic beakers of beer to cater for young revellers. It's cut with water and average tasting – but cheap and free flowing! These fountains of froth are called *minis*.

Other words you'll need when ordering a brew:

cerveza f ...	ther·*ve*·tha ...	... beer
de barril	de ba·*ril*	draught
negra	*neg*·ra	dark
rubia	*roo*·bee·a	light
sin alcohol	sin al·kol	nonalcoholic
botellín m	bo·tel·*yin*	small bottle of beer (250 ml)
litrona f	lee·*tro*·na	litre bottle of beer
mediana f	me·dee·*a*·na	bottle of beer (300 ml)

a bottle/glass of ... wine	*una botella/ copa de vino* ...	*oo*·na bo·*te*·lya/ *ko*·pa de *vee*·no ...
dessert	*dulce*	*dool*·the
red	*tinto*	*teen*·to
rose	*rosado*	ro·*sa*·do
sparkling	*espumoso*	es·poo·*mo*·so
white	*blanco*	*blan*·ko
a ... of beer	*una ... de cerveza*	*oo*·na ... de ther·*ve*·tha
glass	*caña*	*ka*·nya
jug	*jarra*	*kha*·ra
pint	*pinta*	*peen*·ta

one too many?

Cheers!
¡Salud!   sa·*loo*

Thanks, but I don't feel like it.
Lo siento, pero no me   lo *syen*·to *pe*·ro no me
apetece.   a·pe·*te*·the

This is hitting the spot.
Me lo estoy pasando   me lo es·*toy* pa·*san*·do
muy bien.   mooy byen

I'm tired, I'd better go home.
Estoy cansado/a, mejor   es·*toy* kan·*sa*·do/a me·*khor*
me voy a casa. m/f   me voy a *ka*·sa

Where's the toilet?
¿Dónde está el lavabo?   *don*·de es·*ta* el la·*va*·bo

I'm feeling drunk.
Esto me está subiendo   *es*·to me es·*ta* soo·*byen*·do
mucho.   *moo*·cho

I feel fantastic!
¡Me siento fenomenal!   me *syen*·to fe·no·me·*nal*

I really, really love you.
Te quiero muchísimo.   te *kye*·ro moo·*chee*·see·mo

I think I've had one too many.
Creo que he tomado   *kre*·o ke e to·*ma*·do
demasiado.   de·ma·*sya*·do

Can you call a taxi for me?
¿Me puedes pedir un taxi?   me *pwe*·des pe·*deer* oon *tak*·see

I don't think you should drive.
No creo que deberías   no *kre*·o ke de·be·*ree*·as
conducir.   kon·doo·*theer*

I'm pissed.
Estoy borracho/a. m/f   es·*toy* bo·*ra*·cho/a

I feel ill.
Me siento mal.   me *syen*·to mal

key language

lenguaje clave

A piece.	*Un trozo.*	oon *tro*·tho
A slice.	*Una loncha.*	*oo*·na *lon*·cha
That one.	*Ése.*	*e*·se
This.	*Esto.*	*es*·to
A bit more.	*Un poco más.*	oon *po*·ko mas
Less.	*Menos.*	*me*·nos
Enough!	*¡Basta!*	*ba*·sta
cooked	*cocido/a* m/f	ko·*thee*·do/a
dried	*seco/a* m/f	*se*·ko/a
fresh	*fresco/a* m/f	*fres*·ko/a
frozen	*congelado/a* m/f	kon·khe·*la*·do/a
raw	*crudo/a* m/f	*kroo*·do/a

buying food

comprando comida

How much?
¿Cuánto?   *kwan*·to

How many?
¿Cuántos?   *kwan*·tos

How much is (a kilo of cheese)?
*¿Cuánto vale (un kilo   *kwan*·to va·le (oon *kee*·lo
de queso)?*   de *ke*·so)

What's the local speciality?
*¿Cuál es la especialidad   kwal es la es·pe·thya·lee·*da
de la zona?*   de la *tho*·na

What's that?
¿Qué es eso?   ke es *e*·so

listen for ...

en ke le *pwe*·do ser·*veer*
  ¿En qué le puedo servir?   **Can I help you?**

ke ke·*ree*·as
  ¿Qué querías?   **What would you like?**

no *ten*·go
  No tengo.   **I don't have any.**

Can I taste it?
  ¿Puedo probarlo/a? m/f   *pwe*·do pro·*bar*·lo/a

Can I have a bag, please?
  ¿Me da una bolsa, por favor?   me da *oo*·na *bol*·sa por fa·*vor*

I'd like ...	Póngame ...	*pon*·ga·me ...
(three) pieces	*(tres) piezas*	(tres) *pye*·thas
(six) slices	*(seis) lonchas*	(seys) *lon*·chas
(two) kilos	*(dos) kilos*	(dos) *kee*·los
(200) grams	*(doscientos) gramos*	(dos·*thyen*·tos) *gra*·mos

Do you have ...?	*¿Tiene ... ?*	*tye*·ne ...
anything cheaper	*algo más barato*	*al*·go mas ba·*ra*·to
any other kinds	*otros tipos*	*ot*·ros *tee*·pos
Where can I find the ... section?	*¿Dónde está la sección de ...?*	*don*·de es·*ta* la sek·*thyon* de ...
dairy	*productos lácteos*	pro·*dook*·tos *lak*·te·os
frozen goods	*productos congelados*	pro·*dook*·tos kon·khe·*la*·dos
fruit and vegetable	*frutas y verduras*	*froo*·tas ee ver·*doo*·ras
meat	*carne*	*kar*·ne
poultry	*aves*	*a*·ves

FOOD

156

cooking utensils

Could I please borrow a/an ...?
¿Me puede prestar ...?   me *pwe*·de pres·*tar* ...

Where's a/an ...?
¿Dónde hay ...?   *don*·de ai ...

bottle opener	*abrebotellas* m	a·bre·bo·*te*·lyas
bowl	*bol* m	bol
can opener	*abrelatas* m	a·bre·*la*·tas
chopping board	*tabla* f *para cortar*	*tab*·la pa·ra kor·tar
cup	*taza* f	*ta*·tha
corkscrew	*sacacorchos* m	sa·ka·*kor*·chos
fork	*tenedor* m	ten·ne·*dor*
fridge	*nevera* m	ne·*ve*·ra
frying pan	*sartén* f	sar·*ten*
glass	*vaso* m	*va*·so
knife	*cuchillo* m	koo·*chee*·lyo
oven	*horno* m	*or*·no
plate	*plato* m	*pla*·to
saucepan	*cazo* m	*ka*·tho
spoon	*cuchara* f	koo·*cha*·ra
toaster	*tostadora* f	los·ta·*do*·ra

listen for ...

e·so es (oon man·*che*·go) *Eso es (un manchego).*	That's (a manchego).
no *ke*·da mas *No queda más.*	There's none left.
e·so es (*theen*·ko e·oo·ros) *Eso es (cinco euros).*	That's (five euros).
al·go mas *¿Algo más?*	Would you like anything else?

useful amounts

Please give me ...	Por favor, deme ...	por fa·*vor* de·me ...
(100) grams	(cien) gramos	(thyen) *gra*·mos
half a dozen	una media docena	oo·na me·dya do·*the*·na
half a kilo	un medio kilo	oon me·dyo kee·lo
a kilo	un kilo	oon kee·lo
a bottle (of ...)	una botella (de ...)	oo·na bo·*te*·lya (de ...)
a jar	una jarra	oo·na kha·ra
a packet	un paquete	oon pa·*ke*·te
a tin	una lata	oo·na la·ta
(just) a little	(sólo) un poquito	(so·lo) oon po·kee·to
many	muchos/as m/f	moo·chos/as
more	más	mas
some	algunos/as m/f	al·goo·nos/as
less	menos	me·nos

vegetarian & special meals
comidas vegetarianas & platos especiales

ordering food

I'm vegetarian.
Soy vegetariano/a. m/f   soy ve·khe·ta·rya·no/a

Is there a (vegetarian) restaurant near here?
¿Hay un restaurante   ai oon res·tow·ran·te
(vegetariano) por aquí?   (ve·khe·ta·rya·no) por a·kee

Do you have ...   *¿Tienen comida ...?*   tye·nen ko·mee·da ...
food?
    halal   *halal*   a·lal
    kosher   *kosher*   ko·sher
    vegan   *vegetariana*   ve·khe·ta·rya·na
            estricta   es·trik·ta

I don't eat red meat.
No como carne roja.   no ko·mo kar·ne ro·kha

Is it cooked in/with butter?
¿Esta cocinado   es·ta ko·thee·na·do
en/con mantequilla?   en/kon man·te·kee·lya

Could you   *¿Me puede*   me pwe·de
prepare a meal   *preparar una*   pre·pa·rar oo·na
without ...?   *comida sin ...?*   ko·mee·da seen ...
    eggs   *huevo*   we·vo
    fish   *pescado*   pes·ka·do
    meat/fish   *caldo de carne/*   kal·do de kar·ne/
    stock   *pescado*   pes·ka·do
    pork   *cerdo*   ther·do
    poultry   *aves*   a·ves

Is this ...?	¿Esto es ...?	es·to es ...
free of animal produce	*sin productos de animales*	seen pro·*dook*·tos de a·*nee*·ma·les
free-range	*de corral*	de ko·ral
genetically modified	*transgénico*	trans·*khe*·nee·ko
gluten-free	*sin gluten*	seen *gloo*·ten
low in sugar	*bajo en azúcar*	*ba*·kho en a·*thoo*·kar
low-fat	*bajo en grasas*	*ba*·kho en *gra*·sas
organic	*orgánico*	or·*ga*·nee·ko
salt-free	*sin sal*	seen sal

special diets & allergies

regímenes especiales & alergias

I'm on a special diet.
Estoy a régimen especial.   es·*toy* a re·*khee*·men es·pe·*thyal*

I'm allergic to ...	Soy alérgico/a ... m/f	soy a·*ler*·khee·ko/a ...
dairy produce	*a los productos lácteos*	a los pro·*dook*·tos *lak*·te·os
honey	*al miel*	al myel
MSG	*al glutamato monosódico*	al gloo·ta·*ma*·to mo·no·*so*·dee·ko
nuts	*a las nueces*	a las *nwe*·thes
seafood	*a los mariscos*	a los ma·*rees*·kos
shellfish	*a los crustáceos*	a los kroos·*ta*·thyos

---

listen for ...

le pre·goon·ta·*re* al ko·thee·*ne*·ro	
Le preguntaré al cocinero.	**I'll check with the cook.**
pwe·de ko·*mer* ...	
¿Puede comer ...?	**Can you eat ...?**
to·do *lye*·va (*kar*·ne).	
Todo lleva (carne).	**It all has (meat) in it.**

For a more detailed version of this glossary, see Lonely Planet's *World Food Spain*.

A

acebuche ⓜ a·the·*boo*·che *wild olive*
acedía ⓕ a·the·*dee*·a *plaice/flounder*
aceite ⓜ a·*they*·te *oil*
— **de girasol** de khee·ra·*sol*
sunflower oil
— **de oliva** de o·*lee*·va *olive oil*
— **de oliva virgen extra** de o·*lee*·va
veer·khen eks·tra *extra virgin olive oil*
aceituna ⓕ a·they·*too*·na *olive*
— **negra** *ne*·gra *black olive*
— **verde** *ver*·de *green olive*
ácido/a ⓜ/ⓕ a·thee·do/a *tart (of fruit)*
adobo ⓜ a·*do*·bo *marinade*
agrios ⓜ pl a·gryos *citrus fruits*
aguacate ⓜ a·gwa·*ka*·te *avocado*
aguaturma ⓕ a·gwa·*toor*·ma *Jerusalem
artichoke*
ajiaco ⓜ a·*khya*·ko *spicy potato dish*
ajoaceite ⓜ a·kho·a·*they*·te *garlic &
oil sauce* • *garlic mayonnaise*
ajoharina ⓕ a·kho·a·*ree*·na *potatoes
stewed in garlic sauce*
ajoarriero (al) a·kho·a·rye·ro (al) *'mule-
driver's garlic' - anything cooked in a
sauce of onions, garlic & chilli*
ala ⓕ a·la *(chicken) wing*
alajú ⓜ a·la·khoo *honey & almond cake*
albaricoque ⓜ al·ba·ree·*ko*·ke *apricot*
— **seco** *se*·ko *dried apricot*
albóndigas ⓕ pl al·*bon*·dee·gas
meatballs
— **de pescado** de pes·*ka*·do *fish balls*
alcachofas ⓕ pl al·ka·*cho*·fas *artichokes*
— **guisadas a la española** gee·*sa*·das
a la es·*pa*·nyo·la *artichokes in wine*
— **rellenas** re·*lye*·nas *stuffed artichokes*
alcaparra ⓕ al·ka·*pa*·ra *caper*

alloli ⓜ a·lec o lee *garlic mayonnaise*
almejas ⓕ pl al·*me*·khas *clams – superb
eaten raw*
— **a la marinera** a la ma·ree·*ne*·ra
clams in white wine
— **al horno** al *or*·no *baked clams*
almendrado ⓜ al·men·*dra*·do *almond
cake or biscuit* • *chocolate covered
ice cream bar*
almendras ⓕ pl al·*men*·dras *almonds*
alubia ⓕ a·*loo*·bya *haricot bean*
anacardo ⓜ a·na·*kar*·do *cashew nut*
anchoas ⓕ pl an·*cho*·as *anchovies –
mostly eaten fresh, grilled or fried*
angelote ⓜ an·khe·*lo*·te *monkfish*
anguila ⓕ an·*gee*·la *adult eel*
angulas ⓕ pl an·*goo*·las *baby eels –
prized as a delicacy, they resemble
vermicelli*
— **en all i pebre** en al ee *pe*·bre *baby
eels with pepper & garlic*
apio ⓜ a·pyo *celery*
arándano ⓜ a·ran·da·no *blueberry*
arenque ⓜ a·*ren*·ke *herring*
— **ahumado** a·oo·*ma*·do *kipper*
arroz ⓜ a·*roth* *rice*
— **a la Alcireña** a la al·thee·re·nya
baked rice dish
— **abanda (de València)** a·*ban*·da
(de va·*len*·thya) *fish paella*
— **con leche** kon *le*·che *rice pudding*
— **con pollo** kon po·lyo *chicken & rice*
— **integral** een·te·*gral* *brown rice*
— **marinera** ma·ree·*ne*·ra
seafood & rice
— **salvaje** sal·*va*·khe *wild rice*
asadillo ⓜ a·sa·dee·lyo *roasted red
capsicums*

asados ⓜ pl a·sa·dos *roast meats*

atún ⓜ a·toon *tuna – often served marinated & raw*

— al horno al or·no *baked tuna*

avellana ⓕ a·ve·lya·na *hazelnut*

aves ⓕ pl a·ves *poultry*

azúcar ⓜ a·thoo·kar *sugar*

B

bacalao ⓜ ba·ka·low *cod – usually salted & dried*

— a la vizcaína a la veeth·ka·ee·na *cod with chillies & capsicums*

— del convento del kon·ven·to *cod with potatoes & spinach in broth*

bacón ⓜ ba·kon *bacon*

barbo ⓜ bar·bo *red mullet*

barra ⓕ ba·ra *long stick of bread*

batata ⓕ ba·ta·ta *sweet potato*

beicon ⓜ bey·kon *streaky bacon rashers*

berberechos ⓜ pl ber·be·re·chos *cockles*

— en vinagre en vee·na·gre *cockles in vinegar*

berenjenas ⓕ pl be·ren·khe·nas *eggplants*

— a la mallorquina a la ma·lyor·kee·na *eggplants with garlic mayonnaise*

— con setas kon se·tas *eggplants with mushrooms*

berza ⓕ ber·tha *cabbage*

— a la andaluza a la an·da·loo·tha *cabbage & meat hotpot*

besugo ⓜ be·soo·go *red bream*

— a la Donostiarra a la do·nos·tya·ra *barbecued red bream with garlic & paprika*

— estilo San Sebastián es·tee·lo san se·bas·tyan *barbecued red bream with garlic & paprika*

bienmesabe ⓜ byen·me·sa·be *sponge cake, egg & almond confection*

bisbe ⓜ bees·be *black & white blood sausage*

bistec ⓜ bees·tek *steak*

— con patatas kon pa·ta·tas *steak with chips*

bizcocha ⓕ **manchega** beeth·ko·cha man·che·ga *cake soaked in milk, sugar, vanilla & cinnamon*

bizcocho ⓜ beeth·ko·cho *sponge cake*

— de almendra de al·men·dra *almond cake*

— de avellana de a·ve·lya·na *hazelnut cake*

bizcochos ⓜ pl **borrachos** beeth·ko·chos bo·ra·chos *cake soaked in liqueur*

bocadillo ⓜ bo·ka·dee·lyo *bread roll with a filling*

bocas ⓕ pl **de la isla** bo·kas de la ees·la *large crab claws*

bogavante ⓜ bo·ga·van·te *lobster*

bollo ⓜ bo·lyo *crusty bread roll*

bonito ⓜ bo·nee·to *white fleshy tuna*

boquerón ⓜ bo·ke·ron *whitebait*

boquerones ⓜ pl bo·ke·ro·nes *anchovies marinated in wine vinegar*

— fritos free·tos *fried anchovies*

brama ⓕ bra·ma *sea bream*

bróculi ⓜ bro·ko·lee *broccoli*

budín ⓜ **de atún** boo·deen de a·toon *baked tuna pudding*

bull ⓜ **de atún** bool de a·toon *rabbit with garlic & tuna boiled with potatoes*

buñuelitos ⓜ pl boo·nywe·lee·tos *small cheese or ham fritters*

— de San José de san kho·se *lemon & vanilla crepes*

buñuelo ⓜ boo·nywe·lo *fried pastry*

burrida ⓕ **de ratjada** boo·ree·da de rat·kha·da *fish soup with almonds*

butifarra ⓕ **(blanca)** boo·tee·fa·ra (blan·ka) *cured pork sausage*

— con setas kon se·tas *Catalan sausage with mushrooms*

C

caballa ⓕ ka·ba·lya *mackerel*

cabra ⓕ ka·bra *goat*

cabracho ⓜ ka·bra·cho *scorpion fish • mullet*

cacahuete ⓜ ka·ka·we·te *peanut*

cachelos ⓜ pl ka·che·los *potatoes with spicy sausage & pork*

cádiz ⓕ ka·deeth *fresh goats' milk cheese*

calabacín ⓜ ka·la·ba·theen *zucchini*

calabaza ⓕ ka·la·ba·tha *pumpkin*

calamares ⓜ pl ka·la·ma·res *calamari – popular fried or stuffed*
— **fritos a la romana** free·tos a la ro·ma·na *squid rings fried in batter*
— **rellenos** re·lye·nos *stuffed squid*

calçots ⓜ pl kal·sots *spring onion-like vegetables chargrilled and eaten with a romesco dipping sauce*

caldeirada ⓕ kal·dey·ra·da *salted cod & potatoes in a paprika sauce • fish soup*

caldereta ⓕ kal·de·re·ta *stew*
— **asturiana** as·too·rya·na *fish stew*
— **de cordero** de kor·de·ro *lamb stew*

caldillo ⓜ **de perro** kal·dee·lyo de pe·ro *'puppy dog soup' – stew of onions, fresh fish & orange juice*

caldo ⓜ kal·do *broth • clear soup • stock*
— **al estilo del Mar Menor** al es·tee·lo del mar me·nor *fish stew from the Mar Menor*
— **gallego** ga·lye·go *broth with haricot beans, ham & sausage*

callos ⓜ pl ka·lyos *tripe*

camarones fritos ⓜ pl ka·ma·ro·nes free·tos *deep-fried prawns*

anagroc ka·na·grok *mushroom*

añaillas ⓕ pl **de la Isla** ka·nyay·lyas de la ees·la *boiled sea snails*

anelones ⓜ pl ka·ña·lo·nes *squares of pasta for making cannelloni*
— **con espinaca** kon es·pee·na·ka *cannelloni with spinach, anchovies & bechamel*
— **con pescado** kon pes·ka·do *cannelloni with cod, eggs & mushrooms*

anapés ⓜ pl **de fiambres** ka·na·pes de fee·am·bres *mini hors d'oeuvres with ham, anchovies or cheese*

cangrejo ⓜ kan·gre·kho *large-clawed crab usually eaten steamed or boiled*

cantalupo ⓜ kan·ta·loo·po *cantaloupe*

canutillos ⓜ pl ka·noo·tee·lyos *cream biscuits*

capones ⓜ pl **de Villalba** ka·po·nes de vee·lyal·ba *Christmas dish of chicken marinated in brandy*

caracoles ⓜ ka·ra·ko·les *snails*

caramelos ⓜ pl ka·ra·me·los *caramels • confection*

cardos ⓜ pl **fritos** kar·dos free·tos *fried thistles*

carne ⓕ kar·ne *meat*
— **de membrillo** de mem·bree·lyo *quince 'cheese'*
— **molida** mo·lee·da *minced meat*

cassolada ⓕ ka·so·la·da *potato & vegetable stew with bacon & ribs*

castaña ⓕ kas·ta·nya *chestnut*

caviar ⓜ ka·vyar *caviar*

caza ⓕ ka·tha *game*

cazón ⓜ ka·thon *dogfish or shark with a sweet scallop-like flavour*

cazuelitas ⓕ pl **de langostinos San Rafael** ka·thwe·lee·tas de lan·gos·tee·nos san ra·fa·el *baked rice with seafood*

cebolla ⓕ the·bo·lya *onion*

cecina ⓕ the·thee·na *cured meat*

cerdo ⓜ ther·do *pork*

cereales ⓜ pl the·re·a·les *cereal*

cereza ⓕ the·re·tha *cherry*
— **silvestre** seel·ves·tre *wild cherry*

ciervo ⓜ thyer·vo *deer*

cigala ⓕ thee·ga·la *crayfish*

ciruela ⓕ thee·rwe·la *plum*
— **pasa** pa·sa *prune*

civet ⓜ **de llebre** see·vet de le·bre *hare stew*

cochifrito ⓜ **de cordero** ko·chee·free·to de kor·de·ro *lamb fried with garlic & lemon*

cochinillo ⓜ ko·chee·nee·lyo *suckling pig*
— **asado** a·sa·do *roast suckling pig*
— **de pelotas** de pe·lo·tas *meatball stew*
coco ⓜ *ko·*ko *coconut*
codornices ⓕ pl **a la plancha** ko·dor·nee·thes a la *plan·*cha *grilled quail*
codorniz ⓕ ko·dor·neeth *quail*
— **con pimientos** kon pee·*myen·*tos *capsicums stuffed with quail*
col ⓕ kol *cabbage*
— **lombarda** lom·*bar·*da *red cabbage*
coles ⓕ pl **de bruselas** ko·les de broo·se·las *Brussels sprouts*
coliflor ⓕ ko·lee·*flor cauliflower*
conejo ⓜ ko·ne·kho *rabbit*
— **de monte** de mon·te *wild rabbit*
coquina ⓕ ko·kee·na *large clam*
corazón ⓜ ko·ra·*thon heart*
cordero ⓜ kor·de·ro *lamb*
— **al chilindrón** al chee·leen·dron *lamb in tomato & capsicum sauce*
— **con almendras** kon al·*men·*dras *lamb in almond sauce*
costillas ⓕ pl kos·tee·lyas *ribs*
crema ⓕ *kre·*ma *cream*
— **catalana** ka·ta·*la·*na *creme brulee*
— **de espinacas** de es·pee·na·kas *cream of spinach soup*
— **de naranja** de na·*ran·*kha *orange cream dessert*
— **de San José** de san kho·se *egg custard flavoured with cinnamon*
— **de verduras** de ver·doo·ras *cream of vegetable soup*
crocante ⓜ kro·kan·te *ice cream with chopped nuts & chocolate*

CH

chalote ⓜ cha·lo·te *shallot*
champiñones ⓜ pl cham·pee·*nyo·*nes *cultivated white mushrooms*
chanquetes ⓜ pl chan·ke·tes *whitebait • baby anchovies*

chilindrón (al) chee·leen·dron (al) *cooked in a tomato & red pepper sauce*
chipirón ⓜ chee·pee·ron *baby squid – very popular in the Basque Country*
chocolate ⓜ cho·ko·la·te *chocolate*
— **caliente** ka·lee·en·te *thick hot chocolate*
chocos ⓜ pl cho·kos *squid*
chorizo ⓜ cho·ree·tho *spicy red cooked sausage, similar to salami*
— **de Pamplona** de pam·*plo·*na *fine-textured, hard chorizo*
— **de Salamanca** de sa·la·*man·*ka *chunky chorizo from Salamanca*
chuletas ⓕ pl choo·le·tas *chops • cutlets*
— **al sarmiento** al sar·*myen·*to *chops prepared over wood from vines*
— **de buey** de bwey *ox chops*
— **de cerdo a la aragonesa** de *ther·*do a la a·ra·go·ne·sa *baked pork chops with wine & onion*
churros ⓜ choo·ros *fried doughnut strips bought from street-sellers or in cafes*

D

de soja de so·kha *with soya*
despojos ⓜ pl des·po·khos *offal*
dorada ⓕ **a la sal** do·ra·da a la sal *salted sea bream*
dulce ⓜ *dool·*the *sweet*
— **de batata** de ba·ta·ta *sweet potato pudding from Málaga*
dulces ⓜ pl *dool·*thes *sweets*
— **de las monjas** *dool·*thes de las *mon·*khas *confectionery made by nuns & sold in convents or cake shops*

E

embutidos ⓜ pl em·boo·tee·dos *generic name for cured sausages*
empanada ⓕ em·pa·na·da *savoury pie*
— **de carne** de *kar·*ne *spicy meat pie*
— **de espinaca** de es·pee·na·ka *spinach pie*

empanadilla ① em·pa·na·dee·lya *small pie, either sweet or savoury*

empanado ⓜ em·pa·na·do *coated in bread crumbs*

emparedado ⓜ em·pa·re·da·do *sandwich*

— de jamón y espárragos de kha·mon ee es·pa·ra·gos *fried ham & asparagus rolls*

empiñonado ⓜ em·pee·nyo·na·do *small marzipan-filled pastry with pinenuts*

en salsa verde en sal·sa ver·de *in a parsley & garlic sauce*

encurtidos ⓜ pl en·koor·tee·dos *pickles*

ensaimada ① **mallorquina** en·sai·ma·da ma·lyor·kee·na *spiral-shaped bun made with lard*

ensalada ① en·sa·la·da *salad*

— de frutas de froo·tas *fruit salad*

— de patatas de pa·ta·tas *potato salad*

— del tiempo del tyem·po *seasonal salad*

— mixta meeks·ta *mixed salad*

escaldadillas ① pl es·kal·da·dee·lyas *dough soaked in orange juice & fried*

escalivada ① es·ka·lee·va·da *roasted red capsicums in olive oil*

escalopes ⓜ pl **de ternera rellenos** es·ka·lo·pes de ter·ne·ra re·lye·nos *deep fried veal cutlets stuffed with egg & cheese*

espaguetis ⓜ pl es·pa·ge·tees *spaghetti*

espárragos ⓜ pl es·pa·ra·gos *asparagus*

— con dos salsas kon dos sal·sas *asparagus & tomato or paprika mayonnaise*

— en vinagreta en vee·na·gre·ta *asparagus in vinaigrette*

espinacas ① pl es·pee·na·kas *spinach*

— a la catalana a la ka·ta·la·na *spinach with pinenuts & raisins*

esqueixada ① es·kee·sha·da *cod dressed with olives, tomato & onion*

txeko kopa e·che·ko ko·pa *ice cream dessert*

F

fabada ① **asturiana** fa·ba·da as·too·rya·na *stew made with pork, blood sausage & white beans*

faisán ⓜ fai·san *pheasant*

favès Ⓤ pl **a la antalana** fa·ves a la ka·ta·la·na *broad beans with ham*

fiambres ⓜ pl fee·am·bres *cold meats*

— surtidos soor·tee·dos *selection of cold meats*

fideos ⓜ pl fee·de·os *pasta noodles*

fideua ① fee·de·wa *rice or noodles with fish & shellfish*

fideus ⓜ pl **a la cassola** fee·de·oos a la ka·so·la *Catalan noodle dish*

filete ⓜ fee·le·te *steak • any boneless slice of meat*

— a la parrilla a la pa·ree·lya *grilled beef steak*

— de ternera de ter·ne·ra *veal steak*

filloas ① pl fee·lyo·as *Galician pancakes filled with cream*

flan ⓜ flan *creme caramel*

flaó ① fla·o *sweet cheese flan*

flor manchega ① flor man·che·ga *deep-fried sweet wafers*

frambuesa ① fram·bwe·sa *raspberry*

frangellos ⓜ pl fran·khe·lyos *sweet made from cornmeal, milk & honey*

fresa ① fre·sa *strawberry*

fricandó ⓜ **de langostinos** free·kan·do de lan·gos·tee·nos *shrimp in almond sauce*

frite ① free·te *lamb stew, served on festive occasions*

fritos ⓜ pl free·tos *fritters*

— con miel kon myel *honey-roasted fritters*

fritura ① free·too·ra *mixed fried fish*

fruta ① froo·ta *fruit*

— variada va·ree·a·da *selection of fresh fruit*

frutas ① pl **en almibar** froo·tas en al·mee·bar *fruit in syrup*

frutos ⓜ pl **secos** froo·tos se·kos *nuts & dried fruit*

fuet ① foo·et *thin pork sausage*

G

gachas ⓕ pl **manchegas** *ga*·chas
man·*che*·gas *flavoured porridge*

galleta ⓕ ga·*lye*·ta *biscuit*

gambas ⓕ pl *gam*·bas *prawns*
— **a la plancha** a la *plan*·cha *grilled
prawns*
— **en gabardina** en ga·bar·*dee*·na
prawns in batter

Gamonedo ⓜ ga·mo·*ne*·do *sharp-
tasting cheese, smoked & cured*

garbanzos ⓜ pl gar·*ban*·thos *chickpeas*
— **con cebolla** kon the·*bo*·lya *chickpeas
in onion sauce*
— **tostados** tos·*ta*·dos *roasted
chickpeas (sold as a snack)*

garbure ⓕ gar·*boo*·re *green vegetable
soup • pork & ham dish*

garúm ⓜ ga·*room* *olive & anchovy dip*

Gata-Hurdes ga·ta·*oor*·des *cheese*

gazpacho ⓜ gath·*pa*·cho *cold tomato
soup*
— **andaluz** an·da·*looz* *cold tomato
soup with chopped salad vegetables*
— **pastoril** pas·to·*reel* *rabbit stew
with tomato & garlic*

gazpachos ⓜ pl **manchegos**
gath·*pa*·chos man·*che*·gos *game &
vegetable hotpot*

Gaztazarra ⓜ gath·ta·*tha*·ra *cheese*

gitano ⓜ khee·*ta*·no *Andalusian
chickpea & tripe stew*

gofio ⓜ go·*fyo* *toasted cornmeal or
barley*

granadilla ⓕ gra·na·*dee*·lya *passion
fruit*

grano ⓜ *gra*·no *grain*
— **largo** *lar*·go *long-grain (rice)*

gratinado ⓜ **de berenjenas**
gra·tee·*na*·do de be·ren·*khe*·nas
eggplant gratin

Grazalema ⓕ gra·tha·*le*·ma *semi-cured
sheep's milk cheese*

guindilla ⓕ geen·*dee*·lya *mild green
chilli*

guisado ⓜ gee·*sa*·do *stew*
— **de cordero** de kor·*de*·ro
lamb ragout
— **de ternera** de ter·*ne*·ra *veal ragout*

guisante ⓜ gee·*san*·te *pea*
— **seco** *se*·ko *split pea*
— **mollar** mo·*lyar* *snow pea*

guisantes ⓜ pl **con jamón a la
española** gee·*san*·tes kon kha·*mon* a
la es·pa·*nyo*·la *pea & ham dish*

guisat ⓜ **de marisco** gee·*sat* de
ma·*rees*·ko *stew made with seafood*

guiso ⓜ **de conejo estilo canario** gee·so
de ko·*ne*·kho es·*tee*·lo ka·*na*·ryo
rabbit stew

guiso ⓜ **de rabo de toro** gee·so de *ra*·bo
de *to*·ro *stewed bull's tail with potatoe*

H

habas ⓕ pl *a*·bas *broad beans*
— **a la granadina** a la gra·na·*dee*·na
broad beans with eggs & ham
— **fritas** *free*·tas *fried broad beans
(sold as a snack)*

habichuela ⓕ a·bee·*chwe*·la *white bean*

hamburguesa ⓕ am·boor·*ge*·sa
hamburger

harina ⓕ a·*ree*·na *flour*
— **integral** een·te·*gral* *wholemeal flour*

helado ⓜ e·*la*·do *ice cream*

hígado ⓜ *ee*·ga·do *liver*

higo ⓜ *ee*·go *fig*
— **seco** *se*·ko *dried fig*

hogaza ⓕ o·*ga*·tha *dense, thick-
crusted bread*

hoja ⓕ **de parra** o·kha de *pa*·ra
vine leaf

hojaldres ⓜ pl o·*khal*·dres *small flaky
pastries covered in sugar*

hojas ⓕ pl **verdes** o·khas *ver*·des *green
vegetables*

hornazo ⓜ or·*na*·tho *bread stuffed
with sausage*

hortalizas ⓕ pl or·ta·*lee*·thas
vegetables

huevo m *we*·vo *egg*
— **cocido** ko·*thee*·do *boiled egg*
— **de chocolate** de cho·ko·*la*·te *chocolate egg*
— **frito** *free*·to *fried egg*

huevos m pl *we*·vos *egg dishes*
— **a la flamenca** a la fla·*men*·ka *baked vegetables with egg & ham*
— **al estilo Sóller** al es·*tee*·lo so·lyer *fried eggs served with a milk & vegetable sauce*
— **en salsa agria** en *sal*·sa a·*grya boiled eggs in wine & vinegar*
— **escalfados** es·kal·*fa*·dos *poached eggs*
— **revueltos** re·*vwel*·tos *scrambled eggs*

J

jabalí m kha·ba·*lee wild boar*
— **con salsa de castaños** kon *sal*·sa de kas·*ta*·nyos *wild boar in chestnut sauce*

jamón m kha·*mon ham*
— **cocido** ko·*thee*·do *cooked ham*
— **ibérico** ee·*ber*·ik·o *ham from the Iberian pig, said to be the best in Spain*
— **serrano** se·*ra*·no *cured mountain ham*

jengibre m khen·*gee*·bre *ginger*
jerez (al) khe·*reth* (al) *in a sherry sauce*
judía f khoo·*dee*·a *fresh green bean* • *dried kidney bean*
judías f pl **del tío Lucas** khoo·*dee*·as del *tee*·o *loo*·kas *bean stew with garlic & bacon*
judías f pl **verdes a la castellana** khoo·*dee*·as *ver*·des a la kas·te·*lya*·na *fried capsicums, garlic & green beans*
judiones m pl **de la granja** kho·dee·*o*·nes de la *gran*·kha *pork & bean stew*

K

kiskilla kees·*kee*·lya *shrimp (also spelled quisquilla)*

L

langosta f lan·*gos*·ta *lobster*
— **a la ibicenca** a la ee·bee·*then*·ka *lobster with stuffed squid*

langostinos m pl lan·gos·*tee*·nos *king prawns*
— **a la plancha** a la *plan*·cha *grilled king prawns*

lavanco m la·*van*·ko *wild duck*
lechuga f le·*choo*·ga *lettuce*
legumbres f pl le·*goom*·bres *pulses* • *vegetables* • *vegetable dishes*
— **secas** se·*kas dried pulses*

leguminosas f pl le·goo·mee·*no*·sas *legumes*
lengua f *len*·gwa *tongue*
— **a la aragonesa** a la a·ra·go·*ne*·sa *tongue in tomato & capsicum sauce*

lenguado m len·*gwa*·do *sole*
— **al chacolí con hongos** al cha·ko·*lee* kon *on*·gos *sole with white wine & mushrooms*

lenguados m pl **al plato** len·*gwa*·dos al *pla*·to *sole & mushroom casserole*
lenguas f pl **con salsa de almendras** *len*·gwas kon *sal*·sa de al·*men*·dras *tongue in almond sauce*
lentejas f pl len·te·*khas lentils*
liebre f *lye*·bre *hare*
— **con castañas** kon kas·*ta*·nyas *hare with chestnuts*
— **estofada** es·to·*fa*·da *stewed hare*

lima f *lee*·ma *lime*
limón m lee·*mon lemon*
lomo m *lo*·mo *fillet* • *loin* • *sirloin*
— **curado** koo·*ra*·do *cured pork sausage*
— **de cerdo** de *ther*·do *loin of pork*

longaniza f lon·ga·*nee*·tha *chorizo, long & skinny sausage*
lubina f loo·*bee*·na *sea bass*
— **a la marinera** a la ma·ree·*ne*·ra *sea bass in parsley sauce*

lucio m *loo*·thyo *pike*

LL

llagostí ⓜ **a l'allioli** lyan·gos·tee a la·lyee·o·lee *grilled prawns in garlic mayonnaise*

llenguado ⓜ **a la nyoca** lyen·gwa·do a la *nyo·*ka *sole with pine nuts & raisins*

M

macedonia ⓕ **de frutas** ma·the·*do·*nya de froo·tas *fruit salad*

macedonia ⓕ **de verduras** ma·the·*do·*nya de ver·*doo·*ras *mixed vegetables*

magdalena ⓕ ma·da·*le·*na *small fairy cake to dunk in coffee*

magras ⓕ pl ma·gras *fried eggs, ham, cheese & tomato*

maíz ⓜ ma·*eeth* maize • *corn*
— **tierno** tyer·no *sweetcorn*

mandarina ⓕ man·da·*ree·*na *tangerine* • *mandarin*

mango ⓜ *man·*go *mango*

manitas ⓕ pl **de cerdo** ma·*nee·*tas de ther·do *pig's trotters*

manitas ⓕ pl **de cordero** ma·*nee·*tas de kor·*de·*ro *leg of lamb*

manteca ⓕ man·*te·*ka *lard*

mantecado ⓜ man·te·*ka·*do *a soft lard biscuit* • *dairy ice cream*

mantequilla ⓕ man·te·*kee·*lya *butter*
— **sin sal** seen sal *unsalted butter*

manzana ⓕ man·*tha·*na *apple*

manzanas ⓕ pl **asadas** man·*tha·*nas a·*sa·*das *baked apples*

margarina ⓕ mar·ga·*ree·*na *margarine*

marinera (a la) ma·ree·*ne·*ra (a la) *cooked or served in a white wine sauce*

mariscos ⓜ ma·*rees·*kos *shellfish* • *seafood*

marmitako mar·mee·*ta·*ko *fresh tuna & potato casserole*

marrano ⓜ ma·*ra·*no *pork*

mar y cel ⓜ mar ee sel *dish of sausages, rabbit, shrimp & angler fish*

masa ⓕ *ma·*sa *pastry (dough)*

mayonesa ⓕ ma·yo·*ne·*sa *mayonnaise*

medallones ⓜ pl **de merluza** me·da·*lyo·*nes de mer·*loo·*tha *hake steaks*

mejillones ⓜ pl me·khee·*lyo·*nes *mussels*
— **al vino blanco** al *vee·*no *blan·*ko *mussels in white wine*
— **con salsa** kon *sal·*sa *mussels with tomato sauce*

mel ⓜ **i mató** mel ee ma·*to* *a dessert of curd cheese with honey*

melocotón ⓜ me·lo·ko·*ton* *peach*

melocotones ⓜ pl **al vino** me·lo·ko·*to·*nes al *vee·*no *peaches in red wine*

melón ⓜ me·*lon* *melon*

membrillo ⓜ mem·*bree·*lyo *quince*

menestra ⓕ me·*nes·*tra *mixed vegetable stew*
— **de pollo** de *po·*lyo *chicken & vegetable stew*

merengue ⓜ me·*ren·*ge *meringue*

merluza ⓕ mer·*loo·*tha *hake*

mermelada ⓕ mer·me·*la·*da *marmalade*

mero ⓜ *me·*ro *halibut* • *grouper* • *sea bass*

miel ⓕ myel *honey*
— **de azahar** de a·tha·*ar* *orange blossom honey*
— **de caña** de *ka·*nya *treacle*

migas ⓕ pl *mee·*gas *fried cubes of bread with capsicums*
— **a la aragonesa** a la a·ra·go·*ne·*sa *fried bread with bacon rashers in tomato sauce*
— **mulatas** moo·la·tas *cubes of bread soaked in chocolate & fried*

mojarra ⓕ mo·*kha·*ra *type of sea bream*

moje ⓜ **manchego** *mo·*khe man·*che·*go *cold broth with black olives*

mojete ⓜ mo·*khe·*te *dipping sauce for bread, made from potatoes, garlic, tomatoes & paprika*
— **murciano** moor·*thya·*no *fish & capsicum dish*

mojo ⓜ *mo·*kho *spicy capsicum sauce*

mollejas ⓕ pl mo·*lye·*khas *sweetbreads*

mollete ⓜ mo·lye·te *soft round bap roll*

monas ⓕ pl **de pascua** mo·nas de pas·kwa *Easter cakes • figures made of chocolate*

mongetes ⓕ pl **seques i butifarra** mon·zhe·tes se·kês ee boo tee fa ra *haricot beans with roasted pork sausage*

mora ⓕ mo·ra *blackberry*

moraga ⓕ **de sardina** mo·ra·ga de sar·dee·na *fresh anchovies on a spit*

morcilla ⓕ mor·thee·lya *black pudding, often stewed with beans & vegetables*

mortadela ⓕ mor·ta·de·la *the mortadella sausage*

morteruelo ⓜ mor·te·rwe·lo *pate dish containing offal, game & spices*

mostachones ⓜ pl mos·ta·cho·nes *small cakes for dipping in coffee or hot chocolate (also spelled mostatxones)*

mostaza ⓕ mos·ta·tha *mustard*
— **en grano** en gra·no *mustard seed*

múgil ⓜ moo·kheel *grey mullet*

mujol ⓜ **guisado** moo·khol gee·sa·do *red mullet*

mus ⓜ **de chocolate** moos de cho·ko·la·te *chocolate mousse*

muslo ⓜ moos·lo *(chicken) leg & thigh*

N

nabo ⓜ na·bo *root vegetable • turnip*

naranja ⓕ na·ran·kha *orange*

nata ⓕ na·ta *cream*
— **agria** a·grya *sour cream*
— **montada** mon·ta·da *whipped cream*

natillas ⓕ pl na·tee·lyas *creamy custard dessert*
— **de chocolate** de cho·ko·la·te *chocolate custard*

navaja ⓕ na·va·kha *razor clam*

nécora ⓕ ne·ko·ra *small crab*

nueces ⓕ pl new·thes *nuts*

nuez ⓕ nweth *nut*
— **de América** de a·me·ree·ka *pecan nut*
— **de nogal** de no·gal *walnut*

Ñ

ñora ⓕ nyo·ra *sweet red capsicum (usually dried)*

O

oca ⓕ o·ka *goose*

olla ⓕ o·lya *meat & vegetable stew • cooking pot*

oreja ⓕ **de mar** o·re·kha de mar *abalone*

ostiones ⓜ pl **a la gaditana** os·tyo·nes a la ga·dee·ta·na *Cádiz oysters with garlic, parsley & bread crumbs*

ostra ⓕ os·tra *oyster*

oveja ⓕ o·ve·kha *mutton*

P

pá ⓜ **amb oli** pa amb o·lee *toasted bread with garlic & olive oil*

pacana ⓕ pa·ka·na *pecan*

paella ⓕ pa·e·lya *rice dish which has many regional variations*
— **marinera** ma·ree·ne·ra *paella with fish & seafood*
— **zamorana** tha·mo·ra·na *paella with meat*

palitos ⓜ pl **de queso** pa·lee·tos de ke·so *cheese straws*

palmera ⓕ pal·me·ra *leaf-shaped flaky pastry, often coated in chocolate*

palomitas ⓕ pl pa·lo·mee·tas *popcorn*

pan ⓜ pan *bread*
— **aceite** a·they·te *flat round bread*
— **árabe** a·ra·be *pita bread*
— **de Alá** de a·la *'Allah's Bread' – dessert*
— **de boda** de bo·da *sculpted bread traditionally made for weddings*
— **de centeno** de then·te·no *rye bread*
— **duro** doo·ro *stale bread, used for toasting & eating with olive oil*
— **integral** een·te·gral *wholemeal bread*

panaché ⓜ pa·na·che *mixed vegetable stew*

panallets ⓜ pl pa·na·*lyets marzipan sweets*

panceta ⓕ pan·*the·ta salt-cured, streaky bacon*

panchineta ⓕ pan·chee·*ne·ta almond tart*

panecillo ⓜ pa·ne·*thee·lyo small bread roll*

panojas ⓕ pl **malagueñas** pa·*no·khas ma·la·ge·nyas sardine dish*

papas ⓕ pl **arrugadas** *pa·pas a·roo·ga·das potatoes boiled in their jackets*

pargo ⓜ *par·go sea bream*

parrillada ⓕ pa·ree·*lya·da grilled meat*
  — **de mariscos** de ma·*rees·kos seafood grill*

pastel ⓜ pas·*tel cake*
  — **de boda** de *bo·da wedding cake*
  — **de chocolate** de cho·ko·*la·te chocolate cake*
  — **de cierva** de *thyer·va meat pie*
  — **de cumpleaños** de koom·ple·a·*nyos birthday cake*

pastelitos ⓜ pl **de miel** pas·te·*lee·tos de myel honey fritters*

pataco ⓜ pa·*ta·ko tuna & potato stew*

patatas ⓕ pl pa·*ta·tas potatoes*
  — **a la riojana** a la ree·o·*kha·na potatoes with chorizo & paprika*
  — **alioli** a·lee·o·*lee potatoes in garlic mayonnaise*
  — **bravas** *bra·vas potatoes in spicy tomato sauce*
  — **con chorizo** kon cho·*ree·tho potatoes with chorizo*
  — **estofadas** es·to·*fa·das boiled potatoes*

pato ⓜ *pa·to duck*
  — **a la sevillana** a la se·vee·*lya·na duck with orange sauce*
  — **alcaparrada** al·ka·pa·*ra·da duck with capers & almonds*

pavo ⓜ *pa·vo turkey*

pececillos ⓜ pl pe·the·*thee·lyos small fish*

pechina ⓕ pe·*chee·na scallop*

pecho ⓜ *pe·cho breast of lamb*

pechuga ⓕ pe·*choo·ga breast of poultry*

pepinillo ⓜ pe·pee·*nee·lyo gherkin*

pepino ⓜ pe·*pee·no cucumber*

pepitoria ⓕ pe·pee·*to·rya sauce made with egg & almond*

pepitos ⓜ pl pe·*pee·tos chocolate eclair cakes filled with custard*

pera ⓕ *pe·ra pear*

La Peral ⓕ la pe·*ral soft cheese*

perca ⓕ *per·ka perch*

perdices ⓕ pl per·dee·*thes partridges*
  — **a la manchega** a la man·*che·ga partridge in red wine & capsicums*
  — **con chocolate** kon cho·ko·*la·te partridge with chocolate*

perdiz ⓕ per·*deeth partridge*

peregrina ⓕ pe·re·*gree·na scallop*

pericana ⓕ pe·ree·*ka·na dish of olives, cod oil, capsicums & garlic*

perrito ⓜ **caliente** pe·*ree·to ka·lee·en·te hot dog*

pescada ⓕ **á galega** pes·*ka·da a ga·*le·ga hake fried in olive oil & served with garlic & paprika sauce*

pescadilla ⓕ pes·ka·dee·*lya whiting • young hake*

pescaditos ⓜ pl **rebozados** pes·ka·dee·tos re·bo·*tha·dos small fish fried in batter*

pescado ⓜ pes·*ka·do fish*
  — **a l'all cremat** a lal kre·*mat fish in burnt garlic*

pescaíto ⓜ **frito** pes·ka·ee·to *free·to tiny fried fish*

pestiños ⓜ pl pes·*tee·nyos honey-coated aniseed pastries, fried with filling*

pez ⓕ **espada** peth es·*pa·da swordfish*
  — **frito** *free·to fried swordfish steaks on a skewer*

picada ⓕ pee·ka·da *mixture of garlic, parsley, toasted almonds & nuts, often used to thicken sauces*

picadillo ⓜ pee·ka·dee·lyo *salad consisting of diced vegetables*
— **de atún** de a·toon *salad made with diced tuna & capsicums*
— **de ternera** de ter·ne·ra *minced veal*

pichón ⓜ pee·chon *pigeon*

pichones ⓜ pl **asados** pee·cho·nes a·sa·dos *roast pigeons*

pilotes ⓕ pl pee·lo·tes *Catalan meatballs*

pimiento ⓜ pee·myen·to *capsicum*
— **amarillo** a·ma·ree·lyo *yellow capsicum*
— **rojo** ro·kho *red capsicum*
— **verde** ver·de *green capsicum*

pimientos ⓜ pl pee·myen·tos *capsicums (the ones from El Bierzo are especially good)*
— **a la riojana** a la ree·o·kha·na *roast red capsicum fried in oil & garlic*
— **al chilindrón** al chee·leen·dron *capsicum casserole*

piña ⓕ pee·nya *pineapple*

pinchito ⓜ **moruno** peen·chee·to mo·roo·no *lamb & chicken kebabs*

piñón ⓜ pee·nyon *pinenut*

pinta ⓕ peen·ta *pinto bean*

pintada ⓕ peen·ta·da *guinea fowl*

piquillo ⓜ pee·kee·lyo *sweet & spicy capsicums*

pistacho ⓜ pees·ta·cho *pistachio nut*

pisto ⓜ **manchego** pees·to man·che·go *zucchini with capsicum & tomato, fried or stewed*

plátano ⓜ pla·ta·no *banana*

pochas ⓕ pl po·chas *beans*
— **a la riojana** a la ree·o·kha·na *beans with chorizo in spicy paprika sauce*
— **con almejas** kon al·me·khas *beans with clams*

pollo ⓜ po·lyo *chicken*
— **asado** a·sa·do *roast chicken*
— **con samfaina** kon sam·fai·na *chicken with mixed vegetables*
— **en escabeche** en es·ka·be·che *marinated chicken*
— **en salsa de ajó** en sal·sa de a·kho *chicken in garlic sauce*
— **granadina** gra·na·dee·na *chicken with wine & ham*
— **y langosta** ee lan·gos·ta *chicken with crayfish*

pulpo ⓜ **a feira** pool·po a fey·ra *spicy boiled octopus*

polvorón ⓜ pol·vo·ron *almond shortbread, often eaten at Christmas*

pomelo ⓜ po·me·lo *grapefruit*

postre ⓜ pos·tre *dessert*
— **de naranja** de na·ran·kha *cream-filled oranges*

potaje ⓜ po·ta·khe *broth*
— **castellano** kas·te·lya·no *broth with beans & sausages*
— **de garbanzos** de gar·ban·thos *broth with chickpeas*
— **de lentejas** de len·te·khas *lentil broth*

pote ⓜ **gallego** po·te ga·lye·go *stew*

potito ⓜ po·tee·to *jar of baby food*

pringada ⓕ preen·ga·da *bread dipped in sauce • a marinated sandwich*

productos ⓜ pl **biológicos** pro·dook·tos bee·o·lo·khee·kos *organic produce*

productos ⓜ pl **del mar** pro·dook·tos del mar *seafood products*

productos ⓜ pl **lácteos** pro·dook·tos lak·te·os *dairy products*

puchero ⓜ poo·che·ro *casserole*

pudin ⓜ poo·din *pudding*

puerco ⓜ pwer·ko *pork*

puerro ⓜ pwe·ro *leek*

pulpo ⓜ pool·po *octopus*

punta ⓕ **de diamante** poon·ta de dya·man·te *confection from Valencia*

porrusalda ⓕ po·roo·sal·da *cod & potato stew*

Q

queso ⓜ *ke·so cheese*
— **azul** *a·thool blue cheese*
— **crema** *kre·ma cream cheese*
quisquilla ⓕ *kees·kee·lya shrimp (also spelled kiskilla)*

R

rábano ⓜ *ra·ba·no radish*
rabas ⓕ **en salsa verde** *ra·bas en sal·sa ver·de squid in green sauce*
rabassola ⓕ *ra·ba·so·la mushroom*
rape ⓜ *ra·pe monkfish*
— **a la gallega** *a la ga·lye·ga monkfish with potatoes & garlic sauce*
— **a la Monistrol** *a la mo·nees·trol monkfish with bechamel sauce*
redondo ⓜ *re·don·do round (of beef)*
— **al horno** *al or·no roast beef*
regañaos ⓜ pl *re·ga·nya·os pastry stuffed with sardines & red capsicum*
relleno ⓜ *re·lye·no stuffing*
remolacha ⓕ *re·mo·la·cha beetroot*
reo ⓜ *re·o sea trout*
repollo ⓜ *re·po·lyo cabbage*
repostería ⓕ *re·pos·te·ree·a confectionery*
requesón ⓜ *re·ke·son cottage cheese*
riñón ⓜ *ree·nyon kidney*
róbalo ⓜ *ro·ba·lo haddock • sea bass*
rodaballo ⓜ *ro·da·ba·lyo turbot • brill*
romero ⓜ *ro·me·ro rosemary*
romesco ⓜ *ro·mes·ko sweet red capsicum, almond & garlic sauce*
rosca ⓕ **de carne** *ros·ka de kar·ne meatloaf wrapped in bacon*
rosco ⓜ *ros·ko small sweet bun*
rossejat ⓜ *ro·se·dyat rice with fish & shellfish*
rovellons ⓜ pl **a la plancha** *ro·ve·lyons a la plan·cha garlic mushrooms*
ruibarbo ⓜ *roo·ee·bar·bo rhubarb*

S

salchicha ⓕ *sal·chee·cha pork sausage*
salchichón ⓜ *sal·chee·chon cured & peppery white sausage*
salmón ⓜ *sal·mon salmon*
— **a la ribereña** *a la ree·be·re·nya salmon in a cider sauce*
— **ahumado** *a·oo·ma·do smoked salmon*
salmonete ⓜ *sal·mo·ne·te red mullet*
salmorejo ⓜ *sal·mo·re·kho thick gazpacho soup made from tomato, bread, olive oil, vinegar, garlic & green capsicum*
— **de Córdoba** *de kor·do·ba gazpacho soup made with more vinegar than usual*
salpicón ⓜ *sal·pee·kon fish or meat salad*
salsa ⓕ *sal·sa sauce*
— **alioli** *a·lee·o·lee garlic & olive oil vinaigrette • garlic mayonnaise*
— **de holandesa** *de o·lan·de·sa hollandaise sauce*
— **de mayonesa** *de ma·yo·ne·sa mayonnaise sauce*
— **de tomate** *de to·ma·te tomato sauce*
— **inglesa** *een·gle·sa Worcestershire sauce*
— **tártara** *tar·ta·ra tartar sauce*
— **verde** *ver·de parsley & garlic sauce*
samfaina ⓕ *sam·fai·na grilled vegetable sauce*
sancocho ⓜ *san·ko·cho fish dish served with potatoes*
sandía ⓕ *san·dee·a watermelon*
sándwich ⓜ *san·weech sandwich*
— **mixto** *meeks·to toasted ham & cheese sandwich*
sanocho ⓜ **canario** *sa·no·cho ka·na·ryo baked monkfish with potatoes*
sardinas ⓕ *sar·dee·nas sardines*
— **a la parrilla** *a la pa·ree·lya sardines grilled*
— **en cazuela** *en ka·thwe·la sardines served in a clay pot*

sargo ⓜ sar·go *bream*

sepia ⓕ se·pya *cuttlefish*

sesos ⓜ pl se·sos *brains*

setas ⓕ pl se·tas *wild mushrooms*
— **a la kashera** a la ka·she·ra *sauteed wild mushrooms*
— **rellenas** re·lye·nas *mushrooms stuffed*

sofrit pagés ⓜ so·freet pa·zhes *vegetable stew*

sofrito ⓜ so·free·to *fried tomato sauce*

soja ⓕ so·kha *soya bean*

soldaditos ⓜ pl **de Pavía** sol·da·dee·tos de pa·vee·a *cod fritters*

solomillo ⓜ so·lo·mee·lyo *fillet*

sopa ⓕ so·pa *soup*
— **del día** del dee·a *soup of the day*

sopas ⓕ pl **de leche** so·pas de le·che *pieces of bread soaked in milk & cinnamon*

sopas ⓕ pl **engañadas** so·pas en·ga·nya·das *soup made from capsicum, onion shoots, vinegar, figs & grapes*

sorbete ⓜ sor·be·te *sorbet*

sorroputún ⓜ so·ro·poo·toon *tuna casserole*

suizo ⓜ swee·tho *sugared bun*

sukaldi soo·kal·dee *beef stew*

suquet ⓜ soo·ket *clams in almond sauce*

suquet de peix ⓜ soo·ket de peysh *fish stew*

suspiros ⓜ pl **de monja** soos·pee·ros de mon·kha *'nun's sighs' – custard sweets*

T

tallarines ⓜ pl ta·lya·ree·nes *pasta noodles*

tarta ⓕ tar·ta *cake • tart*
— **de almendra** de al·men·dra *almond tart*
— **de manzana** de man·tha·na *apple tart*

tartaleta ⓕ tar·ta·le·ta *tartlet*

tartaletas ⓕ pl **de huevos revueltos** tar·ta·le·tas de we·vos re·vwel·tos *scrambled egg tartlets*

ternera ⓕ ter·ne·ra *veal*
— **a la sevillana** a la se·vee·lya·na *veal served with wine & olives*
— **en cazuela con berenjenas** en ka·thwe·la kon be·ren·khe·nas *veal & eggplant casserole*

tocino ⓜ to·thee·no *salted pork • bacon*
— **del cielo** del thye·lo *creamy dessert made with egg yolk & sugar, with a caramel topping*

tocrudo ⓜ to·kroo·do *'everything raw'– salad of meat, garlic, onion & green capsicum*

tomate ⓜ to·ma·te *tomatoes*
— **(de) pera** (de) pe·ra *plum tomato*
— **frito** free·to *tinned tomato sauce*

tomates ⓜ pl to·ma·tes
— **enteros y pelados** en·te·ros ee pe·la·dos *tinned whole tomatoes*
— **rellenos de atún** re·lye·nos de a·toon *tomatoes stuffed with tuna*

toro ⓜ to·ro *bull meat*

torrefacto ⓜ to·re·fak·to *dark-roasted coffee beans*

torrija ⓕ to·ree·kha *French toast*

torta ⓕ tor·ta *pie • tart • flat bread*
— **de aceite** de a·they·te *sweet, flat cake or biscuit made with oil*
— **pascualina** pas·kwa·lee·na *spinach & egg pie, eaten at Easter*

tortilla ⓕ tor·tee·lya *omelette*
— **española** es·pa·nyo·la *potato & onion omelette*
— **francesa** fran·the·sa *plain omelette*

tortillas ⓕ pl **de camarones** tor·tee·lyas de ka·ma·ro·nes *shrimp fritters*

tortita ⓕ tor·tee·ta *waffle*

tostada ⓕ tos·ta·da *toasted bread*

tocino ⓜ to·thee·no *bacon*

tripas ⓕ pl tree·pas *intestines • guts*

trucha ⓕ troo·cha *trout*
— **a la marinera** a la ma·ree·ne·ra *trout in a white wine sauce*

truchas ① pl *troo*·chas *trout*
— **a la navarra** a la na·*va*·ra *trout with ham*
— **con vino y romero** kon *vee*·no ee ro·*me*·ro *trout with red wine & rosemary*
trufa ① *troo*·fa *truffle*
— **tarta** *tar*·ta *chocolate truffle cake*
tumbet (de peix) ⑩ toom·*bet* (de peysh) *vegetable souffle, sometimes containing fish*
turrón ⑩ too·*ron* *Spanish nougat*

U

uva ① *oo*·va *grape*
— **de corinto** de ko·*reen*·to *currant*
— **pasa** *pa*·sa *raisin*
— **sultana** sool·*ta*·na *sultana*

V

vacuno ⑩ va·*koo*·no *beef*
venado ⑩ ve·*na*·do *venison*

verduras ① ver·*doo*·ras *vegetables*
vieira ① vee·*ey*·ra *scallop*
villagodio ⑩ vee·lya·go·*dyo* *large steak*
vinagre ⑩ vee·*na*·gre *vinegar*
visita ① vee·*see*·ta *almond cake*

Y

yemas ① pl *ye*·mas *small round cakes*
yogur ⑩ yo·*goor* *yogurt*

Z

zanahoria ① tha·na·o·*rya* *carrot*
zarangollo ⑩ tha·ran·go·*lyo* *fried zucchini*
zarzamora ① thar·tha·*mo*·ra *blackberry*
zarzuela ① **de mariscos** thar·*thwe*·la de ma·*rees*·kos *spicy shellfish stew*
zarzuela ① **de pescado** thar·*thwe*·la de pes·*ka*·do *fish in almond sauce*
zurrukutano thoo·roo·koo·*ta*·no *cod & green capsicum soup*

emergencies

emergencias

Help!	*¡Socorro!*	so·*ko*·ro
Stop!	*¡Pare!*	*pa*·re
Go away!	*¡Váyase!*	va·ya·se
Thief!	*¡Ladrón!*	lad·*ron*
Fire!	*¡Fuego!*	*fwe*·go
Watch out!	*¡Cuidado!*	kwee·*da*·do

It's an emergency.
Es una emergencia. — es oo·na e·mer·*khen*·thya

Call the police!
¡Llame a la policía! — *lya*·me a la po·lee·*thee*·a

Call a doctor!
¡Llame a un médico! — *lya*·me a oon *me*·dee·ko

Call an ambulance!
¡Llame a una ambulancia! — *lya*·me a oo·na am·boo·*lan*·thya

I'm ill.
Estoy enfermo/a. m/f — es·*toy* en·*fer*·mo/a

My friend is ill.
Mi amigo/a está enfermo/a. m/f — mee a·*mee*·go/a es·*ta* en·*fer*·mo/a

Could you help me, please?
¿Me puede ayudar, por favor? — me *pwe*·de a·yoo·*dar* por fa·*vor*

I have to use the telephone.
    Necesito usar el   ne·the·*see*·to oo·*sar* el
    teléfono.   te·*le*·fo·no

I'm lost.
    Estoy perdido/a. m/f   es·toy per·*dee*·do/a

Where are the toilets?
    ¿Dónde están los   *don*·de es·*tan* los
    servicios?   ser·*vee*·thyos

---

the underground

Petty crime is particularly common in Madrid and
Barcelona. Try not to stand near the train doors and
keep money out of sight. If someone attempts to rob
you, try screaming these phrases at the top of your
lungs:

Leave me alone!   *¡Déjame en*   de·kha·me en
                    paz!   path
Help, thief!   *¡Socorro, al*   so·*ko*·ro al
                    ladron!   lad·*ron*

police

la policia

In an emergency, call the police, who will then put you through
to other emergency services (fire brigade and ambulance). For
more on making a call, see **communications**, page 72.

Where's the police station?
    ¿Dónde está la   *don*·de es·*ta* la
    comisaría?   ko·mee·sa·*ree*·a

I want to report an offence.
    Quiero denunciar un   kye·ro de·noon·*thyar* oon
    delito.   de·*lee*·to

He/She tried to assault me.
    Él/Ella intentó   el/e·lya een·ten·*to*
    asaltarme.   a·sal·*tar*·me

He/She tried to rob me.
Él/Ella intentó robarme.   el/*e*·lya een·ten·*to* ro·*bar*·me

I've been robbed.
Me han robado.   me an ro·*ba*·do

I've been raped.
He sido violado/a. m/f   e *see*·do vee·o·*la*·do/a

My ... was stolen.
Mi ... fue robado/a. m/f   mee ... fwe ro·*ba*·do/a

My ... were stolen.
Mis ... fueron robados/as. m/f   mee ... fwe·*ron* ro·*ba*·dos/as

I've lost my ...   *He perdido ...*   e per·*dee*·do ...
   bags   *mis maletas*   mees ma·*le*·tas
   money   *mi dinero*   mee dee·*ne*·ro
   passport   *mi pasaporte*   mee pa·sa·*por*·te

I apologise.
Lo siento.   lo *syen*·to

I didn't realise I was doing anything wrong.
No sabía que estaba   no sa·*bee*·a ke es·*ta*·ba
haciendo algo mal.   a·*thyen*·do *al*·go mal

I'm innocent.
Soy inocente.   soy ee·no·*then*·te

I (don't) understand.
(No) Entiendo.   (no) en·*tyen*·do

I want to contact my embassy/consulate.
Quiero ponerme en   *kye*·ro po·*ner*·me en
contacto con mi   kon·*tak*·to kon mee
embajada/consulado.   em·ba·*kha*·da/kon·soo·*la*·do

Can I call a lawyer?
¿Puedo llamar a un   *pwe*·do lya·*mar* a oon
abogado?   a·bo·*ga*·do

I need a lawyer who speaks English.
*Necesito un abogado
que hable inglés.*

ne·the·*see*·to oon a·bo·*ga*·do
ke *a*·ble een·*gles*

Can I pay an on-the-spot fine?
*¿Podemos pagar una
multa al contado?*

po·*de*·mos pa·*gar* oo·na
mool·ta al kon·*ta*·do

This drug is for personal use.
*Esta droga es para uso
personal.*

es·ta *dro*·ga es *pa*·ra oo·so
per·so·*nal*

I have a prescription for this drug.
*Tengo receta para esta
droga.*

ten·go re·*the*·ta *pa*·ra es·ta
dro·ga

What am I accused of?
¿De qué me acusan?

de ke me a·*ku*·san

the police may say ...

You have overstayed your visa.
*El plazo de tu
visado se ha pasado.*

el *pla*·tho de too
vee·*sa*·do se a pa·*sa*·do

You'll be charged with ...
Será acusado/a de ... m/f

se·ra a·koo·*sa*·do/a de ...

He'll/She'll be charged with ...
*Él/Ella será acusado/a
de ...*

el/e·lya se·ra a·koo·*sa*·do/a
de ...

assault	*asalto*	a·*sal*·to
possession	*posesión*	po·se·*syon*
(of illegal	*(de sustancias*	(de soos·*tan*·thyas
substances)	*ilegales)*	ee·le·*ga*·les)
shoplifting	*ratería*	ra·te·*ree*·a
speeding	*exceso de*	eks·*the*·so de
	velocidad	ve·lo·thee·*da*

doctor

el médico

Where's the nearest ...?	¿Dónde está ... más cercano/a? m/f	don·de es·ta ... mas ther·ka·no/a
chemist	la farmacia f	la far·ma·thya
dentist	el dentista m	el den·tees·ta
doctor	el médico m	el me·dee·ko
hospital	el hospital m	el os·pee·tal
medical centre	el consultorio m	el kon·sool·to·ryo
optometrist	el oculista m	el o·koo·lees·ta

I've been vaccinated for ...	Estoy vacunado/a contra ... m/f	es·toy va·koo·na·do/a kon·tra ...
He's/She's been vaccinated for ...	Está vacunado/a contra ... m/f	es·ta va·koo·na·do/a kon·tra ...
tetanus	el tétano	el te·ta·no
typhoid	la tifus	la tee·foos
hepatitis A/B/C	la hepatitis A/B/C	la e·pa·tee·tees a/be/the
... fever	la fiebre ...	la fye·bre ...

I need a doctor (who speaks English).
Necesito un doctor (que hable inglés). ne·the·see·to oon dok·tor (ke a·ble een·gles)

I'm sick.
Estoy enfermo/a. m/f es·toy en·fer·mo/a

Could I see a female doctor?
¿Puede examinarme una doctora? pwe·de ek·sa·mee·nar·me oo·na dok·to·ra

For women's medical issues, see **women's health**, page 183.

the doctor may say ...

What's the problem?
¿Qué le pasa?   ke le *pa*·sa

Where does it hurt?
¿Dónde le duele?   *don*·de le *dwe*·le

Do you have a temperature?
¿Tiene fiebre?   *tye*·ne *fye*·bre

How long have you been like this?
¿Desde cuándo se   *des*·de *kwan*·do se
siente así?   *syen*·te a·*see*

Have you had this before?
¿Ha tenido esto antes?   a te·*nee*·do *es*·to *an*·tes

Have you had unprotected sex?
¿Ha tenido relaciones   a te·*nee*·do re·la·*thyo*·nes
sexuales sin   sek·*swa*·les seen
protección?   pro·tek·*thyon*

Are you allergic?
¿Tiene usted alergias?   *tye*·ne oos·*te* a·*ler*·khyas

Are you on medication?
¿Se encuentra   se en·*kwen*·tra
bajo medicación?   *ba*·kho me·dee·ka·*thyon*

You need to be admitted to hospital.
Necesita ingresar   ne·the·*see*·ta een·gre·*sar*
en un hospital.   en oon os·pee·*tal*

How long are you travelling for?
Por cuánto tiempo   por *kwan*·to *tyem*·po
está viajando.   es·*ta* vya·*khan*·do

**You should have it checked when
you go home.**
Debería revisarlo   de·be·*ree*·a re·vee·*sar*·lo
cuando vuelva a casa.   *kwan*·do *vwel*·va a *ka*·sa

Do you ...?	*¿Usted ...?*	oos·*te* ...
drink	*bebe*	*be*·be
smoke	*fuma*	*foo*·ma
take drugs	*toma drogas*	*to*·ma *dro*·gas

I've run out of my medication.
Se me terminaron los
medicamentos.

se me ter·mee·*na*·ron los
me·dee·ka·*men*·tos

This is my usual medicine.
Éste es mi medicamento
habitual.

es·te es mee·me·doo·ka·*men*·to
a·bee·too·*al*

My prescription is ...
Mi receta es ...

mee re·*the*·ta es ...

I don't want a blood transfusion.
No quiero que me hagan
una transfusión de
sangre.

no *kye*·ro ke me a·gan
oo·na trans·foo·*syon* de
san·gre

Please use a new syringe.
Por favor, use una
jeringa nueva.

por fa·*vor* oo·se oo·na
khe·*reen*·ga *nwe*·va

I need new ...	*Necesito ...*	ne·the·*see*·to ...
	nuevas.	*nwe*·vas
glasses	*gafas*	*ga*·fas
contact	*lentes de*	*len*·tes de
lenses	*contacto*	kon·*tak*·to

For cost & receipts, see **shopping**, page 64.

symptoms & conditions

I have ...
Tengo ...

ten·go ...

I've recently had ...
Hace poco he tenido ...

a·the *po*·ko e te·*nee*·do ...

There's a history of ...
Hay antecedentes de ...

ai an·te·the·*den*·tes de ...

I'm on regular medication for ...
Estoy bajo
medicación para ...

es·*toy* ba·kho
me·dee·ka·*thyon* pa·ra ...

asthma	*asma* m	*as*·ma
diarrhoea	*diarrea* f	dee·a·*re*·a
fever	*fiebre* f	*fye*·bre
infection	*infección* f	in·fek·*thyon*
sprain	*torcedura* f	tor·the·*doo*·ra

It hurts here.
Me duele aquí.   me *dwe*·le a·*kee*

I've been injured.
He sido herido/a. m/f   e *see*·do e·*ree*·do/a

I've been vomiting.
He estado vomitando.   e es·*ta*·do vo·mee·*tan*·do

I'm dehydrated.
Estoy deshidratado/a. m/f   es·*toy* de·seed·ra·*ta*·do/a

I can't sleep.
No puedo dormir.   no *pwe*·do dor·*meer*

I think it's the medication I'm on.
Me parece que son los   me pa·*re*·the ke son los
medicamentos que   me·dee·ka·*men*·tos ke
estoy tomando.   es·*toy* to·*man*·do

I feel ...	*Me siento ...*	me *syen*·to ...
better	*mejor*	me·*khor*
depressed	*deprimido/a* m/f	de·pree·*mee*·do
dizzy	*mareado/a* m/f	ma·re·*a*·do
shivery	*destemplado/a* m/f	des·tem·*pla*·do
strange	*raro/a* m/f	*ra*·ro
weak	*débil*	*de*·beel
worse	*peor*	pe·*or*

For more symptoms & conditions, see the **dictionary**.

women's health

la salud femenina

I think I'm pregnant.
Creo que estoy embarazada. kre·o ke es·toy em·ba·ra·*tha*·da

I haven't had my period for ... weeks.
Hace … semanas que no a·the … se·*ma*·nas ke no
me viene la regla. me *vye*·ne la *reg*·la

I need a pregnancy test.
Necesito una prueba ne·the·*see*·to *oo*·na *prwe*·ba
de embarazo. de em·ba·*ra*·tho

I'm on the Pill.
Tomo la píldora. to·mo la *peel*·do·ra

I've noticed a lump here.
He notado que tengo e no·*ta*·do ke *ten*·go
un bulto aquí. oon *bool*·to a·*kee*

I need ...	*Quisiera ...*	kee·*sye*·ra ...
contraception	*usar algún*	oo·*sar* al·*goon*
	método anti-	*me*·to·do an·tee·
	conceptivo	kon·thep·*tee*·vo
the morning-	*tomar la*	to·*mar* la
after pill	*píldora del*	*peel*·do·ra del
	día siguiente	*dee*·a see·*gyen*·te

---

the doctor may say ...

Are you pregnant?
¿Está embarazada? es·*ta* em·ba·ra·*tha*·da

You're pregnant.
Está embarazada. es·*ta* em·ba·ra·*tha*·da

When did you last have your period?
¿Cuándo le vino la *kwan*·do le *vee*·no la
regla por última vez? *reg*·la por *ool*·tee·ma veth

Are you using contraception?
¿Usa anticonceptivos? oo·sa an·tee·kon·thep·*tee*·vos

Do you have your period?
¿Tiene la regla? *tye*·ne la *reg*·la

allergies

I'm allergic to ...	Soy alérgico/a ... m/f	soy a·ler·khee·ko/a ...
He's/She's allergic to ...	Es alérgico/a ... m/f	es a·ler·khee·ko/a ...
antibiotics	a los antibióticos	a los an·tee·byo·tee·kos
anti-inflammatories	a los anti-inflamatorios	a los an·tee-een·fla·ma·to·ryos
aspirin	a la aspirina	a la as·pee·ree·na
bees	a las abejas	a las a·be·khas
codeine	a la codeina	a la ko·de·ee·na
nuts	a las nueces	a las nwe·thes
peanuts	a los cacahuetes	a los ka·ka·we·tes
penicillin	a la penicilina	a la pe·nee·thee·lee·na
pollen	al polen	al po·len

For more food-related allergies, see **vegetarian & special meals** page 160.

I have a skin allergy.
> Tengo una alergia en la piel.
> ten·go oo·na a·ler·khya en la pyel

I'm on a special diet.
> Estoy a régimen especial.
> es·toy a re·khee·men es·pe·thyal

inhaler	inhalador m	een·a·la·dor
injection	inyección f	een·yek·thyon
antihistamines	antihista-mínicos m pl	an·tees·ta-mee·nee·kos

alternative treatments

I don't use Western medicine.
   No uso la medicina   no oo·so la me·dee·thee·na
   occidental.   ok·thee·den·*tal*

I prefer ...
   Prefiero ...   pre·*fye*·ro ...

Can I see someone who practises ...?
   ¿Puedo ver a alguien que   *pwe*·do ver al·gyen ke
   practique ...?   prak·*tee*·ke ...

waiting room

Here are some tips on Spanish etiquette in public places.
• Men usually wait for women to be seated before they take a seat themselves, and when they finally do it's the guys who cross their legs at the knees, not the ladies.
• Yawning and stretching when you have an audience, no matter how small, is considered inappropriate.

parts of the body

My ... hurts.
   Me duele ...   me *dwe*·le ...

I can't move my ...
   No puedo mover ...   no *pwe*·do mo·*ver* ...

I have a cramp in my ...
   Tengo calambres en ...   *ten*·go ka·*lam*·bres en ...

My ... is swollen.
   Mi ... está hinchado.   mee ... es·*ta* een·*cha*·do

health

185

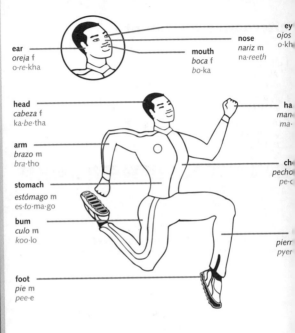

ear
oreja f
o·*re*·kha

nose
nariz m
na·*reeth*

mouth
boca f
bo·ka

ey
ojos
o·kh

head
cabeza f
ka·*be*·tha

arm
brazo m
bra·tho

stomach
estómago m
es·*to*·ma·go

bum
culo m
koo·lo

foot
pie m
pee·e

ha
man
ma·

ch
pecho
pe·c

pierr
pyer

chemist

la farmacia

Is there a (night) chemist nearby?
  ¿*Hay una farmacia (de*   ai oo·na far·*ma*·thya (de
  guardía) por aquí?   gwar·*dee*·a) por a·*kee*

I need something for ...
  Necesito algo para ...   ne·the·*see*·to al·go *pa*·ra ...

Do I need a prescription for ...?
  ¿*Necesito receta*   ne·the·*see*·to re·*the*·ta
  para ...?   *pa*·ra ...

I have a prescription.
Tengo receta médica.   ten·go re·*the*·ta me·dee·ka

How many times a day?
¿Cuántas veces al día?   kwan·tas ve·thes al *dee*·a

listen for ...

a to·*ma*·do es·to an·tes
¿Ha tomado esto antes?   **Have you taken this before?**

de·be ter·mee·*nar* el tra·ta·*myen*·to
Debe terminar el tratamiento.   **You must complete the course.**

dos ve·thes al *dee*·a (kon la ko·*mee*·da)
Dos veces al día (con la comida).   **Twice a day (with food).**

es·ta·*ra lees*·to en (*veyn*·te mee·*noo*·tos)
Estará listo en (veinte minutos).   **It'll be ready to pick up in (20 minutes).**

dentist

el dentista

I have a broken tooth.
Se me ha roto un diente.   se me a *ro*·to oon *dyen*·te

I have a toothache.
Me duele una muela.   me *dwe*·le *oo*·na *mwe*·la

listen for ...

a·bra	*Abra.*	**Open wide.**
no se *mwe*·va	*No se mueva.*	**Don't move.**
en·*khwa*·ge	*¡Enjuague!*	**Rinse!**

I've lost a filling.
Se me ha caído un empaste.
se me a ka·*ee*·do oon em·*pas*·te

My gums hurt.
Me duelen las encías.
me *dwe*·len las en·*thee*·as

I don't want it extracted.
No quiero que me lo saquen.
no *kye*·ro ke me lo *sa*·ken

I need a/an ...	*Necesito ...*	ne·the·*see*·to ...
anaesthetic	*una anestesia*	*oo*·ne a·nes·*te*·sya
filling	*un empaste*	oon em·*pas*·te

signs

Asistencia Sanitaria	a·see·*sten*·thee·a sa·nee·*ta*·ree·a	**First Aid**
Farmacia	far·ma·*thee*·a	**Pharmacy/ Drug Store**
Horas de Visita	o·ras de vee·*see*·ta	**Visiting Hours**
Hospital	o·spee·*tal*	**Hospital**
Médico	*me*·dee·ko	**Doctor**
Planta	*plan*·ta	**Ward**
Urgencias	ur·*khen*·thee·as	**Casualty/ Emergency**

Nouns in the dictionary have their gender indicated by ⑩ or ①. If it's a plural noun, you'll also see pl. Where a word that could be either a noun or a verb has no gender indicated, it's a verb.

A

(to be) able *poder* po·der
aboard *a bordo* a bor·do
abortion *aborto* ⑩ a·bor·to
about *sobre* so·bre
above *arriba* a·ree·ba
abroad *en el extranjero* en el eks·tran·khe·ro
accept *aceptar* a·thep·tar
accident *accidente* ⑩ ak·thee·den·te
accommodation *alojamiento* ⑩ a·lo·kha·myen·to
across *a través* a tra·ves
activist *activista* ⑩&① ak·tee·vees·ta
acupuncture *acupuntura* ① a·koo·poon·too·ra
adaptor *adaptador* ⑩ a·dap·ta·dor
address *dirección* ① dee·rek·thyon
administration *administración* ① ad·mee·nees·tra·thyon
admission price *precio* ⑩ *de entrada* pre·thyo de en·tra·da
admit *admitir* ad·mee·teer
adult *adulto* ⑩ a·dool·to
advertisement *anuncio* ⑩ a·noon·thyo
advice *consejo* ⑩ kon·se·kho
aerobics *aeróbic* ⑩ ai·ro·beek
Africa *África* ① a·free·ka
after *después de* des·pwes de
aftershave *bálsamo de aftershave* bal·sa·mo de ahf·ter·sha·eev
again *otra vez* o·tra veth
age *edad* ① e·da
aggressive *agresivo/a* ⑩/① a·gre·see·vo/a

agree *estar de acuerdo* es·tar de a·kwer·do
agriculture *agricultura* ① a·gree·kul·too·ra
AIDS *SIDA* ⑩ see·da
air *aire* ⑩ ai·re
air mail *por vía aérea* por vee·a a·e·re·a
air-conditioned *con aire acondicionado* kon ai·re a·kon·dee·thyo·na·do
air-conditioning *aire* ⑩ *acondicionado* ai·re a·kon·dee·thyo·na·do
airline *aerolínea* ① ay·ro·lee·nya
airport *aeropuerto* ⑩ ay·ro·pwer·to
airport tax *tasa* ① *del aeropuerto* ta·sa del ay·ro·pwer·to
alarm clock *despertador* ⑩ des·per·ta·dor
alcohol *alcohol* ⑩ al·col
all *todo* to·do
allergy *alergia* ① a·ler·khya
allow *permitir* per·mee·teer
almonds *almendras* ① pl al·men·dras
almost *casi* ka·see
alone *solo/a* ⑩/① so·lo/a
already *ya* ya
also *también* tam·byen
altar *altar* ⑩ al·tar
altitude *altura* ① al·too·ra
always *siempre* syem·pre
amateur *amateur* ⑩&① a·ma·ter
ambassador *embajador/ embajadora* ⑩/① em·ba·kha·dor/ em·ba·kha·do·ra
among *entre* en·tre
anarchist *anarquista* ⑩&① a·nar·kees·ta
ancient *antiguo/a* ⑩/① an·tee·gwo/a
and *y* ee
angry *enfadado/a* ⑩/① en·fa·da·do/a

animal *animal* ⓜ a·nee·*mal*
ankle *tobillo* ⓜ to·*bee*·lyo
answer *respuesta* ⓕ res·*pwes*·ta
answering machine *contestador*
  automático kon·tes·ta·*dor*
  ow·to·ma·tee·ko
ant *hormiga* ⓕ or·*mee*·ga
anthology *antología* ⓕ an·to·lo·*khee*·a
antibiotics *antibióticos* ⓜ pl
  an·tee·*byo*·tee·kos
antinuclear *antinuclear* an·tee·noo·kle·*ar*
antique *antigüedad* ⓕ an·tee·gwe·*da*
antiseptic *antiséptico* ⓜ
  an·tee·*sep*·tee·ko
any *alguno/a* ⓜ/ⓕ al·*goo*·no/a
appendix *apéndice* ⓜ a·*pen*·dee·the
apple *manzana* ⓕ man·*tha*·na
appointment *cita* ⓕ *thee*·ta
apricot *albaricoque* ⓜ al·ba·ree·*ko*·ke
archaeological *arqueológico/a* ⓜ/ⓕ
  ar·keo·*lo*·khee·ko/a
architect *arquitecto/a* ⓜ/ⓕ
  ar·kee·*tek*·to/a
architecture *arquitectura* ⓕ
  ar·kee·tek·*too*·ra
argue *discutir* dees·koo·*teer*
arm *brazo* ⓜ *bra*·tho
army *ejército* ⓜ e·*kher*·thee·to
arrest *detener* de·te·*ner*
arrivals *llegadas* ⓕ pl lye·*ga*·das
arrive *llegar* lye·*gar*
art *arte* ⓜ *ar*·te
art gallery *museo* ⓜ *de arte* moo·*se*·o
  de *ar*·te
artichoke *alcachofa* ⓕ al·ka·*cho*·fa
artist *artista* ⓜ&ⓕ ar·*tees*·ta
ashtray *cenicero* ⓜ the·nee·*the*·ro
Asia *Asia* ⓕ a·sya
ask (a question) *preguntar* pre·goon·*tar*
ask (for something) *pedir* pe·*deer*
aspirin *aspirina* ⓕ as·pee·*ree*·na
assault *asalto* ⓜ a·*sal*·to
asthma *asma* ⓜ *as*·ma
athletics *atletismo* ⓜ at·le·*tees*·mo
atmosphere *atmósfera* ⓕ at·*mos*·fe·ra
aubergine *berenjena* ⓕ be·ren·*khe*·na
aunt *tía* ⓕ *tee*·a

Australia *Australia* ⓕ ow·*stra*·lya
Australian Rules football *fútbol* ⓜ
  australiano foot·bol ow·stra·*lya*·no
automatic teller machine *cajero* ⓜ
  automático ka·*khe*·ro
  ow·to·ma·tee·ko
autumn *otoño* ⓜ o·to·nyo
avenue *avenida* ⓕ a·ve·*nee*·da
avocado *aguacate* ⓜ a·gwa·*ka*·te

B

B&W (film) *blanco y negro* blan·ko
  ee *ne*·gro
baby *bebé* ⓜ be·*be*
baby food *comida* ⓕ *de bebé*
  ko·*mee*·da de be·be
baby powder *talco* ⓜ *tal*·ko
babysitter *canguros* ⓜ kan·*goo*·ros
back (of body) *espalda* ⓕ es·*pal*·da
back (of chair) *respaldo* ⓜ res·*pal*·do
backpack *mochila* ⓕ mo·*chee*·la
bacon *tocino* ⓜ to·*thee*·no
bad *malo/a* ⓜ/ⓕ *ma*·lo/a
bag *bolso* ⓜ *bol*·so
baggage *equipaje* e·kee·*pa*·khe
baggage allowance ⓜ *límite de*
  equipaje lee·mee·te de e·kee·*pa*·khe
baggage claim *recogida* ⓕ *de*
  equipajes re·ko·*khee*·da de
  e·kee·*pa*·khes
bakery *panadería* ⓕ pa·na·de·*ree*·a
balance (account) *saldo* ⓜ *sal*·do
balcony *balcón* ⓜ bal·*kon*
ball *pelota* ⓕ pe·*lo*·ta
ballet *ballet* ⓜ ba·*le*
banana *plátano* ⓜ *pla*·ta·no
band *grupo* ⓜ *groo*·po
bandage *vendaje* ⓜ ven·*da*·khe
band-aids *tiritas* ⓕ pl tee·*ree*·tas
bank *banco* ⓜ *ban*·ko
bank account *cuenta* ⓕ *bancaria*
  kwen·ta ban·ka·rya
banknotes *billetes* ⓜ pl *(de banco)*
  bee·*lye*·tes (de *ban*·ko)
baptism *bautizo* ⓜ bow·*tee*·tho

bar *bar* ⓜ bar
bar (with music) *pub* ⓜ poob
bar work *trabajo* ⓜ *de camarero/a* ⓜ/①
  tra·ba·kho de ka·ma·re·ro/a
baseball *béisbol* ⓜ beys·bol
basket *canasta* ① ka·nas·ta
basketball *baloncesto* ⓜ ba·lon·thes·to
bath *bañera* ① ba·nye·ra
bathing suit *bañador* ⓜ ba·nya·dor
bathroom *baño* ⓜ ba·nyo
battery (car) *batería* ① ba·te·ree·a
battery (small) *pila* ① pee·la
be *ser* ser • *estar* es·tar
beach *playa* ① pla·ya
bean sprouts *brotes* ⓜ pl *de soja*
  bro·tes de so·kha
beans *judías* khoo·dee·as
beautiful *hermoso/a* ⓜ/① er·mo·so/a
beauty salon *salón* ⓜ *de belleza* sa·lon
  de be·lye·tha
because *porque* por·ke
bed *cama* ① ka·ma
bedding *ropa* ① *de cama* ro·pa de ka·ma
bedroom *habitación* ① a·bee·ta·thyon
bee *abeja* ① a·be·kha
beef *carne* ① *de vaca* kar·ne de va·ka
beer *cerveza* ① ther·ve·tha
beetroot *remolacha* ① re·mo·la·cha
before *antes* an·tes
beggar *mendigo/a* ⓜ/① men·dee·go/a
begin *comenzar* ko·men·thar
behind *detrás de* de·tras de
below *abajo* a·ba·kho
best *lo mejor* lo me·khor
bet *apuesta* ① a·pwes·ta
better *mejor* me·khor
between *entre* en·tre
bible *biblia* ① bee·blya
bicycle *bicicleta* ① bee·thee·kle·ta
big *grande* gran·de
bike *bici* ① bee·thee
bike chain *cadena* ① *de bici* ka·de·na
  de bee·thee
bike path *camino* ⓜ *de bici* ka·mee·no
  de bee·thee
bill *cuenta* ① kwen·ta

biodegradable *biodegradable*
  bee·o·de·gra·da·ble
biography *biografía* ① bee·o·gra·fee·a
bird *pájaro* ⓜ pa·kha·ro
birth certificate *partida* ① *de*
  nacimiento par·tee·da de
  na·thee·myen·to
birthday *cumpleaños* ⓜ koom·ple·a·nyos
birthday cake *pastel* ⓜ *de cumpleaños*
  pas·tel de koom·ple·a·nyos
biscuit ① *galleta* ga·lye·ta
bite (dog) *mordedura* ① mor·de·doo·ra
bite (food) *bocado* ⓜ bo·ka·do
bite (insect) *picadura* ① pee·ka·doo·ra
black *negro/a* ⓜ/① ne·gro/a
blanket *manta* ① man·ta
bleed *sangrar* san·grar
blind *ciego/a* ⓜ/① thye·go/a
blister *ampolla* ① am·po·lya
blocked *atascado/a* ⓜ/① a·tas·ka·do/a
blood *sangre* ① san·gre
blood group *grupo* ⓜ *sanguíneo*
  groo·po san·gee·neo
blood pressure *presión* ① *arterial*
  pre·syon ar·te·ryal
blood test *análisis* ⓜ *de sangre*
  a·na·lee·sees de san·gre
blue *azul* a·thool
board (ship, etc) *embarcarse*
  em·bar·kar·se
boarding house *pensión* ① pen·syon
boarding pass *tarjeta* ① *de embarque*
  tar·khe·ta de em·bar·ke
bone *hueso* ⓜ we·so
book *libro* ⓜ lee·bro
book (make a reservation) *reservar*
  re·ser·var
booked out *lleno/a* ⓜ/① lye·no/a
bookshop *librería* ① lee·bre·ree·a
boots *botas* ① pl bo·tas
border *frontera* ① fron·te·ra
boring *aburrido/a* ⓜ/① a·boo·ree·do/a
borrow *tomar prestado* to·mar
  pres·ta·do
botanic garden *jardín* ⓜ *botánico*
  khar·deen bo·ta·nee·ko
both *dos* ⓜ/① pl dos

bottle *botella* ① bo·te·lya
bottle opener *abrebotellas* ⓜ
a·bre·bo·te·lyas
bowl *bol* ⓜ bol
box *caja* ① ka·kha
boxer shorts *calzones* ⓜ kal·*tho*·nes
boxing *boxeo* ⓜ bo·se·o
boy *chico* ⓜ chee·ko
boyfriend *novio* ⓜ no·vyo
bra *sujetador* ⓜ soo·khe·ta·*dor*
Braille *Braille* ⓜ brai·lye
brakes *frenos* ⓜ pl fre·nos
branch office *sucursal* ① soo·koor·*sal*
brandy *coñac* ⓜ ko·*nyak*
brave *valiente* va·*lyen*·te
bread *pan* ⓜ pan
   brown bread *pan moreno* pan mo·re·no
   bread rolls *bollos* bo·lyos
   rye *pan de centeno* pan de then·*te*·no
   sourdough *pan de masa fermentada*
   pan de *ma*·sa fer·men·*ta*·da
   white bread *pan blanco* pan blan·ko
   wholemeal *integral* een·te·*gral*
break *romper* rom·*per*
break down *descomponerse*
des·kom·po·*ner*·se
breakfast *desayuno* des·a·*yoo*·no
breasts *senos* ⓜ pl se·nos
breathe *respirar* res·pee·*rar*
bribe *soborno* ⓜ so·*bor*·no
bribe *sobornar* so·bor·*nar*
bridge *puente* ⓜ *pwen*·te
briefcase *maletín* ⓜ ma·le·*teen*
brilliant *cojonudo/a* ⓜ/①
ko·kho·*noo*·do/a
bring *traer* tra·*er*
brochure *folleto* ⓜ fo·*lye*·to
broken *roto/a* ⓜ/① ro·to/a
bronchitis *bronquitis* ⓜ bron·*kee*·tees
brother *hermano* ⓜ er·ma·no
brown *marrón* ma·*ron*
bruise *cardenal* ⓜ kar·de·*nal*
brussels sprouts *coles* ⓜ pl *de Bruselas*
ko·les de broo·se·las

bucket *cubo* ⓜ koo·bo
Buddhist *budista* ⓜ&① boo·*dees*·ta
buffet *buffet* ⓜ boo·fe
bug *bicho* ⓜ bee·cho
build *construir* kons·troo·*eer*
building *edificio* ⓜ e·dee·fee·thyo
bull *toro* ⓜ to·ro
bullfight *corrida* ① ko·ree·da
bullring *plaza* ① *de toros* pla·tha de
to·ros
bum (of body) *culo* ⓜ koo·lo
burn *quemadura* ① ke·ma·*doo*·ra
bus *autobús* ⓜ ow·to·*boos*
bus (intercity) *autocar* ⓜ ow·to·*kar*
bus station *estación de autobuses/*
autocares ① es·ta·*thyon* de
ow·to·*boo*·ses/ow·to·*ka*·res
bus stop *parada* ① *de autobús* pa·ra·da
de ow·to·*boos*
business *negocios* ⓜ pl ne·go·thyos
business class *clase* ① *preferente*
kla·se pre·fe·*ren*·te
business person *comerciante* ⓜ&①
ko·mer·*thyan*·te
busker *artista callejero/a* ⓜ/①
ar·*tees*·ta ka·lye·*khe*·ro/a
busy *ocupado/a* ⓜ/① o·koo·pa·do/a
but *pero* pe·ro
butcher's shop *carnicería* ①
kar·nee·the·*ree*·a
butter *mantequilla* ① man·te·*kee*·lya
butterfly *mariposa* ① ma·ree·*po*·sa
buttons *botones* ⓜ pl bo·*to*·nes
buy *comprar* kom·*prar*

C

cabbage *col* kol
cable *cable* ⓜ ka·ble
cable car *teleférico* ⓜ te·le·fe·ree·ko
café *café* ⓜ ka·fe
cake *pastel* ⓜ pas·*tel*
cake shop *pastelería* ① pas·te·le·*ree*·a
calculator *calculadora* ① kal·koo·la·do·ra
calendar *calendario* ⓜ ka·len·da·ryo

calf *ternero* ⓜ ter·ne·ro

camera *cámara* ⓕ *(fotográfica)* ka·ma·ra (fo·to·gra·fee·ka)

camera shop *tienda* ⓕ *de fotografía* tyen·da de fo·to·gra·fee·a

camp *acampar* a·kam·par

camping store *tienda* ⓕ *de provisiones de cámping* tyen·da de pro·vee·syo·nes de kam·peen

campsite *cámping* ⓜ kam·peen

can *lata* ⓕ la·ta

can (be able) *poder* po·der

can opener *abrelatas* ⓜ a·bre·la·tas

Canada *Canadá* ⓕ ka·na·da

cancel *cancelar* kan·the·lar

cancer *cáncer* ⓜ kan·ther

candle *vela* ⓕ ve·la

cantaloupe *cantalupo* ⓜ kan·ta·loo·po

capsicum (red/green) *pimiento* ⓜ *rojo/verde* pee·myen·to ro·kho/ver·de

car *coche* ⓜ ko·che

car hire *alquiler* ⓜ *de coche* al·kee·ler de ko·che

car owner's title *papeles* ⓜ pl *del coche* pa·pe·les del ko·che

car registration *matrícula* ⓕ ma·tree·koo·la

caravan *caravana* ⓕ ka·ra·va·na

cards *cartas* ⓕ pl *kar·tas*

care (about something) *preocuparse por* pre·o·koo·par·se por

care (for someone) *cuidar de* kwee·dar de

caring *bondadoso/a* ⓜ/ⓕ bon·da·do·so/a

carpark *aparcamiento* ⓜ a·par·ka·myen·to

carpenter *carpintero/a* ⓜ/ⓕ kar·peen·te·ro/a

carrot *zanahoria* ⓕ tha·na·o·rya

carry *llevar* lye·var

carton *cartón* ⓜ kar·ton

cash *dinero* ⓜ *en efectivo* dee·ne·ro en e·fek·tee·vo

cash (a cheque) *cambiar (un cheque)* kam·byar (oon che·ke)

cash register *caja* ⓕ *registradora* ka·kha re·khees·tra·do·ra

cashew nut *anacardo* ⓜ a·na·kar·do

cashier *caja* ⓕ ka·kha

casino *casino* ⓜ ka·see·no

cassette *casete* ⓜ ka·se·te

castle *castillo* ⓜ kas·tee·lyo

casual work *trabajo* ⓜ *eventual* tra·ba·kho e·ven·twal

cat *gato/a* ⓜ/ⓕ ga·to/a

cathedral *catedral* ⓕ ka·te·dral

Catholic *católico/a* ⓜ/ⓕ ka·to·lee·ko/a

cauliflower *coliflor* ⓕ ko·lee·flor

caves *cuevas* ⓕ pl kwe·vas

CD *cómpact* ⓜ kom·pakt

celebrate (an event) *celebrar* the·le·brar

celebration *celebración* ⓕ the·le·bra·thyon

cemetery *cementerio* ⓜ the·men·te·ryo

cent *centavo* ⓜ then·ta·vo

centimetre *centímetro* ⓜ then·tee·me·tro

central heating *calefacción* ⓕ *central* ka·le·fak·thyon then·tral

centre *centro* ⓜ then·tro

ceramic *cerámica* ⓕ the·ra·mee·ka

cereal *cereales* ⓜ pl the·re·a·les

certificate *certificado* ⓜ ther·tee·fee·ka·do

chair *silla* ⓕ see·lya

champagne *champán* ⓜ cham·pan

chance *oportunidad* ⓕ o·por·too·nee·da

change (money) *cambio* ⓜ kam·byo

change *cambiar* kam·byar

changing rooms *vestuarios* ⓜ pl ves·twa·ryos

charming *encantador/encantadora* ⓜ/ⓕ en·kan·ta·dor/en·kan·ta·do·ra

chat up *ligar* lee·gar

cheap *barato/a* ⓜ/ⓕ ba·ra·to/a

cheat *tramposo/a* ⓜ/ⓕ tram·po·so/a

check *revisar* re·vee·sar

check (bank) *cheque* ⓜ che·ke

check-in *facturación* ⓕ *de equipajes* fak·too·ra·thyon de e·kee·pa·khes

checkpoint *control* ⓜ kon·*trol*

cheese *queso* ⓜ *ke*·so

chef *cocinero* ⓜ ko·thee·*ne*·ro

chemist (person) *farmacéutico/a* ⓜ/ⓕ far·ma·the·*oo*·ti·ko/a

chemist (shop) *farmacia* ⓕ far·*ma*·thya

chess *ajedrez* ⓜ a·khe·*dreth*

chess board *tablero* ⓜ *de ajedrez* ta·*ble*·ro de a·khe·*dreth*

chest *pecho* ⓜ *pe*·cho

chewing gum *chicle* ⓜ *chee*·kle

chicken *pollo* ⓜ *po*·lyo

chicken breast *pechuga* ⓕ pe·*choo*·ga

chickpeas *garbanzos* ⓜ pl gar·*ban*·thos

child *niño/a* ⓜ/ⓕ *nee*·nyo/a

child seat *asiento* ⓜ *de seguridad para bebés* a·*syen*·to de se·goo·ree·*da* pa·ra be·*bes*

childminding service *guardería* ⓕ gwar·de·*ree*·a

children *hijos* ⓜ pl *ee*·khos

chilli *guindilla* ⓕ geen·*dee*·lya

chilli sauce *salsa* ⓕ *de guindilla* *sal*·sa de geen·*dee*·lya

chocolate *chocolate* ⓜ cho·ko·*la*·te

choose *escoger* es·ko·*kher*

Christian *cristiano/a* ⓜ/ⓕ krees·*tya*·no/a

Christian name *nombre* ⓜ *de pila* *nom*·bre de *pee*·la

Christmas *Navidad* ⓕ na·vee·*da*

Christmas Eve *Nochebuena* ⓕ no·che·*bwe*·na

church *iglesia* ⓕ ee·*gle*·sya

cider *sidra* ⓕ *see*·dra

cigar *cigarro* ⓜ thee·*ga*·ro

cigarette *cigarillo* ⓜ thee·ga·*ree*·lyo

cigarette lighter *mechero* ⓜ me·*che*·ro

cigarette machine *máquina* ⓕ *de tabaco* *ma*·kee·na de ta·*ba*·ko

cigarette paper *papel* ⓜ *de fumar* pa·*pel* de foo·*mar*

cinema *cine* ⓜ *thee*·ne

circus *circo* ⓜ *theer*·ko

citizenship *ciudadanía* ⓕ theew·da·da·*nee*·a

city *ciudad* ⓕ theew·*da*

city centre *centro* ⓜ *de la ciudad* *then*·tro de la theew·*da*

city walls *murallas* ⓕ pl moo·*ra*·lyas

civil rights *derechos civiles* ⓜ pl de·*re*·chos thee·*vee*·les

classical *clásico/a* ⓜ/ⓕ *kla*·see·ko/a

clean *limpio/a* ⓜ/ⓕ *leem*·pyo/a

cleaning *limpieza* ⓕ leem·*pye*·tha

client *clienta/e* ⓜ/ⓕ klee·*en*·ta/e

cliff *acantilado* ⓜ a·kan·tee·*la*·do

climb *subir* soo·*beer*

cloak *capote* ⓜ ka·*po*·te

cloakroom *guardarropa* ⓜ gwar·da·*ro*·pa

clock *reloj* ⓜ re·*lokh*

close *cerrar* the·*rar*

closed *cerrado/a* ⓜ/ⓕ the·*ra*·do/a

clothes line *cuerda* ⓕ *para tender la ropa* *kwer*·da pa·ra ten·*der* la *ro*·pa

clothing *ropa* ⓕ *ro*·pa

clothing store *tienda* ⓕ *de ropa* *tyen*·da de *ro*·pa

cloud *nube* ⓕ *noo*·be

cloudy *nublado* noo·*bla*·do

clove (garlic) *diente* ⓜ *(de ajo)* *dyen*·te (de *a*·kho)

cloves *clavos* ⓜ pl *kla*·vos

clutch *embrague* ⓕ em·*bra*·ge

coach *entrenador/entrenadora* ⓜ/ⓕ en·tre·na·*dor*/en·tre·na·*do*·ra

coast *costa* ⓕ *kos*·ta

cocaine *cocaína* ⓕ ko·ka·*ee*·na

cockroach *cucaracha* ⓕ koo·ka·*ra*·cha

cocoa *cacao* ⓜ ka·*kow*

coconut *coco* ⓜ *ko*·ko

codeine *codeína* ⓕ ko·de·*ee*·na

coffee *café* ⓜ ka·*fe*

coins *monedas* ⓕ pl mo·*ne*·das

cold *frío/a* ⓜ/ⓕ *free*·o/a

cold (illness) *resfriado* ⓜ res·free·*a*·do

colleague *colega* ⓜ&ⓕ ko·*le*·ga

collect call *llamada* ① *a cobro revertido* lya·ma·da a ko·bro re·ver·tee·do
college *residencia* ① *de estudiantes* re·see·den·thya de es·too·dyan·tes
colour *color* ⓜ ko·lor
colour (film) *película* ① *en color* pe·lee·koo·la en ko·lor
comb *peine* ⓐ pey·ne
come *venir* ve·neer
come (arrive) *llegar* lye·gar
comedy *comedia* ① ko·me·dya
comfortable *cómodo/a* ⓜ/① ko·mo·do/a
communion *comunión* ① ko·moo·nyon
communist *comunista* ⓜ&① ko·moo·nees·ta
companion *compañero/a* ⓜ/① kom·pa·nye·ro/a
company *compañía* ① kom·pa·nyee·a
compass *brújula* ① broo·khoo·la
complain *quejarse* ke·khar·se
computer *ordenador* ⓜ or·de·na·dor
computer game *juegos* ⓜ pl *de ordenador* khwe·gos de or·de·na·dor
concert *concierto* ① kon·thyer·to
conditioner *acondicionador* ⓜ a·kon·dee·thyo·na·dor
condoms *condones* ⓜ pl kon·do·nes
confession *confesión* ① kon·fe·syon
confirm *confirmar* kon·feer·mar
connection *conexión* ① ko·ne·ksyon
conservative *conservador/ conservadora* ⓜ/① kon·ser·va·dor/ kon·ser·va·do·ra
constipation *estreñimiento* ⓜ es·tre·nyee·myen·to
consulate *consulado* ⓜ kon·soo·la·do
contact lenses *lentes* ⓜ pl *de contacto* len·tes de kon·tak·to
contraceptives *anticonceptivos* ⓜ pl an·tee·kon·thep·tee·vos
contract *contrato* ⓜ kon·tra·to
convenience store *negocio* ⓜ *de artículos básicos* ne·go·thyo de ar·tee·koo·los ba·see·kos

convent *convento* ⓜ kon·ven·to
cook *cocinero* ⓜ ko·thee·ne·ro
cook *cocinar* ko·thee·nar
cookie *galleta* ① ga·lye·ta
corn *maíz* ⓜ ma·eeth
corn flakes *copos* ⓜ pl *de maíz* ko·pos de ma·eeth
corner *esquina* ① es·kee·na
corrupt *corrupto/a* ⓜ/① ko·roop·to/a
cost *costar* kos·tar
cottage cheese *requesón* ⓜ re·ke·son
cotton *algodón* ⓜ al·go·don
cotton balls *bolas* ① pl *de algodón* bo·las de al·go·don
cough *tos* ① tos
cough medicine *jarabe* ⓜ kha·ra·be
count *contar* kon·tar
counter *mostrador* ⓜ mos·tra·dor
country *país* ⓜ pa·ees
countryside *campo* ⓜ kam·po
coupon *cupón* ⓜ koo·pon
courgette *calabacín* ⓜ ka·la·ba·theen
court (tennis) *pista* ① pees·ta
cous cous *cus cus* ⓜ koos koos
cover charge *precio* ⓜ *del cubierto* pre·thyo del koo·byer·to
cow *vaca* ① va·ka
crab *cangrejo* ⓜ kan·gre·kho
crackers *galletas* ① pl *saladas* ga·lye·tas sa·la·das
crafts *artesanía* ① ar·te·sa·nee·a
crash *choque* ⓜ cho·ke
crazy *loco/a* ⓜ/① lo·ko/a
cream (food) *crema* kre·ma
cream (moisturising) *crema* ① *hidratante* kre·ma ee·dra·tan·te
cream cheese *queso* ⓜ *crema* ke·so kre·ma
creche *guardería* ① gwar·de·ree·a
credit card *tarjeta* ① *de crédito* tar·khe·ta de kre·dee·to
cricket *críquet* ⓜ kree·ket
crop *cosecha* ① ko·se·cha
crowded *abarrotado/a* ⓜ/① a·ba·ro·ta·do/a

cucumber *pepino* ⓜ pe·*pee*·no
cuddle *abrazo* ⓜ a·*bra*·tho
cup *taza* ⓕ *ta*·tha
cupboard *armario* ⓜ ar·*ma*·ryo
currency exchange *cambio* ⓜ *(de dinero)* *kam*·byo (de dee·*ne*·ro)
current (electricity) *corriente* ⓕ ko·*ryen*·te
current affairs *informativo* ⓜ een·for·ma·*tee*·vo
curry *curry* ⓜ *koo*·ree
curry powder *curry en polvo* ⓜ *koo*·ree en *pol*·vo
customs *aduana* ⓕ a·*dwa*·na
cut *cortar* kor·*tar*
cutlery *cubiertos* ⓜ pl koo·*byer*·tos
CV *historial profesional* ⓜ ees·to·*ryal* pro·fe·syo·*nal*
cycle *andar en bicicleta* an·*dar* en bee·thee·*kle*·ta
cycling *ciclismo* ⓜ thee·*klees*·mo
cyclist *ciclista* ⓜ&ⓕ thee·*klees*·ta
cystitis *cistitis* ⓕ thees·*tee*·tees

D

dad *papá* ⓜ pa·*pa*
daily *diariamente* dya·rya·*men*·te
dance *bailar* bai·*lar*
dancing *bailar* ⓜ bai·*lar*
dangerous *peligroso/a* ⓜ/ⓕ pe·lee·*gro*·so/a
dark *oscuro/a* ⓜ/ⓕ os·*koo*·ro/a
date *citarse* thee·*tar*·se
date (a person) *salir con* sa·*leer* kon
date (time) *fecha* ⓕ *fe*·cha
date of birth *fecha de nacimiento* ⓕ *fe*·cha de na·thee·*myen*·to
daughter *hija* ⓕ *ee*·kha
dawn *alba* ⓕ *al*·ba
day *día* ⓜ *dee*·a
day after tomorrow *pasado mañana* pa·*sa*·do ma·*nya*·na
day before yesterday *anteayer* an·te·a·*yer*
dead *muerto/a* ⓜ/ⓕ *mwer*·to/a

deaf *sordo/a* ⓜ/ⓕ *sor*·do/a
deal (cards) *repartir* re·par·*teer*
decide *decidir* de·thee·*deer*
deep *profundo/a* ⓜ/ⓕ pro·*foon*·do/a
deforestation *deforestación* ⓕ de·fo·res·ta·*thyon*
degree *título* ⓜ *tee*·too·lo
delay *demora* ⓕ de·*mo*·ra
delirious *delirante* de·lee·*ran*·te
deliver *entregar* en·tre·*gar*
democracy *democracia* ⓕ de·mo·*kra*·thya
demonstration *manifestación* ⓕ ma·nee·fes·ta·*thyon*
dental floss *hilo dental* ⓜ *ee*·lo den·*tal*
dentist *dentista* ⓜ&ⓕ den·*tees*·ta
deny *negar* ne·*gar*
deodorant *desodorante* ⓜ de·so·do·*ran*·te
depart *salir de* sa·*leer* de
department store *grande almacen* ⓜ *gran*·de al·*ma*·then
departure *salida* ⓕ sa·*lee*·da
deposit *depósito* ⓜ de·*po*·see·to
descendant *descendiente* ⓜ des·then·*dyen*·te
desert *desierto* ⓜ de·*syer*·to
design *diseño* ⓜ dee·*se*·nyo
destination *destino* ⓜ des·*tee*·no
destroy *destruir* des·troo·*eer*
detail *detalle* ⓜ de·*ta*·lye
diabetes *diabetes* ⓕ dee·a·*be*·tes
diaper *pañal* ⓜ pa·*nyal*
diaphragm *diafragma* ⓜ dee·a·*frag*·ma
diarrhoea *diarrea* ⓕ dee·a·*re*·a
diary *agenda* ⓕ a·*khen*·da
dice (die) *dados* ⓜ pl *da*·dos
dictionary *diccionario* ⓜ deek·thyo·*na*·ryo
die *morir* mo·*reer*
diet *régimen* ⓜ *re*·khee·men
different *diferente* ⓜ/ⓕ dee·fe·*ren*·te
difficult *difícil* ⓜ/ⓕ dee·*fee*·theel
dining car *vagón restaurante* va·*gon* res·tow·*ran*·te

dinner *cena* ① the·na
direct *directo/a* ⓜ/① dee·rek·to/a
direct-dial *marcar directo* mar·kar
dee·rek·to
director *director/directora* ⓜ/①
dee·rek·tor/dee·rek·to·ra
dirty *sucio/a* ⓜ/① soo·thyo/a
disabled *minusválido/a* ⓜ/①
mee·noos·va·lee·do/a
disco *discoteca* ① dees·ko·te·ka
discount *descuento* ⓜ des·kwen·to
discover *descubrir* des·koo·breer
discrimination *discriminación* ①
dees·kree·mee·na·thyon
disease *enfermedad* ① en·fer·me·da
disk *disco* ⓜ dees·ko
dive *bucear* boo·the·ar
diving *submarinismo* ⓜ
soob·ma·ree·nees·mo
diving equipment *equipo* ⓜ
de inmersión e·kee·po de
ee·mer·syon
dizzy *mareado/a* ⓜ/① ma·re·a·do/a
do *hacer* a·ther
doctor *doctor/doctora* ⓜ/① dok·tor/
dok·to·ra
documentary *documental* ⓜ
do·koo·men·tal
dog *perro/a* ⓜ/① pe·ro/a
dole *paro* ⓜ pa·ro
doll *muñeca* ① moo·nye·ka
dollar *dólar* ⓜ do·lar
domestic flight *vuelo* ⓜ *doméstico*
vwe·lo do·mes·tee·ko
donkey *burro* ⓜ boo·ro
door *puerta* ① pwer·ta
dope *droga* ① dro·ga
double *doble* ⓜ/① do·ble
double bed *cama* ① *de matrimonio*
ka·ma de ma·tree·mo·nyo
double room *habitación* ① *doble*
a·bee·ta·thyon do·ble
down *abajo* a·ba·kho
downhill *cuesta abajo* kwes·ta a·ba·kho
dozen *docena* ① do·the·na

drama *drama* ⓜ dra·ma
draw *dibujar* dee·boo·khar
dream *soñar* so·nyar
dress *vestido* ⓜ ves·tee·do
dried fruit *fruto* ⓜ *seco* froo·to se·ko
drink *bebida* ① be·bee·da
drink *beber* be·ber
drive *conducir* kon·doo·theer
drivers licence *carnet* ⓜ *de conducir*
kar·ne de kon·doo·theer
drug *droga* ① dro·ga
drug addiction *drogadicción* ①
dro·ga·deek·thyon
drug dealer *traficante* ⓜ *de drogas*
tra·fee·kan·te de dro·gas
drums *batería* ① ba·te·ree·a
drumstick (chicken) *muslo* moos·lo
drunk *borracho/a* ⓜ/① bo·ra·cho/a
dry *secar* se·kar
duck *pato* ⓜ pa·to
dummy (pacifier) *chupete* ⓜ choo·pe·te

E

each *cada* ka·da
ear *oreja* ① o·re·kha
early *temprano* tem·pra·no
earn *ganar* ga·nar
earplugs *tapones* ⓜ pl *para los oídos*
ta·po·nes pa·ra los o·ee·dos
earrings *pendientes* ⓜ pl pen·dyen·tes
Earth *Tierra* ① tye·ra
earthquake *terremoto* ⓜ te·re·mo·to
east *este* es·te
Easter *Pascua* ① pas·kwa
easy *fácil* fa·theel
eat *comer* ko·mer
economy class *clase* ① *turística* kla·se
too·rees·tee·ka
eczema *eczema* ① ek·the·ma
editor *editor/editora* ⓜ/① e·dee·tor/
e·dee·to·ra
education *educación* ① e·doo·ka·thyon
eggplant *berenjenas* ① pl
be·ren·khe·nas

egg *huevo* ⓜ we·vo
elections *elecciones* ⓕ pl
e·lek·thyo·nes
electrical store *tienda* ⓕ *de productos
eléctricos* tyen·da de pro·dook·tos
e·lek·tree·kos
electricity *electricidad* ⓕ
e·lek·tree·thee·da
elevator *ascensor* ⓜ as·then·sor
embarrassed *avergonzado/a* ⓜ/ⓕ
a·ver·gon·tha·do/a
embassy *embajada* ⓕ em·ba·kha·da
emergency *emergencia* ⓕ
e·mer·khen·thya
emotional *emocional* e·mo·thyo·nal
employee *empleado/a* ⓜ/ⓕ
em·ple·a·do/a
employer *jefe/a* ⓜ/ⓕ khe·fe/a
empty *vacío/a* ⓜ/ⓕ va·thee·o/a
end *fin* ⓜ feen
end *acabar* a·ka·bar
endangered species *especies* ⓕ pl *en
peligro de extinción* es·pe·thyes en
pe·lee·gro de eks·teen·thyon
engagement *compromiso* ⓜ
kom·pro·mee·so
engine *motor* ⓜ mo·tor
engineer *ingeniero/a* ⓜ/ⓕ
een·khe·nye·ro/a
engineering *ingeniería* ⓕ
een·khe·nye·ree·a
England *Inglaterra* ⓕ een·gla·te·ra
English *inglés* ⓜ een·gles
enjoy (oneself) *divertirse* dee·ver·teer·se
enough *suficiente* ⓜ/ⓕ
soo·fee·thyen·te
enter *entrar* en·trar
entertainment guide *guía* ⓕ *del ocio*
gee·a del o·thyo
envelope *sobre* ⓜ so·bre
environment *medio* ⓜ *ambiente*
me·dyo am·byen·te
epilepsy *epilepsia* ⓕ e·pee·lep·sya
equal opportunity *igualdad* ⓕ *de
oportunidades* ee·gwal·da de
o·por·too·nee·da·des

equality *igualdad* ⓕ ee·gwal·da
equipment *equipo* ⓜ e·kee·po
escalator *escaleras* ⓕ pl *mecánicas*
es·ka·le·ras me·ka·nee·kas
euro *euro* ⓜ e·oo·ro
Europe *Europa* ⓕ e·oo·ro·pa
euthanasia *eutanasia* ⓕ e·oo·ta·na·sya
evening *noche* ⓕ no·che
everything *todo* to·do
example *ejemplo* ⓜ e·khem·plo
excellent *excelente* ⓜ/ⓕ eks·the·len·te
exchange *cambio* ⓜ kam·byo
exchange (money) *cambiar* kam·byar
exchange rate *tipo* ⓜ *de cambio*
tee·po de kam·byo
exchange (give gifts) *regalar* re·ga·lar
excluded *no incluido* no een·kloo·ee·do
exhaust *tubo* ⓜ *de escape* too·bo de
es·ka·pe
exhibit *exponer* eks·po·ner
exhibition *exposición* ⓕ
eks·po·see·thyon
exit *salida* ⓕ sa·lee·da
expensive *caro/a* ⓜ/ⓕ ka·ro/a
experience *experiencia* ⓕ
eks·pe·ryen·thya
express *expreso/a* ⓜ/ⓕ eks·pre·so/a
express mail *correo* ⓜ *urgente* ko·re·o
oor·khen·te
extension (visa) *prolongación* ⓕ
pro·lon·ga·thyon
eye *ojo* ⓜ o·kho
eye drops *gotas* ⓕ pl *para los ojos*
go·tas pa·ra los o·khos

F

fabric *tela* ⓕ te·la
face *cara* ⓕ ka·ra
face cloth *toallita* ⓕ to·a·lyee·ta
factory *fábrica* ⓕ fa·bree·ka
factory worker *obrero/a* ⓜ/ⓕ o·bre·ro/a
fall *caída* ⓕ ka·ee·da
family *familia* ⓕ fa·mee·lya
family name *apellido* ⓜ a·pe·lyee·do
famous *famoso/a* ⓜ/ⓕ fa·mo·so/a

fan (hand held) abanico ⓜ a·ba·nee·ko
fan (electric) ventilador ⓜ
    ven·tee·la·dor
fanbelt correa ⓕ del ventilador ko·re·a
    del ven·tee·la·dor
far lejos le·lhos
farm granja ⓕ gran·kha
farmer agricultor/agricultora ⓜ/ⓕ
    a·gree·kool·tor/a·gree·kool·to·ra
fast rápido/a ⓜ/ⓕ ra·pee·do/a
fat gordo/a ⓜ/ⓕ gor·do/a
father padre ⓜ pa·dre
father-in-law suegro ⓜ swe·gro
fault falta ⓕ fal·ta
faulty defectuoso/a ⓜ/ⓕ
    de·fek·too·o·so/a
feed dar de comer dar de ko·mer
feel sentir sen·teer
feelings sentimientos ⓜ pl
    sen·tee·myen·tos
fence cerca ⓕ ther·ka
fencing esgrima ⓕ es·gree·ma
festival festival ⓜ fes·tee·val
fever fiebre ⓕ fye·bre
few pocos po·kos
fiance prometido ⓜ pro·me·tee·do
fiancee prometida ⓕ pro·me·tee·da
fiction ficción ⓕ feek·thyon
field campo ⓜ kam·po
fig higo ⓜ ee·go
fight pelea ⓕ pe·le·a
fight against luchar contra loo·char
    kon·tra
fill llenar lye·nar
fillet filete ⓜ fee·le·te
film película ⓕ pe·lee·koo·la
film speed sensibilidad ⓕ
    sen·see·bee·lee·da
filtered con filtro kon feel·tro
find encontrar en·kon·trar
fine multa ⓕ mool·ta
finger dedo ⓜ de·do
finish terminar ter·mee·nar
fire fuego ⓜ fwe·go
firewood leña ⓕ le·nya
first primero/a ⓜ/ⓕ pree·me·ro/a

first-class de primera clase de
    pree·me·ra kla·se
first-aid kit maletín ⓜ de primeros
    auxilios ma·le·teen de pree·me·ros
    ow·ksee·lyos
fish nez ⓜ peth
fish (as food) pescado ⓜ pes·ka·do
fish shop pescadería ⓕ pes·ka·de·ree·a
fishing pesca ⓕ pes·ka
flag bandera ⓕ ban·de·ra
flannel franela ⓕ fra·ne·la
flashlight linterna ⓕ leen·ter·na
flat llano/a ⓜ/ⓕ lya·no/a
flea pulga ⓕ pool·ga
flooding inundación ⓕ ee·noon·da·thyon
floor suelo ⓜ swe·lo
florist florista ⓜ&ⓕ flo·rees·ta
flour harina ⓕ a·ree·na
flower flor ⓕ flor
flower seller vendedor/vendedora ⓜ/ⓕ
    de flores ⓜ/ⓕ ven·de·dor/
    ven·de·do·ra de flo·res
fly volar vo·lar
foggy brumoso/a ⓜ/ⓕ broo·mo·so
follow seguir se·geer
food comida ⓕ ko·mee·da
food supplies víveres ⓜ pl vee·ve·res
foot pie ⓜ pye
football fútbol ⓜ foot·bol
footpath acera ⓕ a·the·ra
foreign extranjero/a ⓜ/ⓕ
    eks·tran·khe·ro/a
forest bosque ⓜ bos·ke
forever para siempre pa·ra syem·pre
forget olvidar ol·vee·dar
forgive perdonar per·do·nar
fork tenedor ⓜ te·ne·dor
fortnight quincena ⓕ keen·the·na
foul sucio/a ⓜ/ⓕ soo·thee·o/a
foyer vestíbulo ⓜ ves·tee·boo·lo
fragile frágil fra·kheel
free (not bound) libre lee·bre
free (of charge) gratis gra·tees
freeze helarse e·lar·se
friend amigo/a ⓜ/ⓕ a·mee·go/a

frost *escarcha* ① es·kar·cha

frozen foods *productos congelados* ⓜ pl pro·dook·tos kon·khe·la·dos

fruit *fruta* ① froo·ta

fruit picking *recolección* ① *de fruta* re·ko·lek·thyon de froo·ta

fry *freír* free·eer

frying pan *sartén* ① sar·ten

full *lleno/a* ⓜ/① lye·no/a

full-time *a tiempo completo* a tyem·po kom·ple·to

fun *diversión* ① dee·ver·syon

funeral *funeral* ⓜ foo·ne·ral

funny *gracioso/a* ⓜ/① gra·thyo·so/a

furniture *muebles* ⓜ pl mwe·bles

future *futuro* ⓜ foo·too·ro

G

gay *gay* gai

general *general* khe·ne·ral

Germany *Alemania* ① a·le·ma·nya

gift *regalo* ⓜ re·ga·lo

gig *bolo* ⓜ bo·lo

gin *ginebra* ① khee·ne·bra

ginger *jengibre* ⓜ khen·khee·bre

girl *chica* ① chee·ka

girlfriend *novia* ① no·vya

give *dar* dar

glandular fever *fiebre* ① *glandular* fye·bre glan·doo·lar

glass (material) *vidrio* ⓜ vee·dryo

glass (drinking) *vaso* ⓜ va·so

glasses *gafas* ① pl ga·fas

gloves *guantes* ⓜ pl gwan·tes

go *ir* eer

go out with *salir con* sa·leer kon

go shopping *ir de compras* eer de kom·pras

goal *gol* ⓜ gol

goalkeeper *portero/a* ⓜ/① por·te·ro/a

goat *cabra* ① ka·bra

goat's cheese *queso* ⓜ *de cabra* ke·so de ka·bra

god *Dios* ⓜ dyos

goggles *gafas* ① pl *de submarinismo* ga·fas de soob·ma·ree·nees·mo

golf ball *pelota* ① *de golf* pe·lo·ta de golf

golf course *campo* ⓜ *de golf* kam·po de golf

good *bueno/a* ⓜ/① bwe·no/a

government *gobierno* ⓜ go·byer·no

gram *gramo* ⓜ gra·mo

grandchild *nieto/a* ⓜ/① nye·to/a

grandfather *abuelo* ⓜ a·bwe·lo

grandmother *abuela* ① a·bwe·la

grapefruit *pomelo* ⓜ po·me·lo

grapes *uvas* ① pl oo·vas

graphic art *arte* ⓜ *gráfico* ar·te gra·fee·ko

grass *hierba* ① yer·ba

grave *tumba* ① toom·ba

gray *gris* grees

great *fantástico/a* ⓜ/① fan·tas·tee·ko/a

green *verde* ver·de

greengrocery (shop) *verdulería* ① ver·doo·le·ree·a

grocer (shopkeeper) *verdulero/a* ⓜ/① ver·doo·le·ro/a

grey *gris* grees

grocery *tienda* ① *de comestibles* tyen·da de ko·mes·tee·bles

grow *crecer* kre·ther

g-string *tanga* ① tan·ga

guess *adivinar* a·dee·vee·nar

guide (audio) *guía* ① *audio* gee·a ow·dyo

guide (person) *guía* ⓜ&① gee·a

guide dog *perro lazarillo* ⓜ pe·ro la·tha·ree·lyo

guidebook *guía* ① gee·a

guided tour *recorrido* ⓜ *guiado* re·ko·ree·do gee·a·do

guilty *culpable* kool·pa·ble

guitar *guitarra* ① gee·ta·ra

gum *chicle* ⓜ chee·kle

gymnastics *gimnasia* ① *rítmica* kheem·na·sya reet·mee·ka

gynaecologist *ginecólogo* ⓜ khee·ne·ko·lo·go

H

hair *pelo* ⓜ pe·lo
hairbrush *cepillo* ⓜ the·pee·lyo
hairdresser *peluquero/a* ⓜ/ⓕ
pe·loo·ke·ro/a
halal *halal* a·lal
half *medio/a* ⓜ/ⓕ me·dyo/a
half a litre *medio litro* ⓜ me·dyo lee·tro
hallucinate *alucinar* a·loo·thee·nar
ham *jamón* ⓜ kha·mon
hammer *martillo* ⓜ mar·tee·lyo
hammock *hamaca* ⓕ a·ma·ka
hand *mano* ⓕ ma·no
handbag *bolso* ⓜ bol·so
handicrafts *artesanía* ⓕ ar·te·sa·nee·a
handlebar *manillar* ⓜ ma·nee·lyar
handmade *hecho a mano* e·cho a ma·no
handsome *hermoso* ⓜ er·mo·so
happy *feliz* fe·leeth
harassment *acoso* ⓜ a·ko·so
harbour *puerto* ⓜ pwer·to
hard *duro/a* ⓜ/ⓕ doo·ro/a
hardware store *ferretería* ⓕ fe·re·te·ree·a
hash *hachís* ⓕ a·chees
hat *sombrero* ⓜ som·bre·ro
have *tener* te·ner
have a cold *estar constipado/a* ⓜ/ⓕ
es·tar kons·tee·pa·do
have fun *divertirse* dee·ver·teer·se
hay fever *alergia* ⓕ *al polen* a·ler·khya
al po·len
he *él* el
head *cabeza* ⓕ ka·be·tha
headache *dolor* ⓜ *de cabeza* do·lor de
ka·be·tha
headlights *faros* ⓜ pl fa·ros
health *salud* ⓕ sa·loo
hear *oír* o·eer
hearing aid *audífono* ⓜ ow·dee·fo·no
heart *corazón* ⓜ ko·ra·thon
heart condition *condición* ⓕ *cardíaca*
kon·dee·thyon kar·dee·a·ka
heat *calor* ⓜ ka·lor
heater *estufa* ⓕ es·too·fa
heavy *pesado/a* ⓜ/ⓕ pe·sa·do/a

helmet *casco* ⓜ kas·ko
help *ayudar* a·yoo·dar
hepatitis *hepatitis* ⓕ e·pa·tee·tees
her *su* soo
herbalist *herbolario/a* ⓜ/ⓕ
er·bo·la·ree·o/a
herbs *hierbas* ⓕ pl yer·bas
here *aquí* a·kee
heroin *heroína* ⓕ e·ro·ee·na
herring *arenque* ⓜ a·ren·ke
high *alto/a* ⓜ/ⓕ al·to/a
high school *instituto* ⓜ eens·tee·too·to
hike *ir de excursión*
eer de eks·koor·syon
hiking *excursionismo* ⓜ
eks·koor·syo·nees·mo
hiking boots *botas* ⓕ pl *de montaña*
bo·tas de mon·ta·nya
hiking routes *caminos* ⓜ pl *rurales*
ka·mee·nos roo·ra·les
hill *colina* ⓕ ko·lee·na
Hindu *hindú* een·doo
hire *alquilar* al·kee·lar
his *su* soo
historical *histórico/a* ⓜ/ⓕ
ees·to·ree·ko/a
hitchhike *hacer dedo* a·ther de·do
HIV positive *seropositivo/a* ⓜ/ⓕ
se·ro·po·se·tee·vo/a
hockey *hockey* ⓜ kho·kee
holiday *día festivo* ⓜ dee·a fes·tee·vo
holidays *vacaciones* ⓕ pl
va·ka·thyo·nes
Holy Week *Semana* ⓕ *Santa* se·ma·na
san·ta
homemaker *sin hogar* seen o·gar
homemaker *ama* ⓕ *de casa*
a·ma de ka·sa
homosexual *homosexual* ⓜ&ⓕ
o·mo·se·kswal
honey *miel* ⓕ myel
honeymoon *luna* ⓕ *de miel* loo·na
de myel
horoscope *horóscopo* ⓜ o·ros·ko·po
horse *caballo* ⓜ ka·ba·lyo

horse riding *equitación* ① e·kee·ta·*thyon*
horseradish *rábano* ⑩ *picante* ra·ba·no pee·kan·te
hospital *hospital* ⑩ os·pee·*tal*
hospitality *hosteleria* ① os·te·le·*ree*·a
hot *caliente* ka·*lyen*·te
hot water *agua caliente* ⑩ a·gwa ka·*lyen*·te
hotel *hotel* ⑩ o·*tel*
house *casa* ① *ka*·sa
housework *trabajo* ⑩ *de casa* tra·*ba*·kho de *ka*·sa
how *cómo* *ko*·mo
how much *cuánto* *kwan*·to
hug *abrazo* ⑩ a·*bra*·tho
huge *enorme* e·*nor*·me
human rights *derechos* ⑩ pl *humanos* de·*re*·chos oo·*ma*·nos
humanities *humanidades* ① pl oo·ma·nee·*da*·des
hungry *hambriento/a* ⑩/① am·*bryen*·to/a
hungry *tener hambre* te·*ner* am·bre
hunting *caza* ① *ka*·tha
hurt *dañar* da·*nyar*
husband *marido* ⑩ ma·*ree*·do

I

I *yo* yo
ice *hielo* ⑩ *ye*·lo
ice axe *piolet* ⑩ pyo·*le*
ice cream *helado* ⑩ e·la·do
ice cream parlour *heladería* ① e·la·de·*ree*·a
ice hockey *hockey* ⑩ *sobre hielo* kho·kee so·bre *ye*·lo
identification *identificación* ① ee·den·tee·fee·ka·*thyon*
identification card *carnet* ⑩ *de identidad* kar·*net* de ee·den·tee·*da*
idiot *idiota* ⑩&① ee·*dyo*·ta
if *si* see
ill *enfermo/a* ⑩/① en·*fer*·mo/a
immigration *inmigración* ① een·mee·gra·*thyon*

important *importante* eem·por·*tan*·te
in a hurry *de prisa* de *pree*·sa
in front of *enfrente de* en·*fren*·te de
included *incluido* een·kloo·*ee*·do
income tax *impuesto* ⑩ *sobre la renta* eem·*pwes*·to so·bre la *ren*·ta
India *India* ① *een*·dya
indicator *indicador* ⑩ een·dee·ka·*dor*
indigestion *indigestion* ① een·dee·khes·*tyon*
industry *industria* ① een·*doos*·trya
infection *infección* ① een·fek·*thyon*
inflammation *inflamación* ① een·fla·ma·*thyon*
influenza *gripe* ① *gree*·pe
ingredient *ingrediente* ⑩ een·gre·*dyen*·te
inject *inyectarse* een·yek·*tar*·se
injection *inyección* ① een·yek·*thyon*
injury *herida* ① e·*ree*·da
innocent *inocente* ee·no·*then*·te
inside *adentro* a·*den*·tro
instructor *profesor/profesora* ⑩/① pro·fe·*sor*/pro·fe·*so*·ra
insurance *seguro* ⑩ se·*goo*·ro
interesting *interesante* een·te·re·*san*·te
intermission *descanso* ⑩ des·*kan*·so
international *internacional* een·ter·na·thyo·*nal*
Internet *Internet* een·ter·net
Internet cafe *cibercafé* thee·ber·ka·fe
interpreter *intérprete* ⑩&① een·*ter*·pre·te
intersection *cruce* ⑩ *croo*·the
interview *entrevista* ① en·tre·*vees*·ta
invite *invitar* een·vee·*tar*
Ireland *Irlanda* ① *plan*·cha
iron *plancha* ① *plan*·cha
island *isla* ① *ees*·la
IT *informática* ① een·for·ma·tee·ka
itch *picazón* ① pee·ka·*thon*
itemised *detallado/a* ⑩/① de·ta·*lya*·do/a
itinerary *itinerario* ① ee·tee·ne·ra·ryo
IUD *DIU* ⑩ de ee oo

J

jacket *chaqueta* ① cha·ke·ta
jail *cárcel* ① kar·thel
jam *mermelada* ① mer·me·*la*·da
Japan *Japón* ⑩ kha·*pon*
jar *jarra* ① *kha*·ra
jaw *mandíbula* ① man·*dee*·boo·la
jealous *celoso/a* ⑩/① the·*lo*·so/a
jeans *vaqueros* ⑩ pl va·*ke*·ros
jeep *yip* ⑩ yeep
jet lag *jet lag* ⑩ dyet lag
jewellery shop *joyería* ① kho·ye·*ree*·a
Jewish *judío/a* ⑩/① khoo·*dee*·o/a
job *trabajo* ⑩ tra·*ba*·kho
jockey *jockey* ⑩ *dyo*·kee
jogging *footing* ⑩ *foo*·teen
joke *broma* ① *bro*·ma
joke *bromear* bro·me·*ar*
journalist *periodista* ⑩&①
    pe·ryo·*dees*·ta
judge *juez* ⑩&① khweth
juice *jugo* ⑩ *khoo*·go • *zumo* ⑩
    thoo·mo
jump *saltar* sal·*tar*
jumper (sweater) *jersey* ⑩ kher·*say*
jumper leads *cables* ⑩ pl *de arranque*
    ka·bles de a·*ran*·ke

K

ketchup *salsa* ① *de tomate* *sal*·sa de
    to·*ma*·te
key *llave* ① *lya*·ve
keyboard *teclado* ⑩ te·*kla*·do
kick *dar una patada* dar oo·na pa·*ta*·da
kick (a goal) *meter (un gol)* me·*ter*
    (oon gol)
kill *matar* ma·*tar*
kilogram *kilogramo* ⑩ kee·lo·*gram*·o
kilometre *kilómetro* ⑩ kee·*lo*·me·tro
kind *amable* a·*ma*·ble
kindergarten *escuela* ① *de párvulos*
    es·*kwe*·la de *par*·voo·los
king *rey* ⑩ rey

kiss *beso* ⑩ *be*·so
kiss *besar* be·*sar*
kitchen *cocina* ① ko·*thee*·na
kitten *gatito/a* ⑩/① ga·*tee*·to/a
kiwifruit *kiwi* ⑩ *kee*·wee
knapsack *mochila* ① mo·*chee*·la
knee *rodilla* ① ro·*dee*·lya
knife *cuchillo* ⑩ koo·*chee*·lyo
know (someone) *conocer* ko·no·*ther*
know (something) *saber* sa·*ber*
Kosher *kosher* ko·sher

L

labourer *obrero/a* ⑩/① o·*bre*·ro/a
lace *encaje* ① en·*ka*·khe
lager *cerveza* ① *rubia* ther·*ve*·tha
    roo·bya
lake *lago* ⑩ *la*·go
lamb *cordero* ⑩ kor·*de*·ro
land *tierra* ① *tye*·ra
landlady *propietaria* ① pro·pye·*ta*·rya
landlord *propietario* ⑩ pro·pye·*ta*·ryo
languages *idiomas* ⑩ pl ee·*dyo*·mas
laptop *ordenador* ⑩ *portátil*
    or·de·na·*dor* por·*ta*·teel
lard *manteca* ① man·*te*·ka
large *grande* *gran*·de
late *tarde* *tar*·de
laugh *reírse* re·*eer*·se
laundrette *lavandería* ① la·van·de·*ree*·a
laundry *lavadero* ⑩ la·va·*de*·ro
law *ley* ① ley
lawyer *abogado/a* ⑩/① a·bo·*ga*·do/a
leader *líder* ⑩&① *lee*·der
leaf *hoja* ① *o*·kha
learn *aprender* a·pren·*der*
leather *cuero* ⑩ *kwe*·ro
leave *dejar* de·*khar*
lecturer *profesor/profesora* ⑩/①
    pro·fe·*sor*/pro·fe·*so*·ra
ledge *saliente* ⑩ sa·*lyen*·te
leek *puerro* ⑩ *pwe*·ro
left *izquierda* ① eeth·*kyer*·da

M

left (behind/over) *quedar* ke·*dar*
left luggage *consigna* ① kon·*seeg*·na
left-wing *de izquierda* de eeth·*kyer*·da
leg *pierna* ① *pyer*·na
legal *legal* le·*gal*
legislation *legislación* ①
le·khees·la·*thyon*
lemon *limón* ⓜ lee·*mon*
lemonade *limonada* ① lee·mo·*na*·da
lens *objetivo* ⓜ ob·khe·*tee*·vo
Lent *Cuaresma* ① kwa·*res*·ma
lentils *lentejas* ① pl len·*te*·khas
lesbian *lesbiana* ① les·bee·*a*·na
less *menos* *me*·nos
letter *carta* ① *kar*·ta
lettuce *lechuga* ① le·*choo*·ga
liar *mentiroso/a* ⓜ/① men·tee·ro·*so*/a
library *biblioteca* ① bee·blyo·*te*·ka
lice *piojos* ⓜ pl *pyo*·khos
license plate number *matrícula* ①
ma·*tree*·koo·la
lie (not stand) *tumbarse* toom·*bar*·se
life *vida* ① *vee*·da
lifejacket *chaleco* ⓜ *salvavidas*
cha·*le*·ko sal·va·*vee*·das
lift *ascensor* ⓜ as·then·*sor*
light (weight) *leve* *le*·ve
light *luz* ① looth
light bulb *bombilla* ① bom·*bee*·lya
light meter *fotómetro* ⓜ fo·*to*·me·tro
lighter *encendedor* ⓜ en·then·de·*dor*
like *gustar(le)* goos·*tar*(le)
lime *lima* ① *lee*·ma
line *línea* ① *lee*·ne·a
lip balm *bálsamo* ⓜ *de labios*
bal·sa·mo de *la*·byos
lips *labios* ⓜ pl *la*·byos
lipstick *pintalabios* ⓜ peen·ta·*la*·byos
liquor store *bodega* ① bo·*de*·ga
listen *escuchar* es·koo·*char*
live (life) *vivir* vee·*veer*
live (somewhere) *ocupar* o·koo·*par*
liver *hígado* ⓜ *ee*·ga·do
lizard *lagartija* ① la·gar·*tee*·kha

local *de cercanías* de ther·ka·*nee*·as
lock *cerradura* ① the·ra·*doo*·ra
lock *cerrar* the·*rar*
locked *cerrado/a* ⓜ/① *con llave*
the·*ra*·do/a kon *lya*·ve
lollies *caramelos* ⓜ pl ka·ra·*me*·los
long *largo/a* ⓜ/① *lar*·go/a
long-distance *a larga distancia* a *lar*·ga
dees·*tan*·thya
look *mirar* mee·*rar*
look after *cuidar* kwee·*dar*
look for *buscar* boos·*kar*
lookout *mirador* ⓜ mee·ra·*dor*
lose *perder* per·*der*
lost *perdido/a* ⓜ/① per·*dee*·do/a
lost property office *oficina* ① *de*
objetos perdidos o·fee·*thee*·na de
ob·*khe*·tos per·*dee*·dos
loud *ruidoso/a* ⓜ/① rwee·do·*so*/a
love *querer* ke·*rer*
lover *amante* ⓜ&① a·*man*·te
low *bajo/a* ⓜ/① *ba*·kho/a
lubricant *lubricante* ⓜ loo·bree·*kan*·te
luck *suerte* ① *swer*·te
lucky *afortunado/a* ⓜ/①
a·for·too·*na*·do/a
luggage *equipaje* ⓜ e·kee·*pa*·khe
luggage lockers *consigna* ①
automática kon·*seeg*·na
ow·to·ma·*tee*·ka
luggage tag *etiqueta* ① *de equipaje*
e·tee·*ke*·ta de e·kee·*pa*·khe
lump *bulto* ⓜ *bool*·to
lunch *almuerzo* ⓜ al·*mwer*·tho
lungs *pulmones* ⓜ pl pool·*mo*·nes
luxury *lujo* ⓜ *loo*·kho

M

machine *máquina* ① *ma*·kee·na
made of (cotton) *hecho a de (algodón)*
e·cho a de (al·go·*don*)
magazine *revista* ① re·*vees*·ta
magician *mago/a* ⓜ/① *ma*·go/a
mail *correo* ⓜ ko·*re*·o

DICTIONARY

204

mailbox *buzón* ⓜ boo·*thon*

main *principal* preen·thee·*pal*

make *hacer* a·*ther*

make fun of *burlarse de* boor·*lar*·se de

make-up *maquillaje* ⓜ ma·kee·*lya*·khe

mammogram *mamograma* ⓕ
ma·mo·*gra*·ma

man *hombre* ⓜ *om*·bre

manager *gerente* ⓜ&ⓕ khe·*ren*·te

mandarin *mandarina* ⓕ man·da·*ree*·na

mango *mango* ⓜ *man*·go

manual worker *obrero/a* ⓜ/ⓕ o·*bre*·ro/a

many *muchas/os* ⓜ/ⓕ pl *moo*·chas/os

map *mapa* ⓜ *ma*·pa

margarine *margarina* ⓕ mar·ga·*ree*·na

marijuana *marihuana* ⓕ ma·ree·*wa*·na

marital status *estado* ⓜ *civil* es·*ta*·do
thee·*veel*

market *mercado* ⓜ mer·*ka*·do

marmalade *mermelada* ⓕ
mer·me·*la*·da

marriage *matrimonio* ⓜ ma·tree·*mo*·nyo

marry *casarse* ka·*sar*·se

martial arts *artes* pl *marciales* ar·tes
mar·*thya*·les

mass *misa* ⓕ *mee*·sa

massage *masaje* ⓜ ma·*sa*·khe

masseur/masseuse *masajista* ⓜ&ⓕ
ma·sa·*khees*·ta

mat *esterilla* ⓕ es·te·*ree*·lya

match *partido* ⓜ par·*tee*·do

matches *cerillas* ⓕ pl the·*ree*·lyas

mattress *colchón* ⓜ kol·*chon*

maybe *quizás* kee·*thas*

mayonnaise *mayonesa* ⓕ ma·yo·*ne*·sa

mayor *alcalde* ⓜ&ⓕ al·*kal*·de

measles *sarampión* ⓜ sa·ram·*pyon*

meat *carne* ⓕ *kar*·ne

mechanic *mecánico/a* ⓜ/ⓕ
me·*ka*·nee·ko

media *medios* ⓜ pl *de comunicación*
me·dyos de ko·moo·nee·ka·*thyon*

medicine *medicina* ⓕ me·dee·*thee*·na

meet *encontrar* en·kon·*trar*

melon *melón* ⓜ me·*lon*

member *miembro* ⓜ *myem*·bro

menstruation *menstruación* ⓕ
mens·trwa·*thyon*

menu *menú* ⓜ me·*noo*

message *mensaje* ⓜ men·*sa*·khe

metal *metal* ⓜ me·*tal*

metre *metro* ⓜ *me*·tro

metro station *estación* ⓕ *de metro*
es·ta·*thyon* de *me*·tro

microwave *microondas* ⓜ
mee·kro·on·das

midnight *medianoche* ⓕ me·dya·*no*·che

migraine *migraña* ⓕ mee·*gra*·nya

military service *servicio* ⓜ *militar*
ser·*vee*·thyo mee·lee·*tar*

milk *leche* ⓕ *le*·che

millimetre *milímetro* ⓜ mee·*lee*·me·tro

million *millón* ⓜ mee·*lyon*

mince (meat) *carne* ⓜ *molida* *kar*·ne
mo·*lee*·da

mind (object) *cuidar* kwee·*dar*

mineral water *agua* ⓜ *mineral* a·gwa
mee·ne·*ral*

mints *pastillas* ⓕ pl *de menta*
pas·*tee*·lyas de *men*·ta

minute *minuto* ⓜ mee·*noo*·to

mirror *espejo* ⓜ es·*pe*·kho

miscarriage *aborto* ⓜ *natural* a·*bor*·to
na·too·*ral*

miss (feel sad) *echar de menos* e·*char*
de *me*·nos

mistake *error* ⓜ e·*ror*

mix *mezclar* meth·*klar*

mobile phone *teléfono* ⓜ *móvil*
te·*le*·fo·no *mo*·veel

modem *módem* ⓜ *mo*·dem

moisturiser *crema* ⓕ *hidratante* kre·ma
ee·dra·*tan*·te

monastery *monasterio* ⓜ mo·nas·*te*·ryo

money *dinero* ⓜ dee·*ne*·ro

month *mes* ⓜ mes

monument *monumento* ⓜ
mo·noo·*men*·to

(full) moon *luna* ① *(llena)* loo·na
(lye·na)

morning (6am - 1pm) *mañana* ①
ma·nya·na

morning sickness *náuseas* ① pl *del
embarazo* now·se·as del em·ba·ra·tho

mosque *mezquita* ① meth·kee·ta

mosquito *mosquito* ⓜ mos·kee·to

mosquito coil *rollo* ⓜ *repelente contra
mosquitos* ro·lyo re·pe·len·te kon·tra
mos·kee·tos

mosquito net *mosquitera* ①
mos·kee·te·ra

mother *madre* ① ma·dre

mother-in-law *suegra* ① swe·gra

motorboat *motora* ① mo·to·ra

motorcycle *motocicleta* ①
mo·to·thee·kle·ta

motorway *autovía* ① ow·to·vee·a

mountain *montaña* ① mon·ta·nya

mountain bike *bicicleta* ① *de montaña*
bee·thee·kle·ta de mon·ta·nya

mountain path *sendero* ⓜ sen·de·ro

mountain range *cordillera* ①
kor·dee·lye·ra

mountaineering *alpinismo* ⓜ
al·pee·nees·mo

mouse *ratón* ⓜ ra·ton

mouth *boca* ① bo·ka

movie *película* ① pe·lee·koo·la

mud *lodo* ⓜ lo·do

muesli *muesli* ⓜ mwes·lee

mum *mamá* ① ma·ma

muscle *músculo* ⓜ moos·koo·lo

museum *museo* ⓜ moo·se·o

mushroom *champiñón* ⓜ
cham·pee·nyon

music *música* ① moo·see·ka

musician *músico/a* ⓜ/① moo·see·ko/a

Muslim *musulmán/musulmána* ⓜ/①
moo·sool·man/moo·sool·ma·na

mussels *mejillones* ⓜ pl
me·khee·lyo·nes

mustard *mostaza* ① mos·ta·tha

mute *mudo/a* ⓜ/① moo·do/a

my *mi* mee

N

nail clippers *cortauñas* ⓜ pl
kor·ta·oo·nyas

name *nombre* ⓜ nom·bre

napkin *servilleta* ① ser·vee·lye·ta

nappy *pañal* ⓜ pa·nyal

nappy rash *irritación* ① *de pañal*
ee·ree·ta·thyon de pa·nyal

national park *parque* ⓜ *nacional*
par·ke na·thyo·nal

nationality *nacionalidad* ①
na·thyo·na·lee·da

nature *naturaleza* ① na·too·ra·le·tha

naturopathy *naturopatía* ①
na·too·ro·pa·tya

nausea *náusea* ① now·se·a

near *cerca* ther·ka

nearby *cerca* ther·ka

nearest *más cercano/a* ⓜ/①
mas ther·ka·no/a

necessary *necesario/a* ⓜ/①
ne·the·sa·ryo/a

neck *cuello* ⓜ kwe·lyo

necklace *collar* ⓜ ko·lyar

need *necesitar* ne·the·see·tar

needle (sewing) *aguja* ① a·goo·kha

needle (syringe) *jeringa* ① khe·reen·ga

neither *tampoco* tam·po·ko

net *red* ① red

Netherlands *Holanda* ① o·lan·da

never *nunca* noon·ka

new *nuevo/a* ⓜ/① nwe·vo/a

New Year *Año Nuevo* ⓜ a·nyo nwe·vo

New Year's Eve *Nochevieja* ①
no·che·vye·kha

New Zealand *Nueva Zelanda* ①
nwe·va the·lan·da

news *noticias* ① pl no·tee·thyas

news stand *quiosco* ⓜ kyos·ko

newsagency *quiosco* ⓜ kyos·ko

newspaper *periódico* ⓜ pe·ryo·dee·ko

next (month) *el próximo (mes)* el
prok·see·mo (mes)

next to *al lado de* al la·do de

nice *simpático/a* ⓜ/ⓕ seem·pa·tee·ko/a
nickname *apodo* ⓜ a·po·do
night *noche* ⓕ no·che
no *no* no
noisy *ruidoso/a* ⓜ/ⓕ rwee·do·so/a
none *nada* na·da
non-smoking *no fumadores* no foo·ma·do·res
noodles *fideos* ⓜ pl fee·de·os
noon *mediodía* ⓜ me·dyo·dee·a
north *norte* ⓜ nor·te
nose *nariz* ⓕ na·reeth
notebook *cuaderno* ⓜ kwa·der·no
nothing *nada* na·da
now *ahora* a·o·ra
nuclear energy *energía* ⓕ *nuclear* e·ner·khee·a noo·kle·ar
nuclear testing *pruebas* ⓕ pl *nucleares* prwe·bas noo·kle·a·res
nuclear waste *desperdicios* ⓜ pl *nucleares* des·per·dee·thyos noo·kle·a·res
number *número* ⓜ noo·me·ro
nun *monja* ⓕ mon·kha
nurse *enfermero/a* ⓜ/ⓕ en·fer·me·ro/a
nuts *nueces* ⓕ pl nwe·thes
nuts (raw) *nueces* ⓕ pl *(crudas)* nwe·thes (kroo·das)
nuts (roasted) *nueces* ⓕ pl *(tostadas)* nwe·thes (tos·ta·das)

O

oats *avena* ⓕ a·ve·na
ocean *océano* ⓜ o·the·a·no
off (food) *pasado/a* ⓜ/ⓕ pa·sa·do/a
office *oficina* ⓕ o·fee·thee·na
office worker *oficinista* ⓜ&ⓕ o·fee·thee·nees·ta
offside *fuera de juego* fwe·ra de khwe·go
often *a menudo* a me·noo·do
oil *aceite* ⓜ a·they·te
old *viejo/a* ⓜ/ⓕ vye·kho/a
olive oil *aceite* ⓜ *de oliva* a·they·te de o·lee·va

Olympic Games *juegos* ⓜ pl *olímpicos* khwe·gos o·leem·pee·kos
on *en* en
once *vez* ⓕ veth
one-way ticket *billete* ⓜ *sencillo* bee·lye·te sen·thee·lyo
onion *cebolla* ⓕ the·bo·lya
only *sólo* so·lo
open *abierto/a* ⓜ/ⓕ a·byer·to/a
open *abrir* a·breer
opening hours *horas* ⓕ pl *de abrir* o·ras de a·breer
opera *ópera* ⓕ o·pe·ra
opera house *teatro* ⓜ *de la ópera* te·a·tro de la o·pe·ra
operation *operación* ⓕ o·pe·ra·thyon
operator *operador/operadora* ⓜ/ⓕ o·pe·ra·dor/o·pe·ra·do·ra
opinion *opinión* ⓕ o·pee·nyon
opposite *frente a* fren·te a
or *o* o
orange (fruit) *naranja* ⓕ na·ran·kha
orange (colour) *naranja* na·ran·kha
orange juice *zumo* ⓜ *de naranja* thoo·mo de na·ran·kha
orchestra *orquesta* ⓕ or·kes·ta
order *orden* ⓜ or·den
order *ordenar* or·de·nar
ordinary *corriente* ko·ryen·te
orgasm *orgasmo* ⓜ or·gas·mo
original *original* o·ree·khee·nal
other *otro/a* ⓜ/ⓕ o·tro/a
our *nuestro/a* ⓜ/ⓕ nwes·tro/a
outside *exterior* ⓜ eks·te·ryor
ovarian cyst *quiste* ⓜ *ovárico* kees·te o·va·ree·ko
oven *horno* ⓜ or·no
overcoat *abrigo* ⓜ a·bree·go
overdose *sobredosis* ⓕ so·bre·do·sees
owe *deber* de·ver
owner *dueño/a* ⓜ/ⓕ dwe·nyo/a
oxygen *oxígeno* ⓜ o·ksee·khe·no
oyster *ostra* os·tra
ozone layer *capa* ⓕ *de ozono* ka·pa de o·tho·no

P

pacemaker *marcapasos* ⓜ mar·ka·*pa*·sos
pacifier *chupete* ⓜ choo·*pe*·te
package *paquete* ⓜ pa·*ke*·te
packet *paquete* ⓜ pa·*ke*·te
padlock *candado* ⓜ kan·*da*·do
page *página* ⓕ *pa*·khee·na
pain *dolor* ⓜ do·*lor*
painful *doloroso/a* ⓜ/ⓕ do·lo·*ro*·so/a
painkillers *analgésicos* ⓜ pl
   a·nal·*khe*·see·kos
paint *pintar* peen·*tar*
painter *pintor/pintora* ⓜ/ⓕ peen·*tor*/
   peen·*to*·ra
painting *pintura* ⓕ peen·*too*·ra
pair (couple) *pareja* ⓕ pa·*re*·kha
palace *palacio* ⓜ pa·*la*·thyo
pan *cazuela* ⓕ ka·*thwe*·la
pants *pantalones* ⓜ pl pan·ta·*lo*·nes
panty liners *salvaeslips* ⓜ pl
   sal·va·es·*sleeps*
pantyhose *medias* ⓕ pl *me*·dyas
pap smear *citología* ⓕ thee·to·lo·*khee*·a
paper *papel* ⓜ pa·*pel*
paperwork *trabajo* ⓜ *administrativo*
   tra·*ba*·kho ad·mee·nees·tra·*tee*·vo
paraplegic *parapléjico/a* ⓜ/ⓕ
   pa·ra·*ple*·khee·ko/a
parasailing *esquí* ⓜ *acuático con*
   paracaídas es·kee a·*kwa*·tee·ko kon
   pa·ra·ka·*ee*·das
parcel *paquete* ⓜ pa·*ke*·te
parents *padres* ⓜ pl *pa*·dres
park *parque* ⓜ *par*·ke
park (car) *estacionar* es·ta·thyo·*nar*
parliament *parlamento* ⓜ
   par·la·*men*·to
parsley *perejil* ⓜ pe·re·*kheel*
part *parte* ⓕ *par*·te
part-time *a tiempo parcial* a *tyem*·po
   par·*thyal*
party *fiesta* ⓕ *fyes*·ta
party (political) *partido* ⓜ par·*tee*·do
pass *pase* ⓜ *pa*·se

passenger *pasajero/a* ⓜ/ⓕ
   pa·sa·*khe*·ro
passport *pasaporte* ⓜ pa·sa·*por*·te
passport number *número* ⓜ *de pasaporte*
   noo·me·ro de pa·sa·*por*·te
past *pasado* ⓜ pa·*sa*·do
pasta *pasta* ⓕ *pas*·ta
pate (food) *paté* ⓜ pa·*te*
path *sendero* ⓜ sen·*de*·ro
pay *pagar* pa·*gar*
payment *pago* ⓜ *pa*·go
peace *paz* ⓕ path
peach *melocotón* ⓜ me·lo·ko·*ton*
peak *cumbre* ⓕ *koom*·bre
peanuts *cacahuetes* ⓜ pl ka·ka·*we*·tes
pear *pera* ⓕ *pe*·ra
peas *guisantes* ⓜ pl gee·*san*·tes
pedal *pedal* ⓜ pe·*dal*
pedestrian *peatón* ⓜ&ⓕ pe·a·*ton*
pedestrian crossing *paso* ⓜ *de cebra*
   pa·so de *the*·bra
pen *bolígrafo* ⓜ bo·*lee*·gra·fo
pencil *lápiz* ⓜ *la*·peeth
penis *pene* ⓜ *pe*·ne
penknife *navaja* ⓕ na·*va*·kha
pensioner *pensionista* ⓜ&ⓕ
   pen·syo·*nees*·ta
people *gente* ⓕ *khen*·te
pepper (vegetable) *pimiento* ⓜ
   pee·*myen*·to
pepper (spice) *pimienta* ⓕ
   pee·*myen*·ta
per (day) *por (día)* por (*dee*·a)
percent *por ciento* por *thyen*·to
performance *actuación* ⓕ ak·twa·*thyon*
perfume *perfume* ⓜ per·*foo*·me
period pain *dolor* ⓜ *menstrual* do·*lor*
   mens·*trwal*
permission *permiso* ⓜ per·*mee*·so
permit *permiso* ⓜ per·*mee*·so
permit *permitir* per·mee·*teer*
person *persona* ⓕ per·*so*·na
perspire *sudar* soo·*dar*
petition *petición* ⓕ pe·tee·*thyon*
petrol *gasolina* ⓕ ga·so·*lee*·na

pharmacy farmacia ⓕ far·ma·thya

phone book guía ⓕ telefónica gee·a te·le·fo·nee·ka

phone box cabina ⓕ telefónica ka·bee·ka te·le·fo·nee·ka

phone card tarjeta ⓕ de teléfono tar·khe·ta de te·le·fo·no

photo foto ⓕ fo·to

photographer fotógrafo/a ⓜ/ⓕ fo·to·gra·fo/a

photography fotografía ⓕ fo·to·gra·fee·a

phrasebook libro ⓜ de frases lee·bro de fra·ses

pick up ligar lee·gar

pickaxe piqueta ⓕ pee·ke·ta

pickles encurtidos ⓜ pl en·koor·tee·dos

picnic comida ⓕ en el campo ko·mee·da en el kam·po

pie pastel ⓜ pas·tel

piece pedazo ⓜ pe·da·tho

pig cerdo ⓜ ther·do

pill pastilla ⓕ pas·tee·lya

pillow almohada ⓕ al·mwa·da

pillowcase funda ⓕ de almohada foon·da de al·mwa·da

pineapple piña ⓕ pee·nya

pink rosa ro·sa

pistachio pistacho ⓜ pees·ta·cho

place lugar ⓜ loo·gar

place of birth lugar ⓜ de nacimiento loo·gar de na·thee·myen·to

plane avión ⓜ a·vyon

planet planeta ⓕ pla·ne·ta

plant planta ⓕ plan·ta

plant sembrar sem·brar

plastic plástico ⓜ plas·tee·ko

plate plato ⓜ pla·to

plateau meseta ⓕ me·se·ta

platform plataforma ⓕ pla·ta·for·ma

play obra ⓕ o·bra

play (musical instrument) tocar to·kar

play (sport/games) jugar khoo·gar

plug tapar ta·par

plum ciruela thee·rwe·la

pocket bolsillo ⓜ bol·see·lyo

poetry poesía ⓕ po·e·see·a

point apuntar a·poon·tar

point (tip) punto ⓜ poon·to

poisonous venenoso/a ⓜ/ⓕ ve·ne·no·so/a

poker póquer ⓜ po·ker

police policía ⓕ po·lee·thee·a

police station comisaría ⓕ ko·mee·sa·ree·a

policy política ⓕ po·lee·tee·ka

policy (insurance) póliza ⓕ po·lee·tha

politician político ⓜ po·lee·tee·ko

politics política ⓕ po·lee·tee·ka

pollen polen ⓜ po·len

polls sondeos ⓜ pl son·de·os

pollution contaminación ⓕ kon·ta·mee·na·thyon

pool (swimming) piscina ⓕ pees·thee·na

poor pobre po·bre

popular popular po·poo·lar

pork cerdo ⓜ ther·do

pork sausage chorizo ⓜ cho·ree·tho

port puerto ⓜ pwer·to

port (wine) oporto ⓜ o·por·to

possible posible po·see·ble

post code código postal ⓜ ko·dee·go pos·tal

post office correos ⓜ ko·re·os

postage franqueo ⓜ fran·ke·o

postcard postal ⓕ pos·tal

poster póster ⓜ pos·ter

pot (kitchen) cazuela ⓕ ka·thwe·la

pot (plant) tiesto ⓜ tyes·to

potato patata ⓕ pa·ta·ta

pottery alfarería ⓕ al·fa·re·ree·a

pound (money) libra ⓕ lee·bra

poverty pobreza ⓕ po·bre·tha

power poder ⓜ po·der

prawns gambas ⓕ pl gam·bas

prayer oración ⓕ o·ra·thyon

prayer book devocionario ⓜ de·vo·thyo·na·ryo

prefer *preferir* pre·fe·reer
pregnancy test *prueba* ① *del embarazo* prwe·ba del em·ba·ra·tho
pregnant *embarazada* ① em·ba·ra·tha·da
premenstrual tension *tensión* ① *premenstrual* ten·syon pre·mens·trwal
prepare *preparar* pre·pa·rar
president *presidente/a* ⑩/① pre·see·den·te/a
pressure *presión* ① pre·syon
pretty *bonito/a* ⑩/① bo·nee·to/a
prevent *prevenir* pre·ve·neer
price *precio* ⑩ pre·thyo
priest *sacerdote* ① sa·ther·do·te
prime minister *primer ministro/ primera ministra* ⑩/① pree·mer mee·nees·tro/pree·me·ra mee·nees·tra
prison *cárcel* ① kar·thel
prisoner *prisionero/a* ⑩/① pree·syon·ne·ro/a
private *privado/a* ⑩/① pree·va·do/a
private hospital *clínica* ① klee·nee·ka
produce *producir* pro·doo·theer
profit *beneficio* ⑩ be·ne·fee·thyo
programme *programa* ⑩ pro·gra·ma
projector *proyector* ⑩ pro·yek·tor
promise *promesa* ① pro·me·sa
protect *proteger* pro·te·kher
protected (species) *protegido/a* ⑩/① pro·te·khee·do/a
protest *protesta* ① pro·tes·ta
protest *protestar* pro·tes·tar
provisions *provisiones* ① pl pro·bee·syo·nes
prune *ciruela* ① pasa thee·rwe·la pa·sa
pub *pub* ⑩ poob
public telephone *teléfono* ⑩ *público* te·le·fo·no poo·blee·ko
public toilet *servicios* ⑩ pl ser·vee·thyos
pull *tirar* tee·rar
pump *bomba* ① bom·ba

pumpkin *calabaza* ① ka·la·ba·tha
puncture *pinchar* peen·char
punish *castigar* kas·tee·gar
puppy *cachorro* ⑩ ka·cho·ro
pure *puro/a* ⑩/① poo·ro/a
purple *lila* lee·la
push *empujar* em·poo·khar
put *poner* po·ner

Q

qualifications *cualificaciones* ① pl kwa·lee·fee·ka·thyo·nes
quality *calidad* ① ka·lee·da
quarantine *cuarentena* ① kwa·ren·te·na
quarrel *pelea* ① pe·le·a
quarter *cuarto* ⑩ kwar·to
queen *reina* ① rey·na
question *pregunta* ① pre·goon·ta
question *cuestionar* kwes·tyo·nar
queue *cola* ① ko·la
quick *rápido/a* ⑩/① ra·pee·do/a
quiet *tranquilo/a* ⑩/① tran·kee·lo/a
quiet *tranquilidad* ① tran·kee·lee·da
quit *dejar* de·khar

R

rabbit *conejo* ⑩ ko·ne·kho
race (people) *raza* ① ra·tha
race (sport) *carrera* ① ka·re·ra
racetrack (bicycles) *velódromo* ⑩ ve·lo·dro·mo
racetrack (cars) *circuito* ⑩ *de carreras* theer·kwee·to de ka·re·ras
racetrack (horses) *hipódromo* ⑩ ee·po·dro·mo
racetrack (runners) *pista* ① pees·ta
racing bike *bicicleta* ① *de carreras* bee·thee·kle·ta de ka·re·ras
racquet *raqueta* ① ra·ke·ta
radiator *radiador* ⑩ ra·dya·dor
radish *rábano* ⑩ ra·ba·no
railway station *estación* ① *de tren* es·ta·thyon de tren
rain *lluvia* ① lyoo·vya

raincoat *impermeable* ⓜ
eem·per·me·a·ble

raisin *uva* ⓕ *pasa* oo·va pa·sa

rally *concentración* ⓕ
kon·then·tra·thyon

rape *violar* vyo·lar

rare *raro/a* ⓜ/ⓕ ra·ro/a

rash *irritación* ⓕ ee·ree·ta·thyon

raspberry *frambuesa* ⓕ fram·bwe·sa

rat *rata* ⓕ ra·ta

rate of pay *salario* ⓜ sa·la·ryo

raw *crudo/a* ⓜ/ⓕ kroo·do/a

razor *afeitadora* ⓕ a·fey·ta·do·ra

razor blades *cuchillas* ⓕ pl *de afeitar*
koo·chee·lyas de a·fey·tar

read *leer* le·er

ready *listo/a* ⓜ/ⓕ lees·to/a

real estate agent *agente inmobiliario* ⓜ
a·khen·te een·mo·bee·lya·ryo

realise *darse cuenta de* dar·se kwen·ta de

realistic *realista* re·a·lees·ta

reason *razón* ⓕ ra·thon

receipt *recibo* ⓜ re·thee·bo

receive *recibir* re·thee·beer

recently *recientemente* re·thyen·te·men·te

recognise *reconocer* re·ko·no·ther

recommend *recomendar* re·ko·men·dar

recording *grabación* ⓕ gra·ba·thyon

recyclable *reciclable* re·thee·kla·ble

recycle *reciclar* re·thee·klar

red *rojo/a* ⓜ/ⓕ ro·kho/a

referee *árbitro* ⓜ ar·bee·tro

reference *referencias* ⓕ pl
re·fe·ren·thyas

refrigerator *nevera* ⓕ ne·ve·ra •
frigerífico ⓜ free·ge·ree·fee·ko

refugee *refugiado/a* ⓜ/ⓕ
re·foo·khya·do/a

refund *reembolso* ⓜ re·em·bol·so

refund *reembolsar* re·em·bol·sar

refuse *negar* ne·gar

registered mail *correo* ⓜ *certificado*
ko·re·o ther·tee·fee·ka·do

regret *lamentar* la·men·tar

relationship *relación* ⓕ re·la·thyon

relax *relajarse* re·la·khar·se

relic *reliquia* ⓕ re·lee·kya

religion *religión* ⓕ re·lee·khyon

religious *religioso/a* ⓜ/ⓕ
re·lee·khyo·so/a

remember *recordar* re·kor·dar

remote *remoto/a* ⓜ/ⓕ re·mo·to/a

remote control *mando* ⓜ *a distancia*
man·do a dees·tan·thya

rent *alquiler* ⓜ al·kee·ler

rent *alquilar* al·kee·lar

repair *reparar* re·pa·rar

repeat *repetir* re·pe·teer

republic *república* ⓕ re·poo·blee·ka

reservation *reserva* ⓕ re·ser·va

reserve *reservar* re·ser·var

rest *descansar* des·kan·sar

restaurant *restaurante* ⓜ res·tow·ran·te

resumé *currículum* ⓜ
koo·ree·koo·loom

retired *jubilado/a* ⓜ/ⓕ khoo·bee·la·do/a

return *volver* vol·ver

return ticket *billete* ⓜ *de ida y vuelta*
bee·lye·te de ee·da ee vwel·ta

review *crítica* ⓕ kree·tee·ka

rhythm *ritmo* ⓜ reet·mo

rice *arroz* ⓜ a·roth

rich *rico/a* ⓜ/ⓕ ree·ko/a

ride *paseo* ⓜ pa·se·o

ride *montar* mon·tar

right (correct) *correcto/a* ⓜ/ⓕ
ko·rek·to/a

right (not left) *derecha* de·re·cha

right-wing *derechista* de·re·chees·ta

ring *llamada* ⓕ lya·ma·da

ring *llamar por telefono* lya·mar por
te·le·fo·no

rip-off *estafa* ⓕ es·ta·fa

risk *riesgo* ⓜ ryes·go

river *río* ⓜ ree·o

road *carretera* ⓕ ka·re·te·ra

rob *robar* ro·bar

rock (stone) *roca* ⓕ ro·ka

rock (music) *rock* ⓜ rok
rock climbing *escalada* ⓕ es·ka·la·da
rock group *grupo* ⓜ *de rock* groo·po
  de rok
rollerblading *patinar* pa·tee·nar
romantic *romántico/a* ⓜ/ⓕ
  ro·man·tee·ko/a
room *habitación* ⓕ a·bee·ta·thyon
room number *número* ⓜ *de la
  habitación* noo·me·ro de la
  a·bee·ta·thyon
rope *cuerda* ⓕ kwer·da
round *redondo/a* ⓜ/ⓕ re·don·do/a
roundabout *glorieta* ⓕ glo·rye·ta
route *ruta* ⓕ roo·ta
rowing *remo* ⓜ re·mo
rubbish *basura* ⓕ ba·soo·ra
rug *alfombra* ⓕ al·fom·bra
rugby *rugby* ⓜ roog·bee
ruins *ruinas* ⓕ pl rwee·nas
rules *reglas* ⓕ pl re·glas
rum *ron* ron
run *correr* ko·rer
run out of *quedarse sin* ke·dar·se seen

S

sad *triste* trees·te
saddle *sillín* ⓜ see·lyeen
safe *seguro/a* ⓜ/ⓕ se·goo·ro/a
safe *caja* ⓕ *fuerte* ka·kha fwer·te
safe sex *sexo* ⓜ *seguro* se·kso se·goo·ro
saint *santo/a* ⓜ/ⓕ san·to/a
salad *ensalada* ⓕ en·sa·la·da
salami (Spanish sausage) *chorizo*
  cho·ree·tho
salary *salario* ⓜ sa·la·ryo
sales tax *IVA* ⓜ ee·va
salmon *salmón* ⓜ sal·mon
salt *sal* ⓕ sal
same *igual* ee·gwal
sand *arena* ⓕ a·re·na
sandals *sandalias* ⓕ pl san·da·lyas
sanitary napkins *compresas* ⓕ pl
  kom·pre·sas

sauna *sauna* ⓕ sow·na
sausage *salchicha* ⓕ sal·chee·cha
save *salvar* sal·var
save (money) *ahorrar* a·o·rar
say *decir* de·theer
scale/climb *trepar* tre·par
scarf *bufanda* ⓕ boo·fan·da
school *escuela* ⓕ es·kwe·la
science *ciencias* ⓕ pl thyen·thyas
scientist *científico/a* ⓜ/ⓕ
  thyen·tee·fee·ko/a
scissors *tijeras* ⓕ pl tee·khe·ras
score *marcar* mar·kar
scoreboard *marcador* ⓜ mar·ka·dor
Scotland *Escocia* ⓕ es·ko·thya
screen *pantalla* ⓕ pan·ta·lya
script *guión* ⓜ gee·on
sculpture *escultura* ⓕ es·kool·too·ra
sea *mar* ⓜ mar
seasick *mareado/a* ⓜ/ⓕ ma·re·a·do/a
seaside *costa* ⓕ kos·ta
season *estación* ⓕ es·ta·thyon
season (in sport) *temporada* ⓕ
  tem·po·ra·da
seat *asiento* ⓜ a·syen·to
seatbelt *cinturón* ⓜ *de seguridad*
  theen·too·ron de se·goo·ree·da
second *segundo/a* ⓜ/ⓕ se·goon·do/a
second *segundo* ⓜ se·goon·do
second-hand *de segunda mano* de
  se·goon·da ma·no
secretary *secretario/a* ⓜ/ⓕ
  se·kre·ta·ryo/a
see *ver* ver
selfish *egoísta* e·go·ees·ta
self-service *autoservicio* ⓜ
  ow·to·ser·vee·thyo
sell *vender* ven·der
send *enviar* en·vee·ar
sensible *prudente* proo·den·te
sensual *sensual* sen·swal
separate *separado/a* ⓜ/ⓕ se·pa·ra·do/a
separate *separar* se·pa·rar
series *serie* ⓕ se·rye

serious *serio/a* ⓜ/ⓕ se·ryo/a
service station *gasolinera* ⓕ
ga·so·lee·ne·ra
service charge *carga* ⓕ kar·ga
several *varias/os* ⓜ/ⓕ va·ryas/os
sew *coser* ko·ser
sex *sexo* ⓜ se·kso
sexism *machismo* ⓜ ma·chees·mo
sexy *sexy* se·ksee
shadow *sombra* ⓕ som·bra
shampoo *champú* ⓜ cham·poo
shape *forma* ⓕ for·ma
share (a dorm) *compartir (un dormitorio)*
kom·par·teer (oon dor·mee·to·ryo)
share (with) *compartir* kom·par·teer
shave *afeitarse* a·fey·tar·se
shaving cream *espuma* ⓕ *de afeitar*
es·poo·ma de a·fey·tar
she *ella* ⓕ e·lya
sheep *oveja* ⓕ o·ve·kha
sheet (bed) *sábana* ⓕ sa·ba·na
sheet (of paper) *hoja* ⓕ o·kha
shelf *estante* ⓜ es·tan·te
ship *barco* ⓜ bar·ko
ship *enviar* en·vee·ar
shirt *camisa* ⓕ ka·mee·sa
shoe shop *zapatería* ⓕ tha·pa·te·ree·a
shoes *zapatos* ⓜ pl tha·pa·tos
shoot *disparar* dees·pa·rar
shop *tienda* ⓕ tyen·da
shoplifting *ratería* ⓕ ra·te·ree·a
shopping centre *centro* ⓜ *comercial*
then·tro ko·mer·thyal
short (height) *bajo/a* ⓜ/ⓕ ba·kho/a
short (length) *corto/a* ⓜ/ⓕ kor·to/a
shortage *escasez* ⓕ es·ka·seth
shorts *pantalones* ⓜ pl *cortos*
pan·ta·lo·nes
shoulders *hombros* ⓜ pl om·bros
shout *gritar* gree·tar
show *espectáculo* ⓜ es·pek·ta·koo·lo
show *mostrar* mos·trar
show *enseñar* en·se·nyar
shower *ducha* ⓕ doo·cha

shrine *capilla* ⓕ ka·pee·lya
shut *cerrado/a* ⓜ/ⓕ the·ra·do/a
shut *cerrar* the·rar
shy *tímido/a* ⓜ/ⓕ tee·mee·do/a
sick *enfermo/a* ⓜ/ⓕ en·fer·mo/a
side *lado* ⓜ la·do
sign *señal* ⓕ se·nyal
sign *firmar* feer·mar
signature *firma* ⓕ feer·ma
silk *seda* ⓕ se·da
silver *plateado/a* ⓜ/ⓕ pla·te·a·do/a
silver *plata* ⓕ pla·ta
similar *similar* see·mee·lar
simple *sencillo/a* ⓜ/ⓕ sen·thee·lyo/a
since *desde (mayo)* des·de (ma·yo)
sing *cantar* kan·tar
Singapore *Singapur* ⓜ seen·ga·poor
singer *cantante* ⓜ&ⓕ kan·tan·te
single *soltero/a* ⓜ/ⓕ sol·te·ro/a
single room *habitación* ⓕ *individual*
a·bee·ta·thyon een·dee·vee·dwal
singlet *camiseta* ⓕ ka·mee·se·ta
sister *hermana* ⓕ er·ma·na
sit *sentarse* sen·tar·se
size (clothes) *talla* ⓕ ta·lya
skateboarding *monopatinaje* ⓜ
mo·no·pa·tee·na·khe
ski *esquiar* es·kee·ar
skiing *esquí* ⓜ es·kee
skimmed milk *leche* ⓕ *desnatada*
le·che des·na·ta·da
skin *piel* ⓕ pyel
skirt *falda* ⓕ fal·da
sky *cielo* ⓜ thye·lo
skydiving *paracaidismo* ⓜ
pa·ra·kai·dees·mo
sleep *dormir* dor·meer
sleeping bag *saco* ⓜ *de dormir* sa·ko
de dor·meer
sleeping car *coche cama* ⓜ ko·che
ka·ma
sleeping pills *pastillas* ⓕ pl *para
dormir* pas·tee·lyas pa·ra dor·meer
(to be) sleepy *tener sueño*
te·ner swe·nyo

slide *diapositiva* ① dya·po·see·*tee*·va
slow *lento/a* ⓜ/① *len*·to/a
slowly *despacio* des·*pa*·thyo
small *pequeño/a* ⓜ/① pe·ke·nyo/a
smell *olor* ⓜ o·*lor*
smell *oler* o·*ler*
smile *sonreír* son·re·*eer*
smoke *fumar* foo·*mar*
snack *tentempié* ⓜ ten·tem·*pye*
snail *caracol* ⓜ ka·ra·*kol*
snake *serpiente* ① ser·*pyen*·te
snorkel *tubos* ⓜ pl *respiratorios*
snorkel *buceo* ⓜ boo·*the*·o
snow *nieve* ① *nye*·ve
snowboarding *surf* ⓜ *sobre la nieve*
soorf *so*·bre la *nye*·ve
soap *jabón* ⓜ kha·*bon*
soap opera *telenovela* ① te·le·no·*ve*·la
soccer *fútbol* ⓜ *foot*·bol
social welfare *estado* ⓜ *del bienestar*
es·*ta*·do del byen·es·*tar*
socialist *socialista* ⓜ&① so·thya·*lees*·ta
socks *calcetines* ⓜ pl kal·the·*tee*·nes
soft drink *refresco* ⓜ re·*fres*·ko
soldier *soldado* ⓜ sol·*da*·do
some *alguno/a* ⓜ/① al·*goon*
someone *alguien* al·*gyen*
something *algo* al·go
sometimes *de vez en cuando* de veth
en *kwan*·do
son *hijo* ⓜ ee·kho
song *canción* ① kan·*thyon*
soon *pronto* pron·to
sore *dolorido/a* ⓜ/① do·lo·*ree*·do/a
soup *sopa* ① *so*·pa
sour cream *nata* ① *agria* na·ta a·grya
south *sur* ⓜ soor
souvenir *recuerdo* ① re·*kwer*·do
souvenir shop *tienda* ① *de recuerdos*
tyen·da de re·*kwer*·dos
soy milk *leche* ① *de soja* le·che de
so·kha
soy sauce *salsa* ① *de soja* sal·sa de
so·kha

space *espacio* ⓜ es·*pa*·thyo
Spain *España* ① es·*pa*·nya
sparkling *espumoso/a* ⓜ/①
es·poo·*mo*·so
speak *hablar* a·*blar*
special *especial* es·pe·*thyal*
specialist *especialista* ⓜ&①
es·pe·thya·*lees*·ta
speed *velocidad* ① ve·lo·thee·*da*
speeding *exceso* ⓜ *de velocidad*
eks·*the*·so de ve·lo·thee·*da*
speedometer *velocímetro* ⓜ
ve·lo·*thee*·me·tro
spider *araña* ① a·ra·nya
spinach *espinacas* es·pee·na·kas
spoon *cuchara* ① koo·*cha*·ra
sport *deportes* ⓜ pl de·*por*·tes
sports store *tienda* ① *deportiva*
tyen·da de·por·*tee*·va
sportsperson *deportista* ⓜ&①
de·por·*tees*·ta
sprain *torcedura* ① tor·the·*doo*·ra
spring (wire) *muelle* ⓜ *mwe*·lye
spring (season) *primavera* ①
pree·ma·*ve*·ra
square (shape) *cuadrado* ⓜ kwa·*dra*·do
(main) square *plaza* ① *(mayor)* ①
pla·tha ma·*yor*
stadium *estadio* ⓜ es·*ta*·dyo
stage *escenario* ⓜ es·the·*na*·ryo
stairway *escalera* ① es·ka·*le*·ra
stamp *sello* ⓜ *se*·lyo
standby ticket *billete* ⓜ *de lista de*
espera bee·*lye*·te de *lees*·ta de
es·*pe*·ra
stars *estrellas* ① pl es·*tre*·lyas
start *comenzar* ko·men·*thar*
station *estación* ① es·ta·*thyon*
statue *estatua* ① es·*ta*·twa
stay (remain) *quedarse* ke·*dar*·se
stay (somewhere) *alojarse* a·lo·*khar*·se
steak (beef) *bistec* ⓜ bees·*tek*
steal *robar* ro·*bar*
steep *escarpado/a* ⓜ/① es·kar·pa·do/a

step *paso* Ⓜ *pa*·so
stereo *equipo* Ⓜ *de música* e·kee·po de moo·see·ka
stingy *tacaño/a* Ⓜ/Ⓕ ta·ka·nyo/a
stock *caldo* Ⓜ *kal*·do
stockings *medias* Ⓕ pl *me*·dyas
stomach *estómago* Ⓜ es·*to*·ma·go
stomachache *dolor* Ⓜ *de estómago* do·*lor* de es·*to*·ma·go
stone *piedra* Ⓕ *pye*·dra
stoned *colocado/a* Ⓜ/Ⓕ ko·lo·*ka*·do/a
stop *parada* Ⓕ pa·*ra*·da
stop *parar* pa·*rar*
storm *tormenta* Ⓕ tor·*men*·ta
story *cuento* Ⓜ *kwen*·to
stove *cocina* Ⓕ ko·*thee*·na
straight *recto/a* Ⓜ/Ⓕ *rek*·to/a
strange *extraño/a* Ⓜ/Ⓕ eks·*tra*·nyo/a
stranger *desconocido/a* Ⓜ/Ⓕ des·ko·no·*thee*·do/a
strawberry *fresa* Ⓕ *fre*·sa
stream *arroyo* Ⓜ a·*ro*·yo
street *calle* Ⓕ *ka*·lye
string *cuerda* Ⓕ *kwer*·da
strong *fuerte* *fwer*·te
stubborn *testarudo/a* Ⓜ/Ⓕ tes·ta·*roo*·do/a
student *estudiante* Ⓜ&Ⓕ es·too·*dyan*·te
studio *estudio* Ⓜ es·*too*·dyo
stupid *estúpido/a* Ⓜ/Ⓕ es·*too*·pee·do/a
style *estilo* Ⓜ es·*tee*·lo
subtitles *subtítulos* Ⓜ pl soob·*tee*·too·los
suburb *barrio* Ⓜ *ba*·ryo
subway *parada* Ⓕ *de metro* pa·*ra*·da de *me*·tro
suffer *sufrir* soo·*freer*
sugar *azúcar* Ⓜ a·*thoo*·kar
suitcase *maleta* Ⓕ ma·*le*·ta
summer *verano* Ⓜ ve·*ra*·no
sun *sol* Ⓜ sol
sunblock *crema* Ⓕ *solar* *kre*·ma so·*lar*
sunburn *quemadura* Ⓕ *de sol* ke·ma·*doo*·ra de sol

sun-dried tomato *tomate* Ⓜ *secado al sol* to·*ma*·te se·*ka*·do al sol
sunflower oil *aceite* Ⓜ *de girasol* a·*they*·te khee·ra·*sol*
sunglasses *gafas* Ⓕ pl *de sol* ga·fas de sol
(to be) sunny *hace sol* a·the sol
sunrise *amanecer* Ⓜ a·ma·ne·*ther*
sunset *puesta* Ⓕ *del sol* pwes·ta del sol
supermarket *supermercado* Ⓜ soo·per·mer·*ka*·do
superstition *superstición* Ⓕ soo·pers·tee·*thyon*
supporters *hinchas* Ⓜ&Ⓕ pl *een*·chas
surf *hacer surf* a·ther soorf
surface mail *por vía terrestre* por vee·a te·*res*·tre
surfboard *tabla de surf* Ⓕ *la*·bla de soorf
surname *apellido* Ⓜ a·pe·*lyee*·do
surprise *sorpresa* Ⓕ sor·*pre*·sa
survive *sobrevivir* so·bre·vee·*veer*
sweater *jersey* Ⓜ kher·sey
sweet *dulce* dool·the
sweets (candy) *dulces* Ⓜ pl dool·thes
swim *nadar* na·*dar*
swimming pool *piscina* Ⓕ pees·*thee*·na
swimsuit *bañador* Ⓜ ba·nya·*dor*
synagogue *sinagoga* Ⓕ see·na·*go*·ga
synthetic *sintético/a* Ⓜ/Ⓕ seen·*te*·tee·ko/a
syringe *jeringa* Ⓕ khe·*reen*·ga

T

table *mesa* Ⓕ *me*·sa
table tennis *ping pong* Ⓜ peeng pong
tablecloth *mantel* Ⓜ man·*tel*
tail *rabo* Ⓜ *ra*·bo
tailor *sastre* Ⓜ *sas*·tre
take (away) *llevar* lye·*var*
take (the train) *tomar* to·*mar*
take (photo) *sacar* sa·*kar*
take photographs *sacar fotos* sa·kar *fo*·tos

T

DICTIONARY

talk *hablar* a·blar
tall *alto/a* ⓜ/ⓕ al·to/a
tampons *tampones* ⓜ pl tam·po·nes
tanning lotion *bronceador* ⓜ bron·the·a·dor
tap *grifo* ⓜ gree·fo
tasty *sabroso/a* ⓜ/ⓕ sa·bro·so/a
tax *impuestos* ⓜ pl eem·pwes·tos
taxi *taxi* ⓜ tak·see
taxi stand *parada* ⓕ *de taxis* pa·ra·da de tak·sees
tea *té* ⓜ te
teacher *profesor/profesora* ⓜ/ⓕ pro·fe·sor/pro·fe·so·ra
team *equipo* ⓜ e·kee·po
teaspoon *cucharita* ⓕ koo·cha·ree·ta
technique *técnica* ⓕ tek·nee·ka
teeth *dientes* ⓜ pl dyen·tes
telegram *telegrama* ⓜ te·le·gra·ma
telephone *teléfono* ⓜ te·le·fo·no
telephone *llamar (por teléfono)* lya·mar (por te·le·fo·no)
telephone centre *central* ⓕ *telefónica* then·tral te·le·fo·nee·ka
telescope *telescopio* ⓜ te·les·ko·pyo
television *televisión* ⓕ te·le·vee·syon
tell *decir* de·theer
temperature (fever) *fiebre* ⓕ fye·bre
temperature (weather) *temperatura* ⓕ tem·pe·ra·too·ra
temple *templo* ⓜ tem·plo
tennis *tenis* ⓜ te·nees
tennis court *pista* ⓕ *de tenis* pees·ta de te·nees
tent *tienda* ⓕ *(de campaña)* tyen·da (de kam·pa·nya)
tent pegs *piquetas* ⓕ pl pee·ke·tas
terrible *terrible* te·ree·ble
test *prueba* ⓕ prwe·ba
thank *dar gracias* dar gra·thyas
the Pill *píldora* ⓕ peel·do·ra
theatre *teatro* ⓜ te·a·tro
their *su* soo
they *ellos/ellas* ⓜ/ⓕ e·lyos/e·lyas

thief *ladrón/ladrona* ⓜ/ⓕ la·dron/ la·dro·na
thin *delgado/a* ⓜ/ⓕ del·ga·do/a
think *pensar* pen·sar
third *tercio* ⓜ ter·thyo
thirst *sed* ⓕ se
this *éste/a* ⓜ/ⓕ es·te/a
this month *este mes* es·te mes
throat *garganta* ⓕ gar·gan·ta
ticket *billete* ⓜ bee·lye·te
ticket collector *revisor/revisora* ⓜ/ⓕ re·vee·sor/re·vee·so·ra
ticket machine *máquina* ⓕ *de billetes* ma·kee·na de bee·lye·tes
ticket office *taquilla* ⓕ ta·kee·lya
tide *marea* ⓕ ma·re·a
tight *apretado/a* ⓜ/ⓕ a·pre·ta·do/a
time *hora* ⓕ o·ra • *tiempo* ⓜ tyem·po
time difference *diferencia* ⓕ *de horas* dee·fe·ren·thya de o·ras
timetable *horario* ⓜ o·ra·ryo
tin *hojalata* ⓕ o·kha·la·ta
tin opener *abrelatas* ⓜ a·bre·la·tas
tiny *pequeñito/a* ⓜ/ⓕ pe·ke·nyee·to/a
tip *propina* ⓕ pro·pee·na
tired *cansado/a* ⓜ/ⓕ kan·sa·do/a
tissues *pañuelos* ⓜ pl *de papel* pa·nywe·los de pa·pel
toast *tostada* ⓕ tos·ta·da
toaster *tostadora* ⓕ tos·ta·do·ra
tobacco *tabaco* ⓜ ta·ba·ko
tobacconist *estanquero* ⓜ es·tan·ke·ro
tobogganing *ir en tobogán* eer en to·bo·gan
today *hoy* oy
toe *dedo* ⓜ *del pie de*·do del pye
tofu *tofú* ⓜ to·foo
together *juntos/as* ⓜ/ⓕ khoon·tos/as
toilet *servicio* ⓜ ser·vee·thyo
toilet paper *papel* ⓜ *higiénico* pa·pel ee·khye·nee·ko
tomato *tomate* ⓜ to·ma·te
tomato sauce *salsa* ⓕ *de tomate* sal·sa de to·ma·te
tomorrow *mañana* ma·nya·na

216

tomorrow afternoon *mañana por la tarde* ma·nya·na por la *tar*·de

tomorrow evening *mañana por la noche* ma·nya·na por la *no*·che

tomorrow morning *mañana por la mañana* ma·nya·na por la ma·nya·na

tone *tono* ⓜ *to*·no

tonight *esta noche* es·ta *no*·che

too (expensive) *demasiado (caro/a)* ⓜ/ⓕ de·ma·sya·do (ka·ro/a)

tooth *diente* ⓜ *dyen*·te

tooth (back) *muela* ⓕ *mwe*·la

toothache *dolor* ⓜ *de muelas* do·lor de *mwe*·las

toothbrush *cepillo* ⓜ *de dientes* the·*pee*·lyo de *dyen*·tes

toothpaste *pasta* ⓕ *dentífrica* pas·ta den·*tee*·free·ka

toothpick *palillo* ⓜ pa·*lee*·lyo

torch *linterna* ⓕ leen·*ter*·na

touch *tocar* to·*kar*

tour *excursión* ⓕ eks·koor·*syon*

tourist *turista* ⓜ&ⓕ too·*rees*·ta

tourist (slang) *guiri* ⓜ *gee*·ree

tourist office *oficina* ⓕ *de turismo* o·fee·*thee*·na de too·*rees*·mo

towards *hacia* a·thya

towel *toalla* ⓕ to·a·lya

tower *torre* ⓕ *to*·re

toxic waste *residuos* ⓜ pl *tóxicos* re·*see*·dwos *tok*·see·kos

toyshop *juguetería* ⓕ khoo·ge·te·*ree*·a

track (car racing) *autódromo* ⓜ ow·*to*·dro·mo

track (footprints) *rastro* ⓜ *ras*·tro

trade *comercio* ⓜ ko·*mer*·thyo

traffic *tráfico* ⓜ *tra*·fee·ko

traffic lights *semáforos* ⓜ pl se·*ma*·fo·ros

trail *camino* ⓜ ka·*mee*·no

train *tren* ⓜ tren

train station *estación* ⓕ *de tren* es·ta·*thyon* de tren

tram *tranvía* ⓜ tran·*vee*·a

transit lounge *sala* ⓕ *de tránsito* sa·la de *tran*·see·to

translate *traducir* tra·doo·*theer*

transport *medios* ⓜ pl *de transporte* me·dyos de trans·*por*·te

travel *viajar* vya·*khar*

travel agency *agencia* ⓕ *de viajes* a·*khen*·thya de vya·khes

travel books *libros* ⓜ pl *de viajes* lee·bros de vya·khes

travel sickness *mareo* ⓜ ma·re·o

travellers cheque *cheques* ⓜ pl *de viajero* che·kes de vya·*khe*·ro

tree *árbol* ⓜ *ar*·bol

trip *viaje* ⓜ vya·khe

trousers *pantalones* ⓜ pl pan·ta·*lo*·nes

truck *camión* ⓜ ka·*myon*

trust *confianza* ⓕ kon·fee·an·tha

trust *confiar* kon·fee·*ar*

try *probar* pro·*bar*

try (to do something) *intentar (hacer algo)* een·ten·*tar* (a·ther al·go)

T-shirt *camiseta* ⓕ ka·mee·*se*·ta

tube (tyre) *cámara* ⓕ *de aire* ka·ma·ra de ai·re

tuna *atún* ⓜ a·*toon*

tune *melodía* ⓕ me·lo·*dee*·a

turkey *pavo* ⓜ *pa*·vo

turn *doblar* do·*blar*

TV *tele* ⓕ *te*·le

TV series *serie* ⓕ *se*·rye

tweezers *pinzas* ⓕ pl *peen*·thas

twice *dos veces* dos *ve*·thes

twin beds *dos camas* ⓕ pl dos *ka*·mas

twins *gemelos* ⓜ pl khe·*me*·los

type *tipo* ⓜ *tee*·po

type *escribir a máquina* es·kree·*beer* a *ma*·kee·na

typical *típico/a* ⓜ/ⓕ *tee*·pee·ko/a

tyre *neumático* ⓜ ne·oo·*ma*·tee·ko

U

ultrasound *ecografía* ⓕ e·ko·gra·*fee*·a

umbrella *paraguas* ⓜ pa·ra·gwas

umpire *árbitro* ⓜ *ar*·bee·tro

uncomfortable *incómodo/a* ⓜ/ⓕ een·*ko*·mo·do/a

underpants (men) *calzoncillos* ⑩ pl
kal·thon·*thee*·lyos

underpants (women) *bragas* ① pl
bra·gas

understand *comprender* kom·pren·*der*

underwear *ropa interior* ① *ro*·pa
een·te·*ryor*

unemployed *en el paro* en el *pa*·ro

unfair *injusto* een·*khoos*·to

uniform *uniforme* ⑩ oo·nee·*for*·me

universe *universo* ⑩ oo·nee·*ver*·so

university *universidad* ①
oo·nee·ver·see·*da*

unleaded *sin plomo* seen *plo*·mo

unsafe *inseguro/a* ⑩/① een·se·*goo*·ro/a

until (June) *hasta (junio)* as·ta
(*khoo*·nyo)

unusual *extraño/a* ⑩/① eks·*tra*·nyo/a

up *arriba* a·*ree*·ba

uphill *cuesta arriba* kwes·ta a·*ree*·ba

urgent *urgente* oor·*khen*·te

USA *Los Estados* ⑩ pl *Unidos*
los es·*ta*·dos oo·*nee*·dos

useful *útil* oo·*teel*

V

vacant *vacante* va·*kan*·te

vacation *vacaciones* ① pl
va·ka·*thyo*·nes

vaccination *vacuna* ① va·*koo*·na

vagina *vagina* ① va·*khee*·na

validate *validar* va·lee·*dar*

valley *valle* ⑩ *va*·lye

valuable *valioso/a* ⑩/① va·*lyo*·so/a

value *valor* ① va·*lor*

van *caravana* ① ka·ra·*va*·na

veal *ternera* ① ter·*ne*·ra

vegetable *verdura* ① ver·*doo*·ra

vegetables *verduras* ① pl ver·*doo*·ras

vegetarian *vegetariano/a* ⑩/①
ve·khe·ta·*rya*·no/a

vein *vena* ① *ve*·na

venereal disease *enfermedad* ①
venérea en·fer·me·da ve·ne·re·a

venue *local* ⑩ lo·*kal*

very *muy* mooy

video tape *cinta* ① *de vídeo* theen·ta
de *vee*·de·o

view *vista* ① *vees*·ta

village *pueblo* ⑩ *pwe*·blo

vine *vid* ① veed

vinegar *vinagre* ⑩ vee·*na*·gre

vineyard *viñedo* ⑩ vee·*nye*·do

virus *virus* ⑩ *vee*·roos

visa *visado* ⑩ vee·*sa*·do

visit *visitar* vee·see·*tar*

vitamins *vitaminas* ① pl
vee·ta·*mee*·nas

vodka *vodka* ① *vod*·ka

voice *voz* ① voth

volume *volumen* ⑩ vo·*loo*·men

vote *votar* vo·*tar*

W

wage *sueldo* ⑩ *swel*·do

wait *esperar* es·pe·*rar*

waiter *camarero/a* ⑩/① ka·ma·*re*·ro/a

waiting room *sala* ① *de espera* sa·la
de es·*pe*·ra

walk *caminar* ka·mee·*nar*

wall (inside) *pared* ① pa·*re*

wallet *cartera* ① kar·*te*·ra

want *querer* ke·*rer*

war *guerra* ① *ge*·ra

wardrobe *vestuario* ⑩ ves·*twa*·ryo

warm *templado/a* ⑩/① tem·*pla*·do/a

warn *advertir* ad·ver·*teer*

wash (oneself) *lavarse* la·*var*·se

wash (something) *lavar* la·*var*

wash cloth *toallita* ① to·a·*lyee*·ta

washing machine *lavadora* ① la·va·*do*·ra

watch *reloj* ⑩ *de pulsera* re·*lokh* de
pool·se·ra

watch *mirar* mee·*rar*

water *agua* ① *a*·gwa
— **tap** *del grifo* del *gree*·fo
— **bottle** *cantimplora* ①
kan·teem·*plo*·ra

waterfall *cascada* ① kas·ka·da

watermelon ① *sandía* san·dee·a

waterproof *impermeable* eem·per·me·a·ble

waterskiing *esquí* ⑩ *acuático* es·kee a·kwa·tee·ko

wave *ola* ① o·la

way *camino* ⑩ ka·mee·no

we *nosotros/nosotras* ⑩/① no·so·tros/ no·so·tras

weak *débil* de·beel

wealthy *rico/a* ⑩/① ree·ko/a

wear *llevar* lye·var

weather *tiempo* ⑩ tyem·po

wedding *boda* ① bo·da

wedding cake *tarta* ① *nupcial* tar·ta noop·thyal

wedding present *regalo* ⑩ *de bodas* re·ga·lo de bo·das

weekend *fin de semana* ⑩ feen de se·ma·na

weigh *pesar* pe·sar

weight *peso* ⑩ pe·so

weights *pesas* ① pl pe·sas

welcome *bienvenida* ① byen·ve·nee·da

welcome *dar la bienvenida* dar la byen·ve·nee·da

welfare *bienestar* ⑩ byen·es·tar

well *bien* byen

well *pozo* ⑩ po·tho

west *oeste* ⑩ o·es·te

wet *mojado/a* ⑩/① mo·kha·do/a

what *lo que* lo ke

wheel *rueda* ① rwe·da

wheelchair *silla* ① *de ruedas* see·lya de rwe·das

when *cuando* kwan·do

where *donde* don·de

whiskey *güisqui* ⑩ gwees·kee

white *blanco/a* ⑩/① blan·ko/a

white-water rafting *rafting* ⑩ rahf·teen

who *quien* kyen

why *por qué* por ke

wide *ancho/a* ⑩/① an·cho/a

wife *esposa* ① es·po·sa

win *ganar* ga·nar

wind *viento* ⑩ vyen·to

window *ventana* ① ven·ta·na

window-shopping *mirar los escaparates* mee·rar los es·ka·pa·ra·tes

windscreen *parabrisas* ⑩ pa·ra·bree·sas

windsurfing *hacer windsurf* a·ther ween·soorf

wine *vino* ⑩ vee·no

wineglass *copa* ① *de vino* co·pa de vee·no

winery *bodega* ① bo·de·ga

wings *alas* ① pl a·las

winner *ganador/ganadora* ⑩/① ga·na·dor/ga·na·do·ra

winter *invierno* ⑩ een·vyer·no

wire *alambre* ⑩ a·lam·bre

wish *desear* de·se·ar

with *con* kon

within (an hour) *dentro de (una hora)* den·tro de (oo·na o·ra)

without *sin* seen

woman *mujer* ① moo·kher

wonderful *maravilloso/a* ⑩/① ma·ra·vee·lyo·so/a

wood *madera* ① ma·de·ra

wool *lana* ① la·na

word *palabra* ① pa·la·bra

work *trabajo* ⑩ tra·ba·kho

work *trabajar* tra·ba·khar

work experience *experiencia* ① *laboral* eks·pe·ryen·thya la·bo·ral

work permit *permiso* ⑩ *de trabajo* per·mee·so de tra·ba·kho

workout *entreno* ⑩ en·tre·no

workshop *taller* ⑩ ta·lyer

world *mundo* ⑩ moon·do

World Cup *La Copa* ① *Mundial* la ko·pa moon·dyal

worms *lombrices* ① pl lom·bree·thes

worried *preocupado/a* ⑩/① pre·o·koo·pa·do/a

worship *adoración* ① a·do·ra·*thyon*
wrist *muñeca* ① moo·*nye*·ka
write *escribir* es·kree·*beer*
writer *escritor/escritora* ⓜ/①
 es·kree·*tor*/es·kree·*to*·ra
wrong *equivocado/a* ⓜ/①
 e·kee·vo·*ka*·do/a

Y

yellow *amarillo/a* ⓜ/① a·ma·*ree*·lyo/a
yes *sí* see
(not) yet *todavía (no)* to·da·*vee*·a (no)
yesterday *ayer* a·*yer*

yoga *yoga* ⓜ *yo*·ga
yogurt *yogur* ⓜ yo·*goor*
you pol sg *Usted* oos·*te*
you inf sg *tú* too
young *joven* *kho*·ven
your pol sg *su* soo
your inf sg *tu* too
youth hostel *albergue* ⓜ *juvenil*
 al·*ber*·ge khoo·ve·*neel*

Z

zodiac *zodíaco* ⓜ tho·*dee*·a·ko
zoo *zoológico* ⓜ zo·o·*lo*·khee·ko

Nouns in the dictionary have their gender indicated by ⓜ or ⓕ. If it's a plural noun, you'll also see pl. Where a word that could be either a noun or a verb has no gender indicated, it's a verb.

A

abajo a-ba-kho *below*

abanico ⓜ a-ba-nee-ko *fan (hand held)*

abarrotado a-ba-ro-ta-do *crowded*

abeja ⓕ a-be-kha *bee*

abierto/a ⓜ/ⓕ a-byer-to/a *open*

abogado/a ⓜ/ⓕ a-bo-ga-do/a *lawyer*

aborto ⓜ a-bor-to *abortion*

abrazo ⓜ a-bra-tho *hug*

abrebotellas ⓜ a-bre-bo-te-lyas *bottle opener*

abrelatas ⓜ a-bre-la-tas *can opener • tin opener*

abrigo ⓜ a-bree-go *overcoat*

abrir a-breer *open*

abuela ⓕ a-bwe-la *grandmother*

abuelo ⓜ a-bwe-lo *grandfather*

aburrido/a ⓜ/ⓕ a-boo-ree-do/a *bored • boring*

acabar a-ka-bar *end*

acampar a-kam-par *camp*

acantilado ⓜ a-kan-tee-la-do *cliff*

accidente ⓜ ak-thee-den-te *accident*

aceite ⓜ a-they-te *oil*

aceptar a-thep-tar *accept*

acera ⓕ a-the-ra *footpath*

acondicionador ⓜ a-kon-dee-thyo-na-dor *conditioner*

acoso ⓜ a-ko-so *harassment*

activista ⓜ&ⓕ ak-tee-vees-ta *activist*

actuación ⓕ ak-twa-thyon *performance*

acupuntura ⓕ a-koo-poon-too-ra *acupuncture*

adaptador ⓜ a-dap-ta-dor *adaptor*

adentro a-den-tro *inside*

adivinar a-dee-vee-nar *guess*

administración ⓕ ad-mee-nees-tra-thyon *administration*

admitir ad-mee-teer *admit*

adoración ⓕ a-do-ra-thyon *worship*

aduana ⓕ a-dwa-na *customs*

adulto/a ⓜ/ⓕ a-dool-to/a *adult*

aeróbic ⓜ ay-ro-beek *aerobics*

aerolínea ⓕ ay-ro-lee-nya *airline*

aeropuerto ⓜ ay-ro-pwer-to *airport*

afeitadora ⓕ a-fey-ta-do-ra *razor*

afeitarse a-fey-tar-se *shave*

afortunado/a ⓜ/ⓕ a-for-too-na-do/a *lucky*

África ⓕ a-free-ka *Africa*

agencia ⓕ **de viajes** a-khen-thya de vya-khes *travel agency*

agenda ⓕ a-khen-da *diary*

agente ⓜ **inmobiliario** a-khen-te een-mo-bee-lya-ryo *real estate agent*

agresivo/a ⓜ/ⓕ a-gre-see-vo/a *aggressive*

agricultor(a) ⓜ/ⓕ a-gree-kool-tor/ a-gree-kool-to-ra *farmer*

agricultura ⓕ a-gree-kool-too-ra *agriculture*

agua ⓕ a-gwa *water*

  — caliente ka-lyen-te *hot water*

  — mineral mee-ne-ral *mineral water*

aguacate ⓜ a-gwa-ka-te *avocado*

aguja ⓕ a-goo-kha *needle (sewing)*

ahora a-o-ra *now*

ahorrar a-o-rar *save (money)*

aire ⓜ ai-re *air*

  — acondicionado a-kon-dee-thyo-na-do *air-conditioning*

ajedrez ⓜ a-khe-dreth *chess*

al lado de al la-do de *next to*

alambre ⓜ a·*lam*·bre *wire*
alba ① al·ba *dawn*
albaricoque ⓜ al·ba·ree·ko·ke *apricot*
albergue ⓜ **juvenil** al·*ber*·ge khoo·ve·*neel* *youth hostel*
alcachofa ① al·ka·*cho*·fa *artichoke*
alcohol ⓜ al·*col* *alcohol*
Alemania ① a·le·*ma*·nya *Germany*
alérgia ① a·*ler*·khya *allergy*
alérgia ① **al polen** a·*ler*·khya al po·len *hay fever*
alfarería ① al·fa·re·*ree*·a *pottery*
alfombra ① al·*fom*·bra *rug*
algo *al*·go *something*
algodón ⓜ al·go·*don* *cotton*
alguien *al*·gyen *someone*
algún al·*goon* *some*
alguno/a ⓜ/① al·*goo*·no/a *any*
almendras ① pl al·*men*·dras *almonds*
almohada ① al·*mwa*·da *pillow*
almuerzo ⓜ al·*mwer*·tho *lunch*
alojamiento ⓜ a·lo·kha·*myen*·to *accommodation*
alojarse a·lo·*khar*·se *stay (somewhere)*
alpinismo ⓜ al·pee·*nees*·mo *mountaineering*
alquilar al·kee·*lar* *hire* • *rent*
alquiler ⓜ al·kee·*ler* *rent*
— **de coche** de *ko*·che *car hire*
altar ⓜ al·*tar* *altar*
alto/a ⓜ/① *al*·to/a *high* • *tall*
altura ① al·*too*·ra *altitude*
ama ① **de casa** *a*·ma de *ka*·sa *homemaker*
amable a·*ma*·ble *kind*
amanecer ⓜ a·ma·ne·*ther* *sunrise*
amante ⓜ&① a·*man*·te *lover*
amarillo/a ⓜ/① a·ma·*ree*·lyo/a *yellow*
amigo/a ⓜ/① a·*mee*·go/a *friend*
ampolla ① am·*po*·lya *blister*
anacardo a·na·*kar*·do *cashew nut*
analgésicos ⓜ pl a·nal·*khe*·see·kos *painkillers*
análisis de sangre ⓜ a·*na*·lee·sees de *san*·gre *blood test*
anarquista ⓜ/① a·nar·*kees*·ta *anarchist*

ancho/a ⓜ/① *an*·cho/a *wide*
andar an·*dar* *walk*
animal ⓜ a·nee·*mal* *animal*
Año ⓜ **Nuevo** *a*·nyo *nwe*·vo *New Year*
antes *an*·tes *before*
antibióticos ⓜ pl an·tee·*byo*·tee·kos *antibiotics*
anticonceptivos ⓜ pl an·tee·kon·thep·*tee*·vos *contraceptives*
antigüedad ① an·tee·gwe·*da* *antique*
antiguo/a ⓜ/① an·*tee*·gwo/a *ancient*
antiséptico ⓜ an·tee·*sep*·tee·ko *antiseptic*
antología ① an·to·lo·*khee*·a *anthology*
anuncio ⓜ a·*noon*·thyo *advertisement*
aparcamiento ⓜ a·par·ka·*myen*·to *carpark*
apellido ⓜ a·pe·*lyee*·do *surname*
apéndice ⓜ a·*pen*·dee·the *appendix*
apodo ⓜ a·*po*·do *nickname*
aprender a·pren·*der* *learn*
apretado/a ⓜ/① a·pre·*ta*·do/a *tight*
apuesta ① a·*pwes*·ta *bet*
apuntar a·poon·*tar* *point*
aquí a·*kee* *here*
araña ① a·*ra*·nya *spider*
árbitro ⓜ *ar*·bee·tro *referee*
árbol ⓜ *ar*·bol *tree*
arena ① a·*re*·na *sand*
armario ⓜ ar·*ma*·ryo *cupboard*
arqueológico/a ⓜ/① ar·ke·o·lo·*khee*·ko/a *archaeological*
arquitecto/a ⓜ/① ar·kee·*tek*·to/a *architect*
arquitectura ① ar·kee·tek·*too*·ra *architecture*
arriba a·*ree*·ba *above* • *up*
arroyo ⓜ a·*ro*·yo *stream*
arroz ⓜ a·*roth* *rice*
arte ⓜ *ar*·te *art*
— **gráfico** *gra*·fee·ko *graphic art*
artes ⓜ pl **marciales** *ar*·tes mar·*thya*·le *martial arts*
artesanía ① ar·te·sa·*nee*·a *crafts*
artista ⓜ&① ar·*tees*·ta *artist*
ascensor ⓜ as·then·*sor* *elevator*
Asia ① *a*·sya *Asia*

asiento ⓜ a·*syen*·to *seat*
— **de seguridad para bebés** de se·goo·*ree*·da *pa*·ra be·*bes child seat*
asma ⓕ *as*·ma *asthma*
aspirina ⓕ as·pee·*ree*·na *aspirin*
atascado/a ⓜ/ⓕ a·tas·*ka*·do/a *blocked*
atletismo ⓜ at·le·*tees*·mo *athletics*
atmósfera ⓕ at·*mos*·fe·ra *atmosphere*
atún ⓜ a·*toon luna*
audífono ⓜ ow·*dee*·fo·no *hearing aid*
Australia ⓕ ow·*stra*·lya *Australia*
autobús ⓜ ow·to·*boos bus*
autocar ⓜ ow·to·*kar bus (intercity)*
autódromo ⓜ ow·to·*dro*·mo *track (car racing)*
autoservicio ⓜ ow·to·ser·*vee*·thyo *self-service*
autovía ⓕ ow·to·*vee*·a *motorway*
avenida ⓕ a·ve·*nee*·da *avenue*
avergonzado/a ⓜ/ⓕ a·ver·gon·*tha*·do/a *embarrassed*
avión ⓜ a·*vyon plane*
ayer a·*yer yesterday*
ayudar a·yoo·*dar help*
azúcar ⓜ a·*thoo*·kar *sugar*
azul a·*thool blue*

B

bailar bai·*lar dance*
bajo/a ⓜ/ⓕ *ba*·kho/a *short (height)* • *low*
balcón ⓜ bal·*kon balcony*
ballet ⓜ ba·*le ballet*
baloncesto ⓜ ba·lon·*thes*·to *basketball*
bálsamo ⓜ **de aftershave** *bal*·sa·mo de af·ter·*sha*·eev *aftershave*
bálsamo ⓜ **de labios** *bal*·sa·mo de *la*·byos *lip balm*
bañador ⓜ ba·nya·*dor bathing suit*
banco ⓜ *ban*·ko *bank*
bandera ⓕ ban·*de*·ra *flag*
bañera ⓕ ba·*nye*·ra *bath*
baño ⓜ *ba*·nyo *bathroom*
bar ⓜ bar *bar*
barato/a ⓜ/ⓕ ba·*ra*·to/a *cheap*

barco ⓜ *bar*·ko *boat*
barrio ⓜ *ba*·ryo *suburb*
basura ⓕ ba·*soo*·ra *rubbish*
batería ⓕ ba·te·*ree*·a *battery (car)* • *drums*
bebé ⓜ be·*be baby*
béisbol ⓜ *beys*·bol *baseball*
beneficio ⓜ be·ne·*fee*·thyo *profit*
berenjenas ⓕ pl be·ren·*khe*·nas *aubergine* • *eggplant*
besar be·*sar kiss*
beso ⓜ *be*·so *kiss*
biblia ⓕ *bee*·blya *bible*
biblioteca ⓕ bee·blyo·*te*·ka *library*
bicho ⓜ *bee*·cho *bug*
bici ⓕ *bee*·thee *bike*
bicicleta ⓕ bee·thee·*kle*·ta *bicycle*
— **de carreras** de ka·*re*·ras *racing bike*
— **de montaña** de mon·*ta*·nya *mountain bike*
bien byen *well*
bienestar ⓜ byen·es·*tar welfare*
bienvenida ⓕ byen·ve·*nee*·da *welcome*
billete ⓜ bee·*lye*·te *ticket*
— **de ida y vuelta** de *ee*·da ee *vwel*·ta *return ticket*
— **de lista de espera** de *lees*·ta de es·*pe*·ra *standby ticket*
billetes ⓜ pl **de banco** bee·*lye*·tes de *ban*·ko *banknotes*
biografía ⓕ bee·o·gra·*fee*·a *biography*
bistec ⓜ bees·*tek steak (beef)*
blanco y negro *blan*·ko ee *ne*·gro *B&W (film)*
blanco/a ⓜ/ⓕ *blan*·ko/a *white*
boca ⓕ *bo*·ka *mouth*
bocado ⓜ bo·*ka*·do *bite (food)*
boda ⓕ *bo*·da *wedding*
bodega ⓕ bo·*de*·ga *winery* • *liquor store*
bol ⓜ bol *bowl*
bolas ⓕ pl **de algodón** *bo*·las de al·go·*don cotton balls*
bolígrafo ⓜ bo·*lee*·gra·fo *pen*
bollos ⓜ pl *bo*·lyos *rolls (bread)*

B

bolo ⓜ *bo·lo gig*
bolsillo ⓜ *bol·see·lyo pocket*
bolso ⓜ *bol·so bag • handbag*
bomba ① *bom·ba pump • bomb*
bombilla ① *bom·bee·lya light bulb*
bondadoso/a ⓜ/① *bon·da·do·so/a caring*
bonito/a ⓜ/① *bo·nee·to/a pretty*
bordo ⓜ *bor·do edge*
a bordo *a bor·do aboard*
borracho/a ⓜ/① *bo·ra·cho/a drunk*
bosque ⓜ *bos·ke forest*
botas ① pl *bo·tas boots*
  — **de montaña** *de mon·ta·nya hiking boots*
botella ① *bo·te·lya bottle*
botones ⓜ pl *bo·to·nes buttons*
boxeo ⓜ *bo·kse·o boxing*
bragas ① pl *bra·gas underpants (women)*
brazo ⓜ *bra·tho arm*
broma ① *bro·ma joke*
bronceador ⓜ *bron·the·a·dor tanning lotion*
bronquitis ⓜ *bron·kee·tees bronchitis*
brotes ⓜ pl **de soja** *bro·tes de so·kha bean sprouts*
brújula ① *broo·khoo·la compass*
brumoso *broo·mo·so foggy*
buceo ⓜ *boo·the·o snorkelling*
budista ⓜ&① *boo·dees·ta Buddhist*
bueno/a ⓜ/① *bwe·no/a good*
bufanda ① *boo·fan·da scarf*
buffet ⓜ *boo·fe buffet*
bulto ⓜ *bool·to lump*
burlarse de *boor·lar·se de make fun of*
burro ⓜ *boo·ro donkey*
buscar *boos·kar look for*
buzón ⓜ *boo·thon mailbox*

C

caballo ⓜ *ka·ba·lyo horse*
cabeza ① *ka·be·tha head*
cabina ① **telefónica** *ka·bee·na te·le·fo·nee·ka phone box*
cable ⓜ *ka·ble cable*

cables ⓜ pl **de arranque** *ka·bles de a·ran·ke jumper leads*
cabra ① *ka·bra goat*
cacahuetes ⓜ pl *ka·ka·we·tes peanuts*
cacao ⓜ *ka·kow cocoa*
cachorro ⓜ *ka·cho·ro puppy*
cada *ka·da each*
cadena ① **de bici** *ka·de·na de bee·thee bike chain*
café ⓜ *ka·fe coffee • cafe*
caída ① *ka·ee·da fall*
caja ① *ka·kha box • cashier*
  — **fuerte** *fwer·te safe*
  — **registradora** *re·khees·tra·do·ra cash register*
cajero ⓜ **automático** *ka·khe·ro ow·to·ma·tee·ko automatic teller machine*
calabacín ⓜ *ka·la·ba·theen zucchini • courgette*
calabaza ① *ka·la·ba·tha pumpkin*
calcetines ⓜ pl *kal·the·tee·nes socks*
calculadora ① *kal·koo·la·do·ra calculator*
caldo ⓜ *kal·do stock*
calefacción ① **central** *ka·le·fak·thyon then·tral central heating*
calendario ⓜ *ka·len·da·ryo calendar*
calidad ① *ka·lee·da quality*
caliente *ka·lyen·te hot*
calle ① *ka·lye street*
calor ⓜ *ka·lor heat*
calzoncillos ⓜ pl *kal·thon·thee·lyos underpants (men)*
calzones ⓜ pl *kal·tho·nes boxer shorts*
cama ① *ka·ma bed*
  — **de matrimonio** *de ma·tree·mo·nyo double bed*
cámara ① **(fotográfica)** *ka·ma·ra (fo·to·gra·fee·ka) camera*
cámara ① **de aire** *ka·ma·ra de ai·re tube (tyre)*
camarero/a ⓜ/① *ka·ma·re·ro/a waiter*
cambiar *kam·byar change • exchange (money)*
cambio *kam·byo* ⓜ *loose change*
  — **de dinero** *de dee·ne·ro currency exchange*
caminar *ka·mee·nar walk*

camino ⓜ ka·mee·no trail • way
caminos ⓜ pl rurales ka·mee·nos roo·ra·les hiking routes
camión ⓜ ka·myon truck
camisa ⓕ ka·mee·sa shirt
camiseta ⓕ ka·mee·se·ta singlet • T-shirt
camping ⓦ kam·peen campsite
campo ⓜ kam·po countryside • field
Canadá ⓕ ka·na·dá Canada
canasta ⓕ ka·nas·ta basket
cancelar kan·the·lar cancel
cáncer ⓜ kan·ther cancer
canción ⓕ kan·thyon song
candado ⓜ kan·da·do padlock
cangrejo ⓜ kan·gre·kho crab
cansado/a ⓜ/ⓕ kan·sa·do/a tired
cantalupo ⓜ kan·ta·loo·po cantaloupe
cantante ⓜ&ⓕ kan·tan·te singer
cantar kan·tar sing
cantimplora ⓕ kan·teem·plo·ra water bottle
capa ⓕ de ozono ka·pa de o·tho·no ozone layer
capilla ⓕ ka·pee·lya shrine
capote ⓜ ka·po·te cloak
cara ⓕ ka·ra face
caracol ⓜ ka·ra·kol snail
caramelos ⓜ pl ka·ra·me·los lollies
caravana ⓕ ka·ra·va·na caravan • van • traffic jam
cárcel ⓕ kar·thel prison
cardenal ⓜ kar·de·nal bruise
carne ⓕ kar·ne meat
— de vaca de va·ka beef
— molida mo·lee·da mince meat
carnet ⓜ kar·ne licence
— de identidad de ee·den·tee·da identification card
— de conducir de kon·doo·theer drivers licence
carnicería ⓕ kar·nee·the·ree·a butcher's shop
caro/a ⓜ/ⓕ ka·ro/a expensive
carpintero ⓜ kar·peen·te·ro carpenter
carrera ⓕ ka·re·ra race (sport)
carta ⓕ kar·ta letter

cartas ⓕ pl kar·tas cards
cartón ⓜ kar·ton carton • cardboard
casa ⓕ ka·sa house
(en) casa (en) ka·sa (at) home
casarse ka·sar·se marry
cascada ⓕ kas·ka·da waterfall
casco ⓜ kas·ko helmet
casete ⓜ ka·se·te cassette
casi ka·see almost
casino ⓜ ka·see·no casino
castigar kas·tee·gar punish
castillo ⓜ kas·tee·lyo castle
catedral ⓕ ka·te·dral cathedral
católico/a ⓜ/ⓕ ka·to·lee·ko/a Catholic
caza ⓕ ka·tha hunting
cazuela ⓕ ka·thwe·la pot (kitchen)
cebolla ⓕ the·bo·lya onion
celebración ⓕ the·le·bra·thyon celebration
celebrar the·le·brar celebrate (an event)
celoso/a ⓜ/ⓕ the·lo·so/a jealous
cementerio ⓜ the·men·te·ryo cemetery
cena ⓕ the·na dinner
cenicero ⓜ the·nee·the·ro ashtray
centavo ⓜ then·ta·vo cent
centímetro ⓜ then·tee·me·tro centimetre
central ⓕ telefónica then·tral te·le·fo·nee·ka telephone centre
centro ⓜ then·tro centre
— comercial ko·mer·thyal shopping centre
— de la ciudad de la theew·da city centre
cepillo ⓜ the·pee·lyo hairbrush
— de dientes de dyen·tes toothbrush
cerámica ⓕ the·ra·mee·ka ceramic
cerca ⓕ ther·ka fence
cerca ther·ka near • nearby
cerdo ⓜ ther·do pork • pig
cereales ⓜ pl the·re·a·les cereal
cerillas ⓕ pl las the·ree·lyas matches
cerrado/a ⓜ/ⓕ the·ra·do/a closed
— con llave kon lya·ve locked
cerradura ⓕ the·ra·doo·ra lock (padlock)
cerrar the·rar close • lock • shut

certificado ⓜ ther·tee·fee·ka·do *certificate*

cerveza ⓕ ther·ve·tha *beer*
— **rubia** roo·bya *lager*

cibercafé ⓜ thee·ber·ka·fe *Internet cafe*

ciclismo ⓜ thee·klees·mo *cycling*

ciclista ⓜ&ⓕ thee·klees·ta *cyclist*

ciego/a ⓜ/ⓕ thye·go/a *blind*

cielo ⓜ thye·lo *sky*

ciencias ⓕ pl thyen·thyas *science*

científico/a ⓜ/ⓕ thyen·tee·fee·ko/a *scientist*

cigarrillo ⓜ thee·ga·ree·lyo *cigarette*

cigarro ⓜ thee·ga·ro *cigarette*

cine ⓜ thee·ne *cinema*

cinta de vídeo theen·ta de vee·de·o *video tape*

cinturón de seguridad theen·too·ron de se·goo·ree·da *seatbelt*

circuito de carreras theer·kwee·to de ka·re·ras *racetrack (cars)*

ciruela ⓕ thee·rwe·la *plum*
— **pasa** pa·sa *prune*

cistitis ⓕ thees·tee·tees *cystitis*

cita ⓕ thee·ta *appointment*

citarse thee·tar·se *date*

citología ⓕ thee·to·lo·khee·a *pap smear*

ciudad ⓕ theew·da *city*

ciudadanía ⓕ theew·da·da·nee·a *citizenship*

clase preferente kla·se pre·fe·ren·te *business class*

clase turística kla·se too·rees·tee·ka *economy class*

clásico/a ⓜ/ⓕ kla·see·ko/a *classical*

clienta/e ⓜ/ⓕ klee·en·ta/e *client*

clínica ⓕ klee·nee·ka *private hospital*

cobrar (un cheque) ko·brar (oon che·ke) *cash (a cheque)*

coca ⓕ ko·ka *cocaine*

cocaína ⓕ ko·ka·ee·na *cocaine*

coche ⓜ ko·che *car*
— **cama** ka·ma *sleeping car*

cocina ⓕ ko·thee·na *kitchen • stove*

cocinar ko·thee·nar *cook*

cocinero ⓜ ko·thee·ne·ro *chef • cook*

coco ⓜ ko·ko *coconut*

codeína ⓕ ko·de·ee·na *codeine*

código postal ko·dee·go pos·tal *post code*

cojonudo/a ⓜ/ⓕ ko·kho·noo·do/a *fantastic*

col ⓜ kol *cabbage*

cola ⓕ ko·la *queue*

colchón ⓜ kol·chon *mattress*

colega ⓜ&ⓕ ko·le·ga *colleague • mate*

coles de Bruselas ⓕ pl ko·les de broo·se·las *brussels sprouts*

coliflor ⓕ ko·lee·flor *cauliflower*

colina ⓕ ko·lee·na *hill*

collar ⓜ ko·lyar *necklace*

color ⓜ ko·lor *colour*

comedia ⓕ ko·me·dya *comedy*

comenzar ko·men·thar *begin • start*

comer ko·mer *eat*

comerciante ⓜ&ⓕ ko·mer·thyan·te *business person*

comercio ⓜ ko·mer·thyo *trade*

comezón ⓜ ko·me·thon *itch*

comida ⓕ ko·mee·da *food*
— **de bebé** de be·be *baby food*
— **en el campo** en el kam·po *picnic*

comisaría ⓕ ko·mee·sa·ree·a *police station*

cómo ko·mo *how*

cómodo/a ⓜ/ⓕ ko·mo·do/a *comfortable*

cómpact ⓜ kom·pak *CD*

compañero/a ⓜ/ⓕ kom·pa·nye·ro/a *companion*

compañía ⓕ kom·pa·nyee·a *company*

compartir kom·par·teer *share (with)*

comprar kom·prar *buy*

comprender kom·pren·der *understand*

compresas ⓕ pl kom·pre·sas *sanitary napkins*

compromiso ⓜ kom·pro·mee·so *engagement*

comunión ⓕ ko·moo·nyon *communion*

comunista ⓜ&ⓕ ko·moo·nees·ta *communist*

con kon *with*

coñac ⓜ ko·nyak *brandy*

concentración ⓕ kon·then·tra·thyon *rally*

concierto ⓜ kon·*thyer*·to *concert*

condición ⓕ **cardíaca** kon·dee·*thyon* kar·*dee*·a·ka *heart condition*

condones ⓜ pl kon·*do*·nes *condoms*

conducir kon·doo·*theer* *drive*

conejo ⓜ ko·*ne*·kho *rabbit*

conexión ⓕ ko·ne·*ksyon* *connection*

confesión ⓕ kon·fe·*syon* *confession*

confianza ⓕ kon·fee·*an*·tha *trust*

confiar kon·fee·*ar* *trust*

confirmar kon·feer·*mar* *confirm*

conocer ko·no·*ther* *know (someone)*

conocido/a ⓜ/ⓕ ko·no·*thee*·do/a *famous*

consejo ⓜ kon·*se*·kho *advice*

conservador(a) ⓜ/ⓕ kon·ser·va·*dor*/ kon·ser·va·*do*·ra *conservative*

consigna ⓕ kon·*seeg*·na *left luggage*
— **automática** ow·to·ma·*tee*·ka *luggage lockers*

construir kons·troo·*eer* *build*

consulado ⓜ kon·soo·*la*·do *consulate*

contaminación ⓕ kon·ta·mee·na·*thyon* *pollution*

contar kon·*tar* *count*

contestador ⓜ **automático** kon·tes·ta·*dor* ow·to·ma·*tee*·ko *answering machine*

contrato ⓜ kon·*tra*·to *contract*

control ⓜ kon·*trol* *checkpoint*

convento ⓜ kon·*ven*·to *convent*

copa ⓕ *ko*·pa *drink*
— **de vino** de *vee*·no *wineglass*

copos de maíz *ko*·pos de ma·*eeth* *corn flakes*

corazón ⓜ ko·ra·*thon* *heart*

cordero ⓜ kor·*de*·ro *lamb*

cordillera ⓕ kor·dee·*lye*·ra *mountain range*

correcto/a ⓜ/ⓕ ko·*rek*·to/a *right (correct)*

correo ⓜ ko·*re*·o *mail*
— **urgente** oor·*khen*·te *express mail*

correos ko·*re*·os *post office*

correr ko·*rer* *run*

corrida ⓕ **de toros** ko·*ree*·da de *to*·ros *bullfight*

corriente ⓕ ko·*ryen*·te *current (electricity)*

corriente ko·*ryen*·te *ordinary*

corrupto/a ⓜ/ⓕ ko·*roop*·to/a *corrupt*

cortar kor·*tar* *cut*

cortauñas ⓜ pl kor·ta·oo·nyas *nail clippers*

corto/a ⓜ/ⓕ *kor*·to/a *short (length)*

cosecha ⓕ ko·*se*·cha *crop*

coser ko·*ser* *sew*

costa ⓕ *kos*·ta *coast* • *seaside*

costar kos·*tar* *cost*

crecer kre·*ther* *grow*

crema ⓕ *kre*·ma *cream*
— **hidratante** ee·dra·*tan*·te *cream (moisturising)*
— **solar** so·*lar* *sunblock*

críquet ⓜ *kree*·ket *cricket*

cristiano/a ⓜ/ⓕ krees·*tya*·no/a *Christian*

crítica ⓕ *kree*·tee·ka *review*

cruce ⓜ *kroo*·the *intersection*

crudo/a ⓜ/ⓕ *kroo*·do/a *raw*

cuaderno ⓜ kwa·*der*·no *notebook* • *square*

cualificaciones ⓕ pl kwa·lee·fee·ka·*thyo*·nes *qualifications*

cuando *kwan*·do *when*

cuánto *kwan*·to *how much*

cuarentena ⓕ kwa·ren·*te*·na *quarantine*

Cuaresma ⓕ kwa·*res*·ma *Lent*

cuarto ⓜ *kwar*·to *quarter*

cubiertos ⓜ pl koo·*byer*·tos *cutlery*

cubo ⓜ *koo*·bo *bucket*

cucaracha ⓕ koo·ka·ra·cha *cockroach*

cuchara ⓕ koo·*cha*·ra *spoon*

cucharita ⓕ koo·cha·*ree*·ta *teaspoon*

cuchillas ⓕ pl **de afeitar** koo·*chee*·lyas de a·fey·*tar* *razor blades*

cuchillo ⓜ koo·*chee*·lyo *knife*

cuenta ⓕ *kwen*·ta *bill*
— **bancaria** ban·ka·rya *bank account*

cuento ⓜ *kwen*·to *story*

cuerda ⓕ *kwer*·da *rope* • *string*
— **para tender la ropa** pa·ra ten·*der* la *ro*·pa *clothes line*

cuero ⓜ *kwe*·ro *leather*

cuerpo ⓜ *kwer*·po *body*

cuesta abajo *kwes·ta a·ba·kho* downhill

cuesta arriba *kwes·ta a·ree·ba* uphill

cuestionar *kwes·tyo·nar* question

cuevas ① pl *kwe·vas* caves

cuidar *kwee·dar* care for • mind (an object)

cuidar de *kwee·dar de* care (for someone)

culo ⓜ *koo·lo* bum (of body)

culpable *kool·pa·ble* guilty

cumbre ① *koom·bre* peak

cumpleaños ⓜ *koom·ple·a·nyos* birthday

currículum ⓜ *koo·ree·koo·loom* resumé

curry ⓜ *koo·ree* curry

cus cus ⓜ *koos koos* cous cous

CH

chaleco salvavidas *cha·le·ko sal·va·vee·das* lifejacket

champán ⓜ *cham·pan* Champagne

champiñón ⓜ *cham·pee·nyon* mushrooms

champú ⓜ *cham·poo* shampoo

chaqueta ① *cha·ke·ta* jacket

cheque ⓜ *che·ke* check (bank)

cheques ⓜ pl **de viajero** *che·kes de vya·khe·ro* travellers cheque

chica ① *chee·ka* girl

chicle ⓜ *chee·kle* chewing gum

chico ⓜ *chee·ko* boy

chocolate ⓜ *cho·ko·la·te* chocolate

choque ⓜ *cho·ke* crash

chorizo ⓜ *cho·ree·tho* salami (Spanish sausage)

chupete ⓜ *choo·pe·te* dummy • pacifier

D

dados ⓜ pl *da·dos* dice (die)

dañar *da·nyar* hurt

dar *dar* give

— **de comer** de *ko·mer* feed

— **gracias** *gra·thyas* thank

— **la bienvenida** la *byen·ve·nee·da* welcome

— **una patada** *oo·na pa·ta·da* kick

darse cuenta de *dar·se kwen·ta de* realise

de *de* from

— **(cuatro) estrellas** de *(kwa·tro) es·tre·lyas* (four-)star

— **izquierda** de *eeth·kyer·da* left-wing

— **pena** de *pe·na* terrible

— **primera clase** de *pree·me·ra kla·se* first-class

— **segunda mano** de *se·goon·da ma·no* second-hand

— **vez en cuando** de *veth en kwan·do* sometimes

deber *de·ver* owe

débil *de·beel* weak

decidir de·*thee·deer* decide

decir de·*theer* say • tell

dedo ⓜ *de·do* finger

— **del pie** del *pye* toe

defectuoso/a ⓜ/① de·*fek·too·o·so/a* faulty

deforestación ① de·fo·res·ta·*thyon* deforestation

dejar de·*khar* leave • quit

delgado/a ⓜ/① del·*ga·do/a* thin

delirante de·lee·*ran·te* delirious

demasiado caro/a ⓜ/① de·ma·*sya·do ka·ro/a* too (expensive)

democracia ① de·mo·*kra·thya* democracy

demora ① de·*mo·ra* delay

dentista ⓜ&① den·*tees·ta* dentist

dentro de (una hora) *den·tro de (oo·na o·ra)* within (an hour)

deportes ⓜ pl de·*por·tes* sport

deportista ⓜ&① de·por·*tees·ta* sportsperson

depósito ⓜ de·*po·see·to* deposit

derecha ① de·*re·cha* right (not left)

derechista de·re·*chees·ta* right-wing

derechos ⓜ pl **civiles** de·*re·chos thee·vee·les* civil rights

derechos m pl **humanos** de·re·chos oo·ma·nos *human rights*

desayuno m des·a·yoo·no *breakfast*

descansar des·kan·sar *rest*

descanso m des·kan·so *intermission*

descendiente m des·then·dyen·te *descendant*

descomponerse des·kôm·po·ner·se *decompose*

descubrir des·koo·breer *discover*

descuento m des·kwen·to *discount*

desde (mayo) des·de (ma·yo) *since (may)*

desear de·se·ar *wish*

desierto m de·syer·to *desert*

desodorante m de·so·do·ran·te *deodorant*

despacio des·pa·thyo *slowly*

desperdicios m pl **nucleares** des·per·dee·thyos noo·kle·a·res *nuclear waste*

despertador m des·per·ta·dor *alarm clock*

después de des·pwes de *after*

destino m des·tee·no *destination*

destruir des·troo·eer *destroy*

detallado/a m/f de·ta·lya·do/a *itemised*

detalle m de·ta·lye *detail*

detener de·te·ner *arrest*

detrás de de·tras de *behind*

devocionario m de·vo·thyo·na·ryo *prayer book*

día m dee·a *day*
 — **festivo** fes·tee·vo *holiday*

diabetes f dee·a·be·tes *diabetes*

diafragma m dee·a·frag·ma *diaphragm*

diapositiva f dya·po·see·tee·va *slide*

diariamente dya·rya·men·te *daily*

diarrea f dee·a·re·a *diarrhoea*

dieta f dee·e·ta *diet*

dibujar dee·boo·khar *draw*

diccionario m deek·thyo·na·ryo *dictionary*

diente (de ajo) dyen·te (de a·kho) *clove (garlic)*

dientes m pl dyen·tes *teeth*

diferencia f **de horas** dee·fe·ren·thya de o·ras *time difference*

diferente dee·fe·ren·te *different*

difícil dee·fee·theel *difficult*

dinero m dee·ne·ro *money*
 — **en efectivo** en e·fek·tee·vo *cash*

Dios dyos *god*

dirección f dee·rek·thyon *address*

directo/a m/f dee·rek·to/a *direct*

director(a) m/f dee·rek·tôr/ dee·rek·to·ra *director*

disco m dees·ko *disk*

discoteca f dees·ko·te·ka *disco*

discriminación f dees·kree·mee·na·thyon *discrimination*

discutir dees·koo·teer *argue*

diseño m dee·se·nyo *design*

disparar dees·pa·rar *shoot*

DIU m de ee oo *IUD*

diversión f dee·ver·syon *fun*

divertirse dee·ver·teer·se *enjoy (oneself)*

doblar do·blar *turn • bend*

doble do·ble *double*

docena f do·the·na *dozen*

doctor(a) m/f dok·tor/dok·to·ra *doctor*

dólar m do·lar *dollar*

dolor m do·lor *pain*
 — **de cabeza** de ka·be·tha *headache*
 — **de estómago** de es·to·ma·go *stomachache*
 — **de muelas** de mwe·las *toothache*
 — **menstrual** mens·trwal *period pain*

dolorido/a m/f do·lo·ree·do/a *sore*

doloroso/a m/f do·lo·ro·so/a *painful*

donde don·de *where*

dormir dor·meer *sleep*

dos m/f pl dos *two*
 — **camas** ka·mas *twin beds*
 — **veces** ve·thes *twice*

drama m dra·ma *drama*

droga f dro·ga *drug • dope*

drogadicción f dro·ga·deek·thyon *drug addiction*

drogas f pl dro·gas *drugs*

ducha f doo·cha *shower*

dueño/a m/f dwe·nyo/a *owner*

dulce dool·the *sweet*

dulces m pl dool·thes *sweets*

duro/a m/f doo·ro/a *hard*

E

eczema ① ek·*the*·ma *eczema*
edad ① e·*da age*
edificio ⓜ e·dee·*fee*·thyo *building*
editor(a) ⓜ/① e·dee·*tor*/e·dee·*to*·ra *editor*
educación ① e·doo·ka·*thyon education*
egoísta e·go·*ees*·ta *selfish*
ejemplo ⓜ e·*khem*·plo *example*
ejército ⓜ e·*kher*·thee·to *military*
él ⓜ el *he*
elecciones ① pl e·lek·*thyo*·nes *elections*
electricidad ① e·lek·tree·thee·*da electricity*
elegir e·le·*kheer* pick • *choose*
ella ① e·*lya she*
ellos/ellas ⓜ/① e·*lyos*/e·*lyas they*
embajada ① em·ba·*kha*·da *embassy*
embajador(a) ⓜ/① em·ba·kha·*dor*/em·ba·kha·*do*·ra *ambassador*
embarazada em·ba·ra·*tha*·da *pregnant*
embarcarse em·bar·*kar*·se *board (ship, etc)*
embrague ⓜ em·*bra*·ge *clutch*
emergencia ① e·mer·*khen*·thya *emergency*
emocional e·mo·thyo·*nal emotional*
empleado/a ⓜ/① em·ple·a·*do*/a *employee*
empujar em·poo·*khar push*
en en *on*
— **el extranjero** el eks·tran·*khe*·ro *abroad*
— **el paro** el *pa*·ro *unemployed*
encaje ⓜ en·*ka*·khe *lace*
encantador(a) ⓜ/① en·kan·ta·*dor*/en·kan·ta·*do*·ra *charming*
encendedor ⓜ en·then·de·*dor lighter*
encontrar en·kon·*trar find* • *meet*
encurtidos ⓜ pl en·koor·*tee*·dos *pickles*
energía ① **nuclear** e·ner·*khee*·a noo·*kle*·ar *nuclear energy*
enfadado/a ⓜ/① en·fa·*da*·do/a *angry*

enfermedad ① en·fer·me·*da disease*
— **venérea** ve·*ne*·re·a *venereal disease*
enfermero/a ⓜ/① en·fer·*me*·ro/a *nurse*
enfermo/a ⓜ/① en·*fer*·mo/a *sick*
enfrente de en·*fren*·te de *in front of*
enorme e·*nor*·me *huge*
ensalada en·sa·*la*·da *salad*
enseñar en·se·*nyar show* • *teach*
entrar en·*trar enter*
entre en·tre *among* • *between*
entregar en·tre·*gar deliver*
entrenador(a) ⓜ/① en·tre·na·*dor*/en·tre·na·*do*·ra *coach*
entreno ⓜ en·*tre*·no *workout*
entrevista ① en·tre·*vees*·ta *interview*
enviar en·vee·*ar send* • *ship off*
epilepsia ① e·pee·*lep*·sya *epilepsy*
equipaje ⓜ e·kee·*pa*·khe *luggage*
equipo ⓜ e·*kee*·po *equipment* • *team*
— **de inmersión** de een·mer·*syon diving equipment*
— **de música** ⓜ de *moo*·see·ka *stereo*
equitación ① e·kee·ta·*thyon horse riding*
equivocado/a ⓜ/① e·kee·vo·ka·*do*/a *wrong*
error ⓜ e·*ror mistake*
escalada ① es·ka·*la*·da *rock climbing*
escalera ① es·ka·*le*·ra *stairway*
escaleras ① pl **mecánicas** es·ka·*le*·ras me·*ka*·nicas *escalator*
escarcha ① es·*kar*·cha *frost*
escarpado/a ⓜ/① es·kar·*pa*·do/a *steep*
escasez ① es·ka·*seth shortage*
escenario ⓜ es·the·*na*·ryo *stage*
Escocia ① es·*ko*·thya *Scotland*
escoger es·ko·*kher choose*
escribir es·kree·*beer write*
— **a máquina** a *ma*·kee·na *type*
escritor(a) ⓜ/① es·kree·*tor*/es·kree·*to*·ra *writer*
escuchar es·koo·*char listen*
escuela ① es·*kwe*·la *school*
— **de párvulos** de *par*·voo·los *kindergarten*

escultura ① es·kool·*too*·ra *sculpture*

espacio ⓜ es·*pa*·thyo *space*

espalda ① es·*pal*·da *back (body)*

España ① es·*pa*·nya *Spain*

especial es·pe·*thyal* *special*

especialista ⓜ&① es·pe·thya·*lees*·ta *specialist*

especies ① pl **en peligro de extinción** es·*pe*·thyes en pe·*lee*·gro de cks·*teen*·*thyon* *endangered species*

espectáculo ⓜ es·pek·*ta*·koo·lo *show*

espejo ⓜ es·*pe*·kho *mirror*

esperar es·pe·*rar* *wait*

espinaca ① es·pee·*na*·ka *spinach*

esposa ① es·*po*·sa *wife*

espuma ① **de afeitar** es·*poo*·ma de a·*fey*·tar *shaving cream*

espumoso/a ⓜ/①es·poo·*mo*·so/a *sparkling • foamy*

esquí ⓜ es·*kee* *skiing*
— **acuático** a·*kwa*·tee·ko *waterskiing*

esquiar es·kee·*ar* *ski*

esquina ① es·*kee*·na *corner*

esta noche *es*·ta *no*·che *tonight*

éste/a ⓜ/① *es*·te/a *this*

estación ① es·ta·*thyon* *season • station*
— **de autobuses** de ow·to·*boo*·ses *bus station*
— **de metro** de *me*·tro *metro station*
— **de tren** de tren *railway station*

estacionar es·ta·thyo·*nar* *park (car)*

estadio ⓜ es·*ta*·dyo *stadium*

estado ⓜ **civil** es·*ta*·do thee·*veel* *marital status*

estado ⓜ **del bienestar** es·*ta*·do del byen·es·*tar* *social welfare • well being*

estafa ① es·*ta*·fa *rip-off*

estanquero ⓜ es·tan·*ke*·ro *tobacconist*

estante ⓜ es·*tan*·te *shelf*

estar es·*tar* *to be*
— **constipado/a** ⓜ/① kons·tee·*pa*·do/a *have a cold*
— **de acuerdo** de a·*kwer*·do *agree*

estatua ① es·*ta*·twa *statue*

este *es*·te *east*

esterilla ① es·te·*ree*·lya *mat*

estilo ⓜ es·*tee*·lo *style*

estómago ⓜ es·*to*·ma·go *stomach*

estrellas ① pl es·*tre*·lyas *stars*

estreñimiento ⓜ es·tre·nyee·*myen*·to *constipation*

estudiante ⓜ&① es·too·*dyan*·te *student*

estudio ⓜ es·*too*·dyo *studio*

estufa ① es·*too*·fa *heater*

estúpido/a ⓜ/① es·too·*pee*·do/a *stupid*

etiqueta ① **de equipaje** e·tee·*ke*·ta de e·kee·*pa*·khe *luggage tag*

euro ⓜ e·oo·ro *euro*

Europa ① e·oo·*ro*·pa *Europe*

eutanasia ① e·oo·ta·*na*·sya *euthanasia*

excelente eks·the·*len*·te *excellent*

excursión ① eks·koor·*syon* *tour*

excursionismo ⓜ eks·koor·syo·*nees*·mo *hiking*

experiencia ① eks·pe·*ryen*·thya *experience*
— **laboral** ① la·bo·*ral* *work experience*

exponer eks·po·*ner* *exhibit*

exposición ① eks·po·see·*thyon* *exhibition*

expreso eks·*pre*·so *express*

exterior ⓜ eks·te·*ryor* *outside*

extrañar eks·tra·*nyar* *miss (feel sad)*

extranjero/a ⓜ/① eks·tran·*khe*·ro/a *foreign*

F

fábrica ① *fa*·bree·ka *factory*

fácil *fa*·theel *easy*

facturación ① **de equipajes** fak·too·ra·*thyon* de e·kee·*pa*·khes *check-in*

falda ① *fal*·da *skirt*

falta ① *fal*·ta *fault*

familia ① fa·*mee*·lya *family*

fantástico/a ⓜ/① fan·*tas*·tee·ko/a *great*

farmacia ① far·*ma*·thya *chemist (shop) • pharmacy*

farmacéutico ⓜ far·ma·thee·*oo*·tee·ko *chemist (person)*

faros ⓜ pl *fa*·ros *headlights*

fecha ⓕ *fe*·cha *date (time)*
— **de nacimiento** de na·thee·*myen*·to *date of birth*
feliz fe·*leeth* *happy*
ferretería ⓕ fe·re·te·*ree*·a *hardware store*
festival ⓜ fes·tee·*val* *festival*
ficción ⓕ feek·*thyon* *fiction*
fideos ⓜ pl fee·*de*·os *noodles*
fiebre ⓕ *fye*·bre *fever*
— **glandular** glan·doo·*lar* *glandular fever*
fiesta ⓕ *fyes*·ta *party*
filete ⓜ fee·*le*·te *fillet*
film ⓜ feelm *film*
fin ⓜ feen *end*
— **de semana** de se·*ma*·na *weekend*
final fee·*nal* *end*
firma ⓕ *feer*·ma *signature*
firmar feer·*mar* *sign*
flor ⓕ flor *flower*
florista ⓜ&ⓕ flo·*rees*·ta *florist*
follar fo·*lyar* *fuck*
folleto ⓜ fo·*lye*·to *brochure*
footing ⓜ *foo*·teen *jogging*
forma ⓕ *for*·ma *shape*
fotografía ⓕ fo·to·gra·*fee*·a *photograph*
fotógrafo/a ⓜ/ⓕ fo·*to*·gra·fo/a *photographer*
fotómetro ⓜ fo·*to*·me·tro *light meter*
frágil *fra*·kheel *fragile*
frambuesa ⓕ fram·*bwe*·sa *raspberry*
franela ⓕ fra·*ne*·la *flannel*
franqueo ⓜ fran·*ke*·o *postage*
freír fre·*eer* *fry*
frenos ⓜ pl *fre*·nos *brakes*
frente a *fren*·te a *opposite*
fresa ⓕ *fre*·sa *strawberry*
frío/a ⓜ/ⓕ *free*·o/a *cold*
frontera ⓕ fron·*te*·ra *border*
fruta ⓕ *froo*·ta *fruit*
fruto ⓜ *seco* *froo*·to se·ko *dried fruit*
fuego ⓜ *fwe*·go *fire*
fuera de juego *fwe*·ra de *khwe*·go *offside*
fuerte *fwer*·te *strong*

fumar foo·*mar* *smoke*
funda ⓕ **de almohada** *foon*·da de al·*mwa*·da *pillowcase*
funeral ⓜ foo·ne·*ral* *funeral*
fútbol ⓜ *foot*·bol *football* • *soccer*
— **australiano** ow·stra·*lya*·no *Australian Rules football*
futuro ⓜ foo·*too*·ro *future*

G

gafas ⓕ pl *ga*·fas *glasses*
— **de sol** de sol *sunglasses*
— **de submarinismo** de soob·ma·ree·*nees*·mo *goggles*
galleta ⓕ ga·*lye*·ta *biscuit* • *cookie*
galletas ⓕ pl **saladas** ga·*lye*·tas sa·*la*·das *biscuits* • *crackers*
gambas ⓕ pl *gam*·bas *prawns*
ganador(a) ⓜ/ⓕ ga·na·*dor*/ga·na·*do*·ra *winner*
ganar ga·*nar* *earn* • *win*
garbanzos ⓜ pl gar·*ban*·thos *chickpeas*
garganta ⓕ gar·*gan*·ta *throat*
gasolina ⓕ ga·so·*lee*·na *petrol*
gasolinera ⓕ ga·so·lee·*ne*·ra *service station*
gatito/a ⓜ/ⓕ ga·*tee*·to/a *kitten*
gato/a ⓜ/ⓕ *ga*·to/a *cat*
gay gai *gay*
gemelos ⓜ pl khe·*me*·los *twins*
general khe·ne·*ral* *general*
gente ⓕ *khen*·te *people*
gimnasia ⓕ **rítmica** kheem·*na*·sya *reet*·mee·ka *gymnastics*
ginebra ⓕ khee·*ne*·bra *gin*
ginecólogo ⓜ khee·ne·*ko*·lo·go *gynaecologist*
gobierno ⓜ go·*byer*·no *government*
gol ⓜ gol *goal*
goma ⓕ *go*·ma *condom* • *rubber*
gordo/a ⓜ/ⓕ *gor*·do/a *fat*
grabación ⓕ gra·ba·*thyon* *recording*
gracioso/a ⓜ/ⓕ gra·*thyo*·so/a *funny*
gramo ⓜ *gra*·mo *gram*
grande *gran*·de *big* • *large*

grande almacene ⓜ gran·de al·ma·*the*·ne *department store*
granja ⓕ gran·kha *farm*
gratis gra·tees *free (of charge)*
grifo ⓜ gree·fo *tap*
gripe ⓕ gree·pe *influenza*
gris grees *grey*
gritar gree·*tar* *shout*
grupo ⓜ groo·po *group*
— **de rock** de rok *rock band*
— **sanguineo** san·gee·ne·o *blood group*
guantes ⓜ pl gwan·tes *gloves*
guardarropa ⓜ gwar·da·ro·pa *cloakroom*
guardería ⓕ gwar·de·ree·a *childminding service • creche*
guerra ⓕ ge·ra *war*
guía ⓜ&ⓕ gee·a *guide (person)*
guía ⓕ gee·a *guidebook*
— **audio** ow·dyo *guide (audio)*
— **del ocio** del o·thyo *entertainment guide*
— **telefónica** te·le·*fo*·nee·ka *phone book*
guindilla ⓕ geen·dee·lya *chilli*
guión ⓜ gee·on *script*
guiri ⓜ gee·ree *tourist (slang)*
guisantes gee·san·tes *peas*
güisqui gwees·kee *whiskey*
guitarra ⓕ gee·ta·ra *guitar*
gustar(le) goos·tar(·le) *like*

H

habitación ⓕ a·bee·ta·*thyon* *bedroom • room*
— **doble** do·ble *double room*
— **individual** een·dee·vee·*dwal* *single room*
hablar a·*blar* *speak • talk*
hacer a·*ther* *do • make*
— **dedo** de·do *hitchhike*
— **surf** soorf *surf*
— **windsurf** ween·soorf *windsurfing*

hachís ⓜ a·*chees* *hash*
hacia a·thya *towards*
— **abajo** a·ba·kho *down*
halal a·*lal* *Halal*
hamaca ⓕ a·ma·ka *hammock*
hambriento/a ⓜ/ⓕ am·bryen·to/a *hungry*
harina ⓕ a·ree·na *flour*
hasta (junio) as·ta (khoo·nyo) *until (June)*
hecho/a ⓜ/ⓕ e·cho/a *made*
— **a mano** a ma·no *handmade*
— **de (algodón)** de (al·go·don) *made of (cotton)*
heladería ⓕ e·la·de·ree·a *ice cream parlour*
helado ⓜ e·la·do *ice cream*
helar e·*lar* *freeze*
hepatitis ⓕ e·pa·tee·tees *hepatitis*
herbolario ⓜ er·bo·la·ryo *herbalist (shop)*
herida ⓕ e·ree·da *injury*
hermana ⓕ er·ma·na *sister*
hermano ⓜ er·ma·no *brother*
hermoso/a ⓜ/ⓕ er·mo·so/a *beautiful*
heroína ⓕ e·ro·ee·na *heroin*
hielo ⓜ ye·lo *ice*
hierba ⓕ yer·ba *grass*
hierbas ⓕ pl yer·bas *herbs*
hígado ⓜ ee·ga·do *liver*
higos ⓜ pl ee·gos *figs*
hija ⓕ ee·kha *daughter*
hijo ⓜ ee·kho *son*
hijos ⓜ pl ee·khos *children*
hilo ⓜ **dental** ee·lo den·*tal* *dental floss*
hinchas ⓜ&ⓕ pl een·chas *supporters*
hindú een·*doo* *Hindu*
hipódromo ⓜ ee·po·dro·mo *racetrack (horses)*
historial ⓜ **profesional** ees·to·*ryal* pro·fe·syo·*nal* *CV*
histórico/a ⓜ/ⓕ ees·to·ree·ko/a *historical*
hockey ⓜ kho·kee *hockey*
— **sobre hielo** so·bre ye·lo *ice hockey*
hoja ⓕ o·kha *leaf • sheet (of paper)*

hojalata ① o·kha·*la*·ta *tin*

Holanda ① o·*lan*·da *Netherlands*

hombre ⓜ *om*·bre *man*

hombros ⓜ pl *om*·bros *shoulders*

homosexual ⓜ&① o·mo·se·*kswal* *homosexual*

hora ① o·ra *time*

horario ⓜ o·ra·ryo *timetable*

horas ① pl **de abrir** o·ras de a·*breer* *opening hours*

hormiga ① or·*mee*·ga *ant*

horno ⓜ or·no *oven*

horóscopo ⓜ o·*ros*·ko·po *horoscope*

hospital ⓜ os·pee·*tal* *hospital*

hostelería ① os·te·le·*ree*·a *hospitality*

hotel ⓜ o·*tel* *hotel*

hoy oy *today*

hueso ⓜ we·so *bone*

huevo ⓜ we·vo *egg*

humanidades ① pl oo·ma·nee·*da*·des *humanities*

I

identificación ① ee·den·tee·fee·ka·*thyon* *identification*

idiomas ⓜ pl ee·*dyo*·mas *languages*

idiota ⓜ/① ee·*dyo*·ta *idiot*

iglesia ① ee·*gle*·sya *church*

igual ee·*gwal* *same*

igualdad ① ee·gwal·*da* *equality*

impermeable ⓜ eem·per·me·a·ble *raincoat*

impermeable eem·per·me·a·ble *waterproof*

importante eem·por·*tan*·te *important*

impuesto ⓜ eem·*pwes*·to *tax*
— **sobre la renta** so·bre la *ren*·ta *income tax*

incluido een·kloo·ee·do *included*

incómodo/a ⓜ/① een·*ko*·mo·do/a *uncomfortable*

India ① een·dya *India*

indicador ⓜ een·dee·ka·*dor* *indicator*

indigestion ① een·dee·*khes*·tyon *indigestion*

industria ① een·*doos*·trya *industry*

infección ① een·fek·*thyon* *infection*

inflamación ① een·fla·ma·*thyon* *inflammation*

informática ① een·for·*ma*·tee·ka *IT*

ingeniería ① een·khe·nye·*ree*·a *engineering*

ingeniero/a ⓜ/① een·khe·*nye*·ro/a *engineer*

Inglaterra ① een·gla·*te*·ra *England*

inglés ⓜ een·*gles* *English*

ingrediente ⓜ een·gre·*dyen*·te *ingredient*

injusto/a ⓜ/① een·*khoos*·to/a *unfair*

inmigración ① een·mee·gra·*thyon* *immigration*

inocente ee·no·*then*·te *innocent*

inseguro/a ⓜ/① een·se·*goo*·ro/a *unsafe*

instituto ⓜ eens·tee·*too*·to *high school*

intentar (hacer algo) een·ten·*tar* (a·*ther* al·go) *try (to do something)*

interesante een·te·re·*san*·te *interesting*

internacional een·ter·na·thyo·*nal* *international*

Internet ⓜ een·ter·net *Internet*

intérprete ⓜ&① een·*ter*·pre·te *interpreter*

inundación ① ee·noon·da·*thyon* *flooding*

invierno ⓜ een·*vyer*·no *winter*

invitar een·vee·*tar* *invite*

inyección ① een·yek·*thyon* *injection*

inyectar(se) een·yek·*tar*(·se) *inject (oneself)*

ir eer *go*
— **de compras** de kom·pras *go shopping*
— **de excursión** de eks·koor·*syon* *hike*
— **en tobogán** en to·bo·*gan* *tobogganing*

Irlanda ① eer·*lan*·da *Ireland*

irritación ① ee·ree·ta·*thyon* *rash*
— **de pañal** de pa·*nyal* *nappy rash*

isla ① ees·la *island*

itinerario ① ee·tee·ne·*ra*·ryo *itinerary*

IVA ⓜ ee·va *sales tax*

izquierda ① eeth·*kyer*·da *left*

J

jabón ⓜ kha·*bon* soap
jamón ⓜ kha·*mon* ham
Japón ⓜ kha·*pon* Japan
jarabe ⓜ kha·*ra*·be cough medicine
jardín botánico khar·*deen* bo·*ta*·nee·ko botanic garden
jarra ⓕ *kha*·ra jar
jefe/a ⓜ/ⓕ *khe*·te/a boss • leader
 — **de sección** de sek·*thyon* manager
jengibre ⓜ khen·*khee*·bre ginger
jeringa ⓕ khe·*reen*·ga syringe
jersey ⓜ kher·*sey* jumper • sweater
jet lag ⓜ dyet lag jet lag
jockey ⓜ *dyo*·kee jockey
joven *kho*·ven young
joyería ⓕ kho·ye·*ree*·a jeweller (shop)
jubilado/a ⓜ/ⓕ khoo·bee·*la*·do/a retired
judías ⓕ pl khoo·*dee*·as beans
judío/a ⓜ/ⓕ khoo·*dee*·o/a Jewish
juegos ⓜ pl **de ordenador** *khwe*·gos de or·de·na·*dor* computer games
juegos ⓜ pl **olímpicos** *khwe*·gos o·*leem*·pee·kos Olympic Games
juez ⓜ&ⓕ *khweth* judge
jugar khoo·*gar* play (sport • games)
jugo ⓜ *khoo*·go juice
juguetería ⓕ khoo·ge·te·*ree*·a toyshop
juntos/as ⓜ/ⓕ pl *khoon*·tos/as together

K

kilo ⓜ *kee*·lo kilogram
kilómetro ⓜ kee·*lo*·me·tro kilometre
kiwi ⓜ *kee*·wee kiwifruit
kosher *ko*·sher Kosher

L

La Copa Mundial ⓕ la *ko*·pa moon·*dyal* World Cup
labios ⓜ pl *la*·byos lips
lado ⓜ *la*·do side

ladrón la·*dron* thief
lagartija ⓕ la·gar·*tee*·kha lizard
lago ⓜ *la*·go lake
lamentar la·men·*tar* regret
lana ⓕ *la*·na wool
lápiz ⓜ *la*·peeth pencil
 — **de labios** de *la*·byos lipstick
largo/a ⓜ/ⓕ *lar*·go/a long
lata ⓕ *la*·ta can
lavadero ⓜ la·va·*de*·ro laundry
lavadora ⓕ la·va·*do*·ra washing machine
lavandería ⓕ la·van·de·*ree*·a laundrette
lavar la·*var* wash (something)
lavarse la·*var*·se wash (oneself)
leche ⓕ *le*·che milk
 — **de soja** de *so*·kha soy milk
 — **desnatada** des·na·*ta*·da skimmed milk
lechuga ⓕ le·*choo*·ga lettuce
leer le·*er* read
legal le·*gal* legal
legislación ⓕ le·khees·la·*thyon* legislation
legumbre ⓕ le·*goom*·bre legume
lejos *le*·khos far
leña ⓕ *le*·nya firewood
lentejas ⓕ pl len·*te*·khas lentils
lentes ⓜ pl **de contacto** *len*·tes de kon·*tak*·to contact lenses
lento/a ⓜ/ⓕ *len*·to/a slow
lesbiana ⓕ les·bee·*a*·na lesbian
leve *le*·ve light
ley ⓕ ley law
libra ⓕ *lee*·bra pound (money)
libre *lee*·bre free (not bound)
librería ⓕ lee·bre·*ree*·a bookshop
libro ⓜ *lee*·bro book
 — **de frases** de *fra*·ses phrasebook
libros ⓜ pl **de viajes** *lee*·bros de *vya*·khes travel books
líder ⓜ *lee*·der leader
ligar lee·*gar* pick up
lila *lee*·la purple
lima *lee*·ma lime

límite ⓜ **de equipaje** *lee·mee·te de e·kee·pa·khe* baggage allowance
limón ⓜ *lee·mon* lemon
limonada ⓕ *lee·mo·na·da* lemonade
limpio/a ⓜ/ⓕ *leem·pyo/a* clean
línea ⓕ *lee·ne·a* line
linterna ⓕ *leen·ter·na* flashlight • torch
listo/a ⓜ/ⓕ *lees·to/a* ready
lo que *lo ke* what
local ⓜ *lo·kal* venue
local *lo·kal* local
loco/a ⓜ/ⓕ *lo·ko/a* crazy
lodo ⓜ *lo·do* mud
lombrices ⓕ pl *lom·bree·thes* earth worms
los dos *los dos* both
Los Estados ⓜ pl **Unidos** *los es·ta·dos oo·nee·dos* USA
lubricante ⓜ *loo·bree·kan·te* lubricant
luces ⓕ pl *loo·thes* lights
luchar contra *loo·char kon·tra* fight against
lugar ⓜ *loo·gar* place
— **de nacimiento** *de na·thee·myen·to* place of birth
lujo ⓜ *loo·kho* luxury
luna ⓕ *loo·na* moon
— **llena** *lye·na* full moon
— **de miel** *de myel* honeymoon
luz ⓕ *looth* light

LL

llamada ⓕ *lya·ma·da* phone call
— **a cobro revertido** *a ko·bro re·ver·tee·do* collect call
llamar por telefono *lya·mar por te·le·fo·no* to make a phone call
llano/a ⓜ/ⓕ *lya·no/a* flat
llave ⓕ *lya·ve* key
llegadas ⓕ pl *lye·ga·das* arrivals
llegar *lye·gar* arrive
llenar *lye·nar* fill
lleno/a ⓜ/ⓕ *lye·no/a* full
llevar *lye·var* carry • wear
lluvia ⓕ *lyoo·vya* rain

M

machismo ⓜ *ma·chees·mo* sexism
madera ⓕ *ma·de·ra* wood
madre ⓕ *ma·dre* mother
madrugada ⓕ *ma·droo·ga·da* early morning
mago/a ⓜ/ⓕ *ma·go/a* magician
maíz ⓜ *ma·eeth* corn
maleta ⓕ *ma·le·ta* suitcase
maletín ⓜ *ma·le·teen* briefcase
— **de primeros auxilios** ⓜ *de pree·me·ros ow·ksee·lyos* first-aid kit
malo/a ⓜ/ⓕ *ma·lo/a* bad
mamá ⓕ *ma·ma* mum
mamograma ⓜ *ma·mo·gra·ma* mammogram
mañana ⓕ *ma·nya·na* tomorrow • morning (6am - 1pm)
— **por la mañana** *por la ma·nya·na* tomorrow morning
— **por la noche** *por la no·che* tomorrow evening
— **por la tarde** *por la tar·de* tomorrow afternoon
mandarina ⓕ *man·da·ree·na* mandarin
mandíbula ⓕ *man·dee·boo·la* jaw
mando ⓜ **a distancia** *man·do a dees·tan·thya* remote control
mango ⓜ *man·go* mango
manifestación ⓕ *ma·nee·fes·ta·thyon* demonstration
manillar ⓜ *ma·nee·lyar* handlebar
mano ⓕ *ma·no* hand
manta ⓕ *man·ta* blanket
manteca ⓕ *man·te·ka* lard
mantel ⓜ *man·tel* tablecloth
mantequilla ⓕ *man·te·kee·lya* butter
manzana ⓕ *man·tha·na* apple
mapa ⓜ *ma·pa* map
maquillaje ⓜ *ma·kee·lya·khe* make-up
máquina ⓕ *ma·kee·na* machine
— **de billetes** *de bee·lye·tes* ticket machine
— **de tabaco** *de ta·ba·ko* cigarette machine

mar ⑩ mar *sea*

marido ⑩ ma·*ree*·do *husband*

maravilloso/a ⑩/① ma·ra·vee·*lyo*·so/a *wonderful*

marcador ⑩ mar·ka·*dor scoreboard*

marcapasos ⑩ mar·ka·*pa*·sos *pacemaker*

marcar mar *lar score*

marea ① ma·*re*·a *tide*

mareado/a ⑩/① ma·re·*a* do/a *dizzy • seasick*

mareo ⑩ ma·*re*·o *travel sickness*

margarina ① mar·ga·*ree*·na *margarine*

marihuana ① ma·ree·*wa*·na *marijuana*

mariposa ① ma·ree·*po*·sa *butterfly*

marrón ma·*ron brown*

martillo ⑩ mar·*tee*·lyo *hammer*

más cercano/a ⑩/① mas ther·*ka*·no/a *nearest*

masaje ⑩ ma·*sa*·khe *massage*

masajista ⑩&① ma·sa·*khees*·ta *masseur*

matar ma·*tar kill*

matrícula ① ma·*tree*·koo·la *license plate number*

matrimonio ⑩ ma·tree·*mo*·nyo *marriage*

mayonesa ① ma·yo·*ne*·sa *mayonnaise*

mecánico ⑩ me·*ka*·nee·ko *mechanic*

mechero ⑩ me·*che*·ro *lighter*

medianoche ① me·dya·*no*·che *midnight*

medias ① pl *me*·dyas *stockings • pantyhose*

medicina ① me·dee·*thee*·na *medicine*

medico/a ⑩/① *me*·dee·co/a *doctor*

medio ⑩ **ambiente** *me*·dyo am·*byen*·te *environment*

medio/a ⑩/① *me*·dyo/a *half*

mediodía ⑩ me·dyo·*dee*·a *noon*

medios ⑩ pl **de comunicación** *me*·dyos de ko·moo·nee·ka·*thyon media*

medios ⑩ pl **de transporte** *me*·dyos de trans·*por*·te *means of transport*

mejillones ⑩ pl me·khee·*lyo*·nes *mussels*

mejor me·*khor better • best*

melocotón ⑩ me·lo·ko·*ton peach*

melodía ① me·lo·*dee*·a *tune*

melón ⑩ me·*lon melon*

mendigo/a ⑩/① men·*dee*·go/a *beggar*

menos *me*·nos *less*

mensaje ⑩ men·*sa*·khe *message*

menstruación ① mens·trwa·*thyon menstruation*

mentiroso/a ⑩/① men·tee·ro·*so*/a *liar*

menú ⑩ me·*noo menu*

menudo/a ⑩/① me·*noo*·do/a *little*

a menudo a me·*noo*·do *often*

mercado ⑩ mer·*ka*·do *market*

mermelada ① mer·me·*la*·da *jam • marmalade*

mes ⑩ mes *month*

mesa ① *me*·sa *table*

meseta ① me·*se*·ta *plateau*

metal ⑩ me·*tal metal*

meter (un gol) me·*ter* (oon gol) *kick (a goal)*

metro ⑩ *me*·tro *metre*

mezclar meth·*klar mix*

mezquita ① meth·*kee*·ta *mosque*

mi mee *my*

microondas ⑩ mee·kro·*on*·das *microwave*

miel ① myel *honey*

miembro ⑩ *myem*·bro *member*

migraña ① mee·*gra*·nya *migraine*

milímetro ⑩ mee·*lee*·me·tro *millimetre*

millón ⑩ mee·*lyon million*

minusválido/a ⑩/① mee·noos·va·*lee*·do/a *disabled*

minuto ⑩ mee·*noo*·to *minute*

mirador ⑩ mee·ra·*dor lookout*

mirar mee·*rar look • watch*

— **los escaparates** los es·ka·pa·*ra*·tes *window-shopping*

misa ① *mee*·sa *mass*

mochila ① mo·*chee*·la *backpack*

módem ⑩ *mo*·dem *modem*

(carne) molida (kar·ne) mo·*lee*·da *mince (meat)*

mojado/a ⑩/① mo·*kha*·do/a *wet*

monasterio ⑩ mo·nas·*te*·ryo *monastery*

monedas ① pl mo·*ne*·das *coins*

monja ① *mon*·kha *nun*

monopatinaje ⓜ mo·no·pa·tee·*na*·khe *skateboarding*

montaña ① mon·*ta*·nya *mountain*

montar mon·*tar* *ride*

— **en bicicleta** en bee·thee·*kle*·ta *cycle*

monumento ⓜ mo·noo·*men*·to *monument*

mordedura ① mor·de·*doo*·ra *bite (dog)*

morir mo·*reer* *die*

mosquitera ① mos·kee·*te*·ra *mosquito net*

mosquito ⓜ mos·*kee*·to *mosquito*

mostaza ① mos·*ta*·tha *mustard*

mostrador ⓜ mos·tra·*dor* *counter*

mostrar mos·*trar* *show*

motocicleta ① mo·to·thee·*kle*·ta *motorcycle*

motor ⓜ mo·*tor* *engine*

motora ① mo·*to*·ra *motorboat*

muchas/os ⓜ/① pl moo·chas/os *many*

mudo/a ⓜ/① *moo*·do/a *mute*

muebles pl *mwe*·bles *furniture*

muela ① *mwe*·la *tooth (back)*

muelle ⓜ *mwe*·lye *spring*

muerto/a ⓜ/① *mwer*·to/a *dead*

muesli ⓜ *mwes*·lee *muesli*

mujer ① moo·*kher* *woman*

multa ① *mool*·ta *fine*

mundo ⓜ *moon*·do *world*

muñeca ① moo·*nye*·ka *doll • wrist*

murallas ① pl moo·*ra*·lyas *city walls*

músculo ⓜ *moos*·koo·lo *muscle*

museo ⓜ moo·*se*·o *museum*

— **de arte** de *ar*·te *art gallery*

música ① *moo*·see·ka *music*

músico/a ⓜ/① *moo*·see·ko/a *musician*

— **ambulante** am·boo·*lan*·te *busker*

muslo ⓜ *moos*·lo *drumstick (chicken)*

musulmán(a) ⓜ/① moo·sool·*man*/moo·sool·*ma*·na *Muslim*

muy mooy *very*

nacionalidad ① na·thyo·na·lee·*da* *nationality*

nada na·da *none • nothing*

nadar na·*dar* *swim*

naranja ① na·*ran*·kha *orange*

nariz ① na·*reeth* *nose*

nata ① **agria** na·ta a·grya *sour cream*

naturaleza ① na·too·ra·*le*·tha *nature*

naturopatía ① na·too·ro·pa·*tee*·a *naturopathy*

náusea ① *now*·se·a *nausea*

náuseas ① pl **del embarazo** *now*·se·as del em·ba·*ra*·tho *morning sickness*

navaja ① na·*va*·kha *penknife*

Navidad ① na·vee·*da* *Christmas*

necesario/a ⓜ/① ne·the·*sa*·ryo/a *necessary*

necesitar ne·the·see·*tar* *need*

negar ne·*gar* *deny*

negar ne·*gar* *refuse*

negocio ⓜ ne·go·thyo *business*

— **de artículos básicos** de ar·*tee*·koo·los ba·see·kos *convenience store*

negro/a ⓜ/① ne·gro/a *black*

neumático ⓜ ne·oo·ma·tee·ko *tyre*

nevera ① ne·ve·ra *refrigerator*

nieto/a ⓜ/① nye·to/a *grandchild*

nieve ① nye·ve *snow*

niño/a ⓜ/① nee·nyo/a *child*

no no *no*

— **fumadores** foo·ma·*do*·res *non-smoking*

— **incluido** een·kloo·ee·do *excluded*

noche ① no·che *evening • night*

Nochebuena ① no·che·*bwe*·na *Christmas Eve*

Nochevieja ① no·che·*vye*·kha *New Year's Eve*

nombre ⓜ *nom*·bre *name*

— **de pila** de pee·la *Christian name*

norte ⓜ *nor*·te *north*

nosotros/as ⓜ/① pl no·so·tros/no·so·tras *we*

noticias ① pl no·*tee*·thyas *news*
— **de actualidad** de ak·*twal*·ee·*da*
current affairs
novia ① no·*vya girlfriend*
novio ⓜ no·*vyo boyfriend*
nube ① *noo*·be *cloud*
nublado nos *bla* do *cloudy*
nueces nwe·thes *nuts*
— **crudas** *kroo*·das *raw nuts*
— **tostadas** tos·*ta*·das *roasted nuts*
nuestro/a ⓜ/① *nwes*·tro/a *our*
Nueva Zelanda ① *nwe*·va the·*lan*·da
New Zealand
nuevo/a ⓜ/① *nwe*·vo/a *new*
número ⓜ *noo*·me·ro *number*
— **de la habitación** de la
a·bee·ta·*thyon room number*
— **de pasaporte** de pa·sa·*por*·te
passport number
nunca *noon*·ka *never*

O

o o *or*
obra ① o·bra *play • building site*
obrero/a ⓜ/① o·bre·ro/a *factory
worker • labourer*
océano ⓜ o·*the*·a·no *ocean*
ocupado/a ⓜ/① o·koo·*pa*·do/a *busy*
ocupar o·koo·*par live (somewhere)*
oeste ⓜ o·es·te *west*
oficina ① o·fee·*thee*·na *office*
— **de objetos perdidos** de ob·*khe*·tos
per·*dee*·dos *lost property office*
— **de turismo** de too·rees·mo *tourist
office*
oír o·eer *hear*
ojo ⓜ o·kho *eye*
ola ① o·la *wave*
olor ⓜ o·*lor smell*
olvidar ol·vee·*dar forget*
ópera ① o·pe·ra *opera*
operación ① o·pe·ra·*thyon operation*
opinión ① o·pee·*nyon opinion*
oporto ⓜ o·*por*·to *port (wine)*
oportunidad ① o·por·too·nee·*da chance*

oración ① o·ra·*thyon prayer*
orden ⓜ or·den *order (placement)*
ordenador ⓜ or·de·na·*dor computer*
— **portátil** por·*ta*·teel *laptop*
ordenar or·de·*nar order*
oreja ① o·re·kha *ear*
orgasmo ⓜ or·*gas*·mo *orgasm*
original o·ree·khee·*nal original*
orquesta ① or·*kes*·ta *orchestra*
oscuro/a ⓜ/① os·koo·ro/a *dark*
ostra ① os·tra *oyster*
otoño ⓜ o·*to*·nyo *autumn*
otra vez o·tra veth *again*
otro/a ⓜ/① o·tro/a *other • another*
oveja ① o·ve·kha *sheep*
oxígeno ⓜ o·*ksee*·khe·no *oxygen*

P

padre ⓜ *pa*·dre *father*
padres ⓜ pl *pa*·dres *parents*
pagar pa·*gar pay*
página ① *pa*·khee·na *page*
pago ⓜ *pa*·go *payment*
país ⓜ pa·ees *country*
pájaro ⓜ *pa*·kha·ro *bird*
palabra ① pa·*la*·bra *word*
palacio ⓜ pa·*la*·thyo *palace*
palillo ⓜ pa·*lee*·lyo *toothpick*
pan ⓜ pan *bread*
— **integral** in·te·gral *wholemeal
bread*
— **moreno** mo·re·no *brown bread*
panadería ① pa·na·de·*ree*·a *bakery*
pañal ⓜ pa·nyal *diaper • nappy*
pantalla ① pan·*ta*·lya *screen*
pantalones ⓜ pl pan·ta·*lo*·nes *pants •
trousers*
— **cortos** kor·tos *shorts*
pañuelos ⓜ pl **de papel** pa·nywe·los
de pa·pel *tissues*
papá ⓜ pa·pa *dad*
papel ⓜ pa·*pel paper*
— **de fumar** de foo·*mar cigarette
papers*
— **higiénico** ee·*khye*·nee·ko *toilet
paper*

O

paquete ⓜ pa·*ke*·te *packet • package • wear*

para llevar pa·ra lye·*var* *to take away*

parabrisas ⓜ pa·ra·*bree*·sas *windscreen*

paracaidismo ⓜ pa·ra·kai·*dees*·mo *skydiving*

parada ⓕ pa·*ra*·da *stop*
— **de autobús** de ow·to·*boos* *bus stop*
— **de taxis** de ta·*ksees* *taxi stand*

paraguas ⓜ pa·ra·*gwas* *umbrella*

parapléjico/a ⓜ/ⓕ pa·ra·*ple*·khee·ko/a *paraplegic*

parar pa·*rar* *stop*

pared ⓕ pa·*re* *wall (inside)*

pareja ⓕ pa·*re*·kha *pair (couple)*

parlamento ⓜ par·la·*men*·to *parliament*

paro ⓜ *pa*·ro *dole*

parque ⓜ *par*·ke *park*
— **nacional** na·thyo·*nal* *national park*

parte ⓕ *par*·te *part*

partida ⓕ **de nacimiento** par·*tee*·da de na·thee·*myen*·to *birth certificate*

partido ⓜ par·*tee*·do *match (sport) • party (political)*

pasado ⓜ pa·*sa*·do *past*

pasado mañana pa·*sa*·do ma·*nya*·na *day after tomorrow*

pasado/a ⓜ/ⓕ pa·*sa*·do/a *off (food)*

pasajero ⓜ pa·sa·*khe*·ro *passenger*

pasaporte ⓜ pa·sa·*por*·te *passport*

Pascua ⓕ *pas*·kwa *Easter*

pase ⓜ *pa*·se *pass*

paseo ⓜ pa·*se*·o *street*

paso ⓜ *pa*·so *step*
— **de cebra** de the·bra *pedestrian crossing*

pasta ⓕ *pas*·ta *pasta*
— **dentífrica** den·*tee*·free·ka *toothpaste*

pastel ⓜ pas·*tel* *cake • pie*
— **de cumpleaños** de koom·ple·a·*nyos* *birthday cake*

pastelería ⓕ pas·te·le·*ree*·a *cake shop*

pastilla ⓕ pas·*tee*·lya *pill*

pastillas ⓕ pl **de menta** pas·*tee*·lyas de *men*·ta *mints*

pastillas ⓕ pl **para dormir** pas·*tee*·lyas pa·ra dor·*meer* *sleeping pills*

patata ⓕ pa·*ta*·ta *potato*

paté ⓜ pa·*te* *pate (food)*

patinar pa·tee·*nar* *rollerblading • ice skating*

pato ⓜ *pa*·to *duck*

pavo ⓜ *pa*·vo *turkey*

paz ⓕ *path* *peace*

peatón ⓜ&ⓕ pe·a·*ton* *pedestrian*

pecho ⓜ *pe*·cho *chest*

pechuga ⓕ pe·*choo*·ga *breast (poultry)*

pedal ⓜ pe·*dal* *pedal*

pedazo ⓜ pe·*da*·tho *piece*

pedir pe·*deer* *ask (for something)*

peine ⓜ *pey*·ne *comb*

pelea ⓕ pe·*le*·a *fight*

película ⓕ pe·*lee*·koo·la *movie • film (camera)*
— **en color** en ko·*lor* *colour film*

peligroso/a ⓜ/ⓕ pe·lee·*gro*·so/a *dangerous*

pelo ⓜ *pe*·lo *hair*

pelota ⓕ pe·*lo*·ta *ball*
— **de golf** de golf *golf ball*

peluquero/a ⓜ/ⓕ pe·loo·*ke*·ro/a *hairdresser*

pendientes ⓜ pl pen·*dyen*·tes *earrings*

pene ⓜ *pe*·ne *penis*

pensar pen·*sar* *think*

pensión ⓕ pen·*syon* *boarding house*

pensionista ⓜ&ⓕ pen·syo·*nees*·ta *pensioner*

pepino ⓜ pe·*pee*·no *cucumber*

pequeñito/a ⓜ/ⓕ pe·ke·*nyee*·to/a *tiny*

pequeño/a ⓜ/ⓕ pe·*ke*·nyo/a *small*

pera ⓕ *pe*·ra *pear*

perder per·*der* *lose*

perdido/a ⓜ/ⓕ per·*dee*·do/a *lost*

perdonar per·do·*nar* *forgive*

perejil ⓜ pe·re·*kheel* *parsley*

perfume ⓜ per·foo·me *perfume*

periódico ⓜ pe·ryo·*dee*·ko *newspaper*

periodista ⓜ&ⓕ pe·ryo·*dees*·ta *journalist*

permiso ⓜ per·mee·so *permission • permit*

  — de trabajo ⓜ de tra·ba·kho *work permit*

permitir per·mee·teer *allow • permit*

pero pe·ro *but*

perro/a ⓜ/ⓕ pe·ro/a *dog*

perro ⓜ **lazarillo** pe·ro la·tha·ree·lyo *guide dog*

persona ⓕ per·so·na *person*

pesado/a ⓜ/ⓕ pe·sa·do/a *heavy*

pesar pe·sar *weigh*

pesas ⓕ pl pe·sas *weights*

pesca ⓕ pes·ka *fishing*

pescadería ⓕ pes·ka·de·ree·a *fish shop*

pescado ⓜ pes·ka·do *fish (as food)*

peso ⓜ pe·so *weight*

petición ⓕ pe·tee·thyon *petition*

pez ⓜ peth *fish*

picadura ⓕ pee·ka·doo·ra *bite (insect)*

picazón ⓕ pee·ka·thon *itch*

pie ⓜ pee·e *foot*

piedra ⓕ pye·dra *stone*

piel ⓕ pyel *skin*

pierna ⓕ pyer·na *leg*

pila ⓕ pee·la *battery (small)*

píldora ⓕ peel·do·ra *the Pill*

pimienta ⓕ pee·myen·ta *pepper*

pimiento ⓜ pee·myen·to *capsicum • bell pepper*

  — rojo ro·kho *red capsicum*

  — verde ver·de *green capsicum*

piña ⓕ pee·nya *pineapple*

pinchar peen·char *puncture*

ping pong ⓜ peeng pong *table tennis*

pintar peen·tar *paint*

pintor(a) ⓜ/ⓕ peen·tor/peen·to·ra *painter*

pintura ⓕ peen·too·ra *painting*

pinzas ⓕ pl peen·thas *tweezers*

piojos ⓜ pl pee·o·khos *lice*

piqueta ⓕ pee·ke·ta *pickaxe*

piquetas ⓕ pl pee·ke·tas *tent pegs*

piscina ⓕ pees·thee·na *swimming pool*

pista ⓕ pees·ta *court (tennis)*

  — de tenis de te·nees *tennis court*

pistacho ⓜ pees·ta·cho *pistachio*

plancha ⓕ plan·cha *iron*

planeta ⓜ pla·ne·ta *planet*

planta ⓕ plan·ta *plant*

plástico ⓜ plas·tee·ko *plastic*

plata ⓕ pla·ta *silver*

plataforma ⓕ pla·ta·for·ma *platform*

plátano ⓜ pla·ta·no *banana*

plateado/a ⓜ/ⓕ pla·te·a·do/a *silver*

plato ⓜ pla·to *plate*

playa ⓕ pla·ya *beach*

plaza ⓕ pla·tha *square*

  — de toros de to·ros *bullring*

pobre po·bre *poor*

pobreza ⓕ po·bre·tha *poverty*

pocos po·kos *few*

poder po·der *can (be able)*

poder ⓜ po·der *power*

poesía ⓕ po·e·see·a *poetry*

polen ⓜ po·len *pollen*

policía ⓕ po·lee·thee·a *police*

política ⓕ po·lee·tee·ka *policy • politics*

político ⓜ po·lee·tee·ko *politician*

póliza ⓕ po·lee·tha *policy (insurance)*

pollo ⓜ po·lyo *chicken*

pomelo ⓜ po·me·lo *grapefruit*

poner po·ner *put*

popular po·poo·lar *popular*

póquer ⓜ po·ker *poker*

por (día) por (dee·a) *per (day)*

por ciento por thyen·to *percent*

por qué por ke *why*

por vía aérea por vee·a a·e·re·a *air mail*

por vía terrestre por vee·a te·res·tre *surface mail*

porque por·ke *because*

portero/a ⓜ/ⓕ por·te·ro/a *goalkeeper*

posible po·see·ble *possible*

postal ⓕ pos·tal *postcard*

póster ⓜ pos·ter *poster*

potro ⓜ po·tro *foal*

pozo ⓜ po·tho *well*

precio ⓜ pre·thyo *price*

  — de entrada de en·tra·da *admission price*

  — del cubierto del koo·byer·to *cover charge*

preferir pre·fe·*reer* prefer

pregunta ⓕ pre·*goon*·ta *question*

preguntar pre·goon·*tar* ask (a question)

preocupado/a ⓜ/ⓕ pre·o·koo·*pa*·do/a *worried*

preocuparse por pre·o·koo·*par*·se por *care (about something)*

preparar pre·pa·*rar* prepare

presidente/a ⓜ/ⓕ pre·see·*den*·te/a *president*

presión ⓕ pre·*syon* pressure
— **arterial** ar·te·*ryal* blood pressure

prevenir pre·ve·*neer* prevent

primavera ⓕ pree·ma·ve·ra *spring (season)*

primer ministro ⓜ pree·*mer* mee·*nees*·tro prime minister

primera ministra ⓕ pree·*me*·ra mee·*nees*·tra prime minister

primero/a ⓜ/ⓕ pree·*me*·ro/a *first*

principal preen·thee·*pal* main

prisa ⓕ *pree*·sa hurry

prisionero/a ⓜ/ⓕ pree·syon·*ne*·ro/a *prisoner*

privado/a ⓜ/ⓕ pree·*va*·do/a *private*

probar pro·*bar* try

producir pro·doo·*theer* produce

productos ⓜ pl **congelados** pro·*dook*·tos kon·khe·*la*·dos frozen foods

profesor(a) ⓜ/ⓕ pro·fe·*sor*/ pro·fe·*so*·ra lecturer • instructor • teacher

profundo/a ⓜ/ⓕ pro·*foon*·do/a deep

programa ⓜ pro·*gra*·ma programme

prolongación ⓕ pro·lon·ga·*thyon* extension (visa)

promesa ⓕ pro·*me*·sa promise

prometida ⓕ pro·me·*tee*·da fiancee

prometido ⓜ pro·me·*tee*·do fiance

pronto *pron*·to soon

propietaria ⓕ pro·pye·*ta*·rya landlady

propietario ⓜ pro·pye·*ta*·ryo landlord

propina ⓕ pro·*pee*·na tip

proteger pro·te·*kher* protect

protegido/a ⓜ/ⓕ pro·te·*khee*·do/a *protected*

protesta ⓕ pro·*tes*·ta protest

provisiones ⓕ pl pro·bee·*syo*·nes *provisions*

proyector ⓜ pro·yek·*tor* projector

prudente proo·*den*·te sensible

prueba ⓕ *prwe*·ba test
— **del embarazo** del em·ba·*ra*·tho *pregnancy test kit*

pruebas ⓕ pl **nucleares** *prwe*·bas noo·kle·*a*·res *nuclear testing*

pub ⓜ poob bar (with music) • pub

pueblo ⓜ *pwe*·blo village

puente ⓜ *pwen*·te bridge

puerro ⓜ *pwe*·ro leek

puerta ⓕ *pwer*·ta door

puerto ⓜ *pwer*·to port • harbour

puesta ⓕ **del sol** *pwes*·ta del sol sunset

pulga ⓕ *pool*·ga flea

pulmones ⓜ pl pool·*mo*·nes lungs

punto ⓜ *poon*·to point (tip) • point (score)

puro ⓜ *poo*·ro cigar

puro/a ⓜ/ⓕ *poo*·ro/a pure

Q

(el mes) que viene (el mes) ke *vye*·ne next (month)

quedar ke·*dar* leave (behind)

quedarse ke·*dar*·se stay (remain)

quedarse sin ke·*dar*·se seen run out of

quejarse ke·*khar*·se complain

quemadura ⓕ ke·ma·*doo*·ra burn
— **de sol** de sol sunburn

querer ke·*rer* love • want

queso ⓜ *ke*·so cheese
— **crema** *kre*·ma cream cheese
— **de cabra** de *ka*·bra goat's cheese

quien kyen who

quincena ⓕ keen·*the*·na fortnight

quiosco ⓜ *kyos*·ko news stand • newsagency

quiste ⓜ **ovárico** *kees*·te o·va·*ree*·ko *ovarian cyst*

quizás kee·*thas* maybe

R

rábano ⑩ *ra·ba·no* radish
— **picante** *pee·kan·te* horseradish
rápido/a ⑩/① *ra·pee·do/a* fast
raqueta ① *ra·ke·ta* racquet
raro/a ⑩/① *ra·ro/a* rare (item)
rastro ⑩ *ras·tro* track (footprints)
rata ① *ra·ta* rat
ratón ⑩ *ra·ton* mouse
raza ① *ra·tha* race (people)
razón ① *ra·thon* reason
realista *re·a·lees·ta* realistic
recibir *re·thee·beer* receive
recibo ⑩ *re·thee·bo* receipt
reciclable *re·thee·kla·ble* recyclable
reciclar *re·thee·klar* recycle
recientemente *re·thyen·te·men·te* recently
recogida ① **de equipajes** *re·ko·khee·da de e·kee·pa·khes* baggage claim
recolección ① **de fruta** *re·ko·lek·thyon de froo·ta* fruit picking
recomendar *re·ko·men·dar* recommend
reconocer *re·ko·no·ther* recognise
recordar *re·kor·dar* remember
recorrido ⑩ **guiado** *re·ko·ree·do gee·a·do* guided tour
recto/a ⑩/① *rek·to/a* straight
recuerdo ⑩ *re·kwer·do* souvenir
red ① *red* net
redondo/a ⑩/① *re·don·do/a* round
reembolsar *re·em·bol·sar* refund
reembolso ⑩ *re·em·bol·so* refund
referencias ① pl *re·fe·ren·thyas* references
refresco ⑩ *re·fres·ko* soft drink
refugiado/a ⑩/① *re·foo·khya·do/a* refugee
regalar *re·ga·lar* exchange (gifts)
regalo ⑩ *re·ga·lo* gift
— **de bodas** *de bo·das* wedding present
régimen ⑩ *re·khee·men* diet
reglas ① pl *re·glas* rules
reina ① *rey·na* queen

reírse *re·eer·se* laugh
relación ① *re·la·thyon* relationship
relajarse *re·la·khar·se* relax
religión ① *re·lee·khyon* religion
religioso/a ⑩/① *re·lee·khyo·so/a* religious
reliquia ① *re·lee·kya* relic
reloj ⑩ *re·lokh* clock
— **de pulsera** *de pool·se·ra* watch
remo ⑩ *re·mo* rowing
remolacha ① *re·mo·la·cha* beetroot
remoto/a ⑩/① *re·mo·to/a* remote
reparar *re·pa·rar* repair
repartir *re·par·teer* divide up (share)
repetir *re·pe·teer* repeat
república ① *re·poo·blee·ka* republic
requesón ⑩ *re·ke·son* cottage cheese
reserva ① *re·ser·va* reservation
reservar *re·ser var* book (make a reservation)
resfriado ⑩ *res·free·a·do* cold
residencia ① **de estudiantes** *re·see·den·thya de es·too·dyan·tes* college
residuos ⑩ pl **tóxicos** *re·see·dwos to·ksee·kos* toxic waste
respirar *res·pee·rar* breathe
respuesta ① *res·pwes·ta* answer
restaurante ⑩ *res·tow·ran·te* restaurant
revisar *re·vee·sar* check
revisor(a) ⑩/① *re·vee·sor/re·vee·so·ra* ticket collector
revista ① *re·vees·ta* magazine
rey ⑩ *rey* king
rico/a ⑩/① *ree·ko/a* rich
riesgo ⑩ *ryes·go* risk
río ⑩ *ree·o* river
ritmo ⑩ *reet·mo* rhythm
robar *ro·bar* rob • steal
roca ① *ro·ka* rock
rock ⑩ *rok* rock (music)
rodilla ① *ro·dee·lya* knee
rojo/a ⑩/① *ro·kho/a* red
rollo ⑩ **repelente contra mosquitos** *ro·lyo re·pe·len·te kon·tra mos·kee·tos* mosquito coil

romántico/a ⓜ/ⓕ ro·man·tee·ko/a romantic

romper rom·per break

ron ⓜ ron rum

ropa ⓕ ro·pa clothing
— **de cama** de ka·ma bedding
— **interior** een·te·ryor underwear

rosa ro·sa pink

roto/a ⓜ/ⓕ ro·to/a broken

rueda ⓕ rwe·da wheel

rugby ⓜ roog·bee rugby

ruidoso/a ⓜ/ⓕ rwee·do·so/a loud

ruinas ⓕ pl rwee·nas ruins

ruta ⓕ roo·ta route

S

sábado ⓜ sa·ba·do Saturday

sábana ⓕ sa·ba·na sheet (bed)

saber sa·ber know (something)

sabroso/a ⓜ/ⓕ sa·bro·so/a tasty

sacar sa·kar take out • take (photo)

sacerdote ⓜ sa·ther·do·te priest

saco ⓜ **de dormir** sa·ko de dor·meer sleeping bag

sal ⓕ sal salt

sala ⓕ **de espera** sa·la de es·pe·ra waiting room

sala ⓕ **de tránsito** sa·la de tran·see·to transit lounge

salario ⓜ sa·la·ryo rate of pay • salary

salchicha ⓕ sal·chee·cha sausage

saldo ⓜ sal·do balance (account)

salida ⓕ sa·lee·da departure • exit

saliente ⓜ sa·lyen·te ledge

salir con sa·leer kon go out with

salir de sa·leer de depart

salmón ⓜ sal·mon salmon

salón de belleza ⓜ sa·lon de be·lye·tha beauty salon

salsa ⓕ sal·sa sauce
— **de guindilla** de geen·dee·lya chilli sauce
— **de soja** de so·kha soy sauce
— **de tomate** de to·ma·te tomato sauce • ketchup

saltar sal·tar jump

salud ⓕ sa·loo health

salvaeslips ⓜ pl sal·va·e·sleeps panty liners

salvar sal·var save

sandalias ⓕ pl san·da·lyas sandals

sandia ⓕ san·dee·a watermelon

sangrar san·grar bleed

sangre ⓕ san·gre blood

santo/a ⓜ/ⓕ san·to/a saint

sarampión ⓜ sa·ram·pyon measles

sartén ⓕ sar·ten frying pan

sastre ⓜ sas·tre tailor

sauna ⓕ sow·na sauna

secar se·kar dry

secretario/a ⓜ/ⓕ se·kre·ta·ryo/a secretary

sed ⓕ se thirst

seda ⓕ se·da silk

seguir se·geer follow

segundo/a ⓜ/ⓕ se·goon·do/a second

seguro ⓜ se·goo·ro insurance

seguro/a ⓜ/ⓕ se·goo·ro/a safe

sello ⓜ se·lyo stamp

semáforos ⓜ pl se·ma·fo·ros traffic lights

Semana ⓕ **Santa** se·ma·na san·ta Holy Week

sembrar sem·brar plant

semidirecto/a ⓜ/ⓕ se·mee·dee·rek·to/a non-direct

señal ⓕ se·nyal sign

sencillo/a ⓜ/ⓕ sen·thee·lyo/a simple

(un billete) sencillo ⓜ (oon bee·lye·te) sen·thee·lyo one-way (ticket)

sendero ⓜ sen·de·ro mountain path • path

senos ⓜ pl se·nos breasts

sensibilidad ⓕ sen·see·bee·lee·da sensitivity • film speed

sensual sen·swal sensual

sentarse sen·tar·se sit

sentimientos ⓜ pl sen·tee·myen·tos feelings

sentir sen·teer feel

separado/a ⓜ/ⓕ se·pa·ra·do/a separate

separar se·pa·rar separate

ser ser be

serie ① se·rye *series*

serio/a ⑩/① se·ryo/a *serious*

seropositivo/a ⑩/①
se·ro·po·see·tee·vo/a *HIV positive*

serpiente ① ser·pyen·te *snake*

servicio ⑩ ser·vee·thyo *service charge*
  — militar mee·lee·*tar military service*
  — telefónico automático
  te·le·*fo*·nee·ko ow·to·ma·tee·ko
  direct-dial

servicios ⑩ pl ser·vee·thyos *toilets*

servilleta ① ser·vee·*lye*·ta *napkin*

sexo ⑩ se·kso *sex*
  — seguro se·goo·ro *safe sex*

sexy se·ksee *sexy*

si see *if • yes*

SIDA ⑩ see·da *AIDS*

sidra ① see·dra *cider*

siempre syem·pre *always*

silla ① see·lya *chair*
  — de ruedas de rwe·das *wheelchair*

sillín ⑩ see·*lyeen saddle*

similar see·mee·*lar similar*

simpático/a ⑩/① seem·pa·tee·ko/a *nice*

sin seen *without*
  — hogar o·gar *homeless*
  — plomo plo·mo *unleaded*

sinagoga ① see·na·go·ga *synagogue*

Singapur ⑩ seen·ga·poor *Singapore*

sintético/a ⑩/① seen·te·tee·ko/a
  synthetic

soborno ⑩ so·bor·no *bribe*

sobre so·bre *about • on top of*

sobre ⑩ so·bre *envelope*

sobredosis ① so·bre·do·sees *overdose*

sobrevivir so·bre·vee·veer *survive*

socialista ⑩ & ① so·thya·*lees*·ta *socialist*

sol ⑩ sol *sun*

soldado ⑩ sol·da·do *soldier*

sólo so·lo *only*

solo/a ⑩/① so·lo/a *alone*

soltero/a ⑩/① sol·te·ro/a *single*

sombra ① som·bra *shadow*

sombrero ⑩ som·bre·ro *hat*

soñar so·*nyar dream*

sondeos ⑩ pl son·de·os *polls*

sonreír son·re·eer *smile*

sopa ① so·pa *soup*

sordo/a ⑩/① sor·do/a *deaf*

sorpresa ① sor·pre·sa *surprise*

su soo *her • his • their*

subir soo·beer *climb*

submarinismo ⑩ soob·ma·ree·nees·mo
  diving

subtítulos ⑩ pl soob·tee·too·los *subtitles*

sucio/a ⑩/① soo·thyo/a *dirty*

sucursal ① soo·koor·sal *branch office*

sudar soo·dar *perspire*

suegra ① swe·gra *mother-in-law*

suegro ⑩ swe·gro *father-in-law*

sueldo ⑩ swel·do *wage*

suelo ⑩ swe·lo *floor*

suerte ① swer·te *luck*

suficiente soo·fee·thyen·te *enough*

sufrir soo·freer *suffer*

sujetador ⑩ soo·khe·ta·dor *bra*

supermercado ⑩ soo·per·mer·ka·do
  supermarket

superstición ① soo·pers·tee·thyon
  superstition

sur ⑩ soor *south*

surf ⑩ sobre la nieve soorf so·bre la
  nye·ve *snowboarding*

T

tabaco ⑩ ta·ba·ko *tobacco*

tabla ① de surf ta·bla de soorf *surfboard*

tablero ⑩ de ajedrez ta·ble·ro de
  a·khe·dreth *chess board*

tacaño/a ⑩/① ta·ka·nyo/a *stingy*

talco ⑩ tal·ko *baby powder*

talla ① ta·lya *size (clothes)*

taller ⑩ ta·lyer *workshop*

también tam·byen *also*

tampoco tam·po·ko *neither*

tampones ⑩ pl tam·po·nes *tampons*

tanga ① tan·ga *g-string*

tapones ⑩ pl para los oídos ta·po·nes
  pa·ra los o·ee·dos *earplugs*

taquilla ① ta·kee·lya *ticket office*

tarde tar·de *late*

tarjeta tar·khe·ta *card*
— **de crédito** de kre·dee·to *credit card*
— **de embarque** de em·bar·ke *boarding pass*
— **de teléfono** de te·le·fo·no *phone card*
tarta ① **nupcial** tar·ta noop·thyal *wedding cake*
tasa ① **del aeropuerto** ta·sa del ay·ro·pwer·to *airport tax*
taxi ⓜ ta·ksee *taxi*
taza ① ta·tha *cup*
té ⓜ te *tea*
teatro ⓜ te·a·tro *theatre*
teclado ⓜ te·kla·do *keyboard*
técnica ① tek·nee·ka *technique*
tela ① te·la *fabric*
tele ① te·le *TV*
teleférico ⓜ te·le·fe·ree·ko *cable car*
teléfono ⓜ te·le·fo·no *telephone*
— **móvil** mo·veel *mobile phone*
— **público** poo·blee·ko *public telephone*
telegrama ⓜ te·le·gra·ma *telegram*
telenovela ① te·le·no·ve·la *soap opera*
telescopio ⓜ te·les·ko·pyo *telescope*
televisión ① te·le·vee·syon *television*
temperatura ① tem·pe·ra·too·ra *temperature (weather)*
templado/a ⓜ/① tem·pla·do/a *warm*
templo ⓜ tem·plo *temple*
temporada ① tem·po·ra·da *season (in sport)*
temprano tem·pra·no *early*
tenedor ⓜ te·ne·dor *fork*
tener te·ner *have*
— **hambre** am·bre *to be hungry*
— **prisa** pree·sa *to be in a hurry*
— **sed** seth *to be thirsty*
— **sueño** swe·nyo *to be sleepy*
tenis ⓜ te·nees *tennis*
tensión ① **premenstrual** ten·syon pre·mens·trwal *premenstrual tension*
tentempié ⓜ ten·tem·pye *snack*
tercio ⓜ ter·thyo *third*
terminar ter·mee·nar *finish*

ternera ① ter·ne·ra *veal*
ternero ⓜ ter·ne·ro *calf*
terremoto ⓜ te·re·mo·to *earthquake*
testarudo/a ⓜ/① tes·ta·roo·do/a *stubborn*
tía ① tee·a *aunt*
tiempo ⓜ tyem·po *time • weather*
— **a** — a tyem·po *on time*
— **a** — **completo/parcial** a tyem·po kom·ple·to/par·thyal *full-time/part-time*
tienda ① **(de campaña)** tyen·da (de kam·pa·nya) *tent*
tienda ① tyen·da *shop*
— **de comestibles** de ko·mes·tee·bles *grocery*
— **de fotografía** de fo·to·gra·fee·a *camera shop*
— **de eléctrodomésticos** de e·lek·tro·do·mes·tee·kos *electrical store*
— **de provisiones de cámping** de pro·vee·syo·nes de kam·peen *camping store*
— **de recuerdos** de re·kwer·dos *souvenir shop*
— **de ropa** de ro·pa *clothing store*
— **deportiva** de·por·tee·va *sports store*
Tierra ① tye·ra *Earth*
tierra ① tye·ra *land*
tiesto ⓜ tyes·to *pot (plant)*
tijeras ① pl tee·khe·ras *scissors*
tímido/a ⓜ/① tee·mee·do/a *shy*
típico/a ⓜ/① tee·pee·ko/a *typical*
tipo ⓜ tee·po *type*
— **de cambio** de kam·byo *exchange rate*
tirar tee·rar *pull*
tiritas ① pl tee·ree·tas *band-aids*
título ⓜ tee·too·lo *degree*
toalla ① to·a·lya *towel*
toallita ① to·a·lyee·ta *face cloth*
tobillo ⓜ to·bee·lyo *ankle*
tocar to·kar *touch*
— **la guitarra** la gee·ta·ra *play (guitar)*

tocino ⓜ to·*thee*·no *bacon*

todavía (no) to·da·*vee*·a (no) *(not) yet*

todo *to*·do *all • everything*

tofú ⓜ to·*foo* *tofu*

tomar to·*mar* *take • drink (something)*

tomate ⓜ to·*ma*·te *tomato*
— **secado al sol** se·*ka*·do al sol *sun dried tomato*

tono ⓜ *to*·no *tone*

torcedura ① tor·the·*doo*·ra *sprain*

tormenta ① tor·*men*·ta *storm*

toro ⓜ *to*·ro *bull*

torre ① *to*·re *tower*

tos ① tos *cough*

tostada ① tos·*ta*·da *toast*

tostadora ① tos·ta·*do*·ra *toaster*

trabajar tra·ba·*khar* *work*

trabajo ⓜ tra·*ba*·kho *job • work*
— **administrativo** ad·mee·nees·tra·*tee*·vo *paperwork*
— **de camarero/a** ⓜ/① de ka·ma·re·ro/a *bar work*
— **de casa** de *ka*·sa *housework*
— **de limpieza** de leem·*pye*·tha *cleaning*
— **eventual** e·ven·*twal* *casual work*

traducir tra·doo·*theer* *translate*

traer tra·*er* *bring*

traficante ⓜ&① **de drogas** tra·fee·*kan*·te de *dro*·gas *drug dealer*

tráfico ⓜ *tra*·fee·ko *traffic*

tramposo/a ⓜ/① tram·*po*·so/a *cheat*

tranquilo/a ⓜ/① tran·*kee*·lo/a *quiet*

tranvía ⓜ tran·*vee*·a *tram*

a través a tra·*ves* *across*

tren ⓜ tren *train*
— **de cercanías** de ther·ka·*nee*·as *local train*

trepar tre·*par* *scale • climb*

tres en raya tres en *ra*·ya *noughts & crosses*

triste *trees*·te *sad*

tú too *you (informal)*

tu too *your*

tubo ⓜ **de escape** *too*·bo de es·*ka*·pe *exhaust*

tumba ① *toom*·ba *grave*

tumbarse toom·*bar*·se *lie (not stand)*

turista ⓜ&① too·*rees*·ta *tourist*
— **operador(a)** ⓜ/① o·pe·ra·*dor*/ o·pe·ra·*do*·ra *tourist operator*

U

uniforme ⓜ oo·nee·*for*·me *uniform*

universidad ① oo·nee·ver·*see*·da *university*

universo ⓜ oo·nee·*ver*·so *universe*

urgente oor·*khen*·te *urgent*

usted oos·*te* *you (pol)*

útil *oo*·teel *useful*

uvas ① pl *oo*·vas *grapes*
— **pasas** *pa*·sas *raisins*

V

vaca ① *va*·ka *cow*

vacaciones ① pl va·ka·*thyo*·nes *holidays • vacation*

vacante va·*kan*·te *vacant*

vacío/a ⓜ/① va·*thee*·o/a *empty*

vacuna ① va·*koo*·na *vaccination*

vagina ① va·*khee*·na *vagina*

vagón ⓜ **restaurante** va·*gon* res·tow·*ran*·te *dining car*

validar va·lee·*dar* *validate*

valiente va·*lyen*·te *brave*

valioso/a ⓜ/① va·*lyo*·so/a *valuable*

valle ⓜ *va*·lye *valley*

valor va·*lor* *value*

vaqueros ⓜ pl va·*ke*·ros *jeans*

varios/as ⓜ/① pl va·*ryos*/as *several*

vaso ⓜ *va*·so *(drinking) glass*

vegetariano/a ⓜ/① ve·khe·ta·*rya*·no/a *vegetarian*

vela ① *ve*·la *candle*

velocidad ① ve·lo·*thee*·da *speed*

velocímetro ⓜ ve·lo·*thee*·me·tro *speedometer*

velódromo ⓜ ve·*lo*·dro·mo *racetrack (bicycles)*

vena ① *ve*·na *vein*

Y

vendaje ⓜ ven·*da*·khe *bandage*
vendedor(a) ⓜ/ⓕ **de flores**
  ven·de·*dor*/ven·de·*do*·ra de *flo*·res
  florist
vender ven·*der* *sell*
venenoso/a ⓜ/ⓕ ve·ne·*no*·so/a
  poisonous
venir ve·*neer* *come*
ventana ⓕ ven·*ta*·na *window*
ventilador ⓜ ven·tee·la·*dor* *fan (machine)*
ver ver *see*
verano ⓜ ve·*ra*·no *summer*
verde ver·de *green*
verdulería ⓕ ver·doo·le·*ree*·a
  greengrocery (shop)
verdulero/a ⓜ/ⓕ ver·doo·*le*·ro/a
  grocer (shopkeeper)
verduras ⓕ pl ver·*doo*·ras *vegetables*
vestíbulo ⓜ ves·*tee*·boo·lo *foyer*
vestido ⓜ ves·*tee*·do *dress*
vestuario ⓜ ves·*twa*·ryo *wardrobe*
vestuarios ⓜ pl ves·*twa*·ryos
  changing room
vez ⓕ veth *once*
viajar vya·*khar* *travel*
viaje ⓜ *vya*·khe *trip*
vid ⓕ veed *vine*
vida ⓕ *vee*·da *life*
vidrio ⓜ *vee*·dryo *glass*
viejo/a ⓜ/ⓕ *vye*·kho/a *old*
viento ⓜ *vyen*·to *wind*
vinagre ⓜ vee·*na*·gre *vinegar*
viñedo ⓜ vee·*nye*·do *vineyard*
vino ⓜ *vee*·no *wine*
violar vyo·*lar* *rape*

virus ⓜ *vee*·roos *virus*
visado ⓜ vee·*sa*·do *visa*
visitar vee·see·*tar* *visit*
vista ⓕ *vees*·ta *view*
vitaminas ⓕ pl vee·ta·*mee*·nas
  vitamins
víveres ⓜ pl *vee*·ve·res *food supplies*
vivir vee·*veer* *live (life)*
vodka ⓕ *vod*·ka *vodka*
volar vo·*lar* *fly*
volumen ⓜ vo·*loo*·men *volume*
volver vol·*ver* *return*
votar vo·*tar* *vote*
voz ⓕ voth *voice*
vuelo ⓜ *vwe*·lo
  — doméstico do·*mes*·tee·ko *domestic flight*

Y

y ee *and*
ya ya *already*
yip ⓜ yeep *jeep*
yo yo *I*
yoga ⓜ *yo*·ga *yoga*
yogur ⓜ yo·*goor* *yogurt*

Z

zanahoria ⓕ tha·na·o·rya *carrot*
zapatería ⓕ tha·pa·te·*ree*·a *shoe shop*
zapatos ⓜ pl tha·*pa*·tos *shoes*
zodíaco ⓜ tho·*dee*·a·ko *zodiac*
zoológico ⓜ zo·o·*lo*·khee·ko *zoo*
zumo ⓜ *thoo*·mo *juice*
  — de naranja de na·*ran*·kha
  orange juice

Q

R

S

T

V

W

Y